CHANGING LIVES
OF
REFUGEE HMONG WOMEN

CHANGING LIVES
OF
REFUGEE HMONG WOMEN

NANCY D. DONNELLY

UNIVERSITY OF WASHINGTON PRESS
SEATTLE AND LONDON

Copyright © 1994 by the University of Washington Press
First paperback edition, 1997
Printed in the United States of America

Library of Congress Cataloging-in-Publication Data
Donnelly, Nancy D.
    Changing lives of refugee Hmong women / Nancy D. Donnelly.
      p. cm.
    Includes bibliographical references (p.) and index.
    ISBN 0-29597621-7 (acid-free paper)
    1. Hmong American women I. Title.
E184.H55D66   1994   94-5746
305.48'895—dc20   CIP

The paper used in this publication meets the minimum requirements of American National Standard for Information Sciences—Permanence of Paper for
Printed Library Materials, ANSI Z39.48–1984. ∞

CONTENTS

HMONG LANGUAGE, ORTHOGRAPHY, AND NAMES

Hmong words are mostly single syllables, beginning with a consonant and ending with a vowel. Some words are compounds built of monsyllabic words. Hmong language in the United States is generally written using the Romanized Phonetic Alphabet (RPA) in a system developed by G. F. Barney and W. A. Smalley in the 1950s (see Heimbach 1979: xi–xvi for its history). In the Barney/Smalley system, doubled vowels represent nasal sounds. Final consonant letters indicate the tone of the word, and are not pronounced.

The Hmong dialect groups represented in the United States are the White Hmong (*Hmoob Dawb*), who are more numerous, and the Blue-Green Hmong (*Moob Ntsuab*). *Ntsuab* literally means green, or blue-green, but the *Moob Ntsuab* of Seattle prefer the term Blue, which they link with the indigo-dyed clothes that differentiated them in Laos from the White Hmong, who wore white festival skirts. Blue Hmong dialect has fewer initial aspirations (thus *Moob* instead of *Hmoob*) and more nasals (thus *Vang* instead of *Va*). Many vowels follow shifts in pronunciation, so that, for instance *-ia* in White Hmong is pronounced *-a* in Blue Hmong (thus *kuv has tas* instead of *kuv hais tias*). Most of my subjects were Blue Hmong, but a few were White Hmong, and most writing about the Hmong, including the best dictionary available, refers to White Hmong dialect.

In this book, I did not want to convert Blue Hmong into White Hmong, but I wanted to avoid different spellings for the same word from different speakers. Spoken Hmong of either dialect is not easily converted to written form. The seven tones, or pitches, are especially tricky, as a word in a sentence can change its tone depending on the neighboring words. There were many occasions when my best informants stumbled over the spelling of Hmong words. For these reasons, I decided to give Hmong spellings in this book only occasionally (for instance, the nonsense verses in chapter 6). I have usually written the Hmong words as an English speaker would pronounce them, often omitting the Hmong version. It is not necessary here to take a stand between the names *Tsuj* and *Tsus*; I called him Chue.

Though I risk offending some readers, others may even be relieved to find *Nrwg* spelled True.

HMONG NAMES

Almost all Hmong names used in this book are pseudonyms. Exceptions are those who wanted their real names used, especially if their work had been published earlier. Hmong divide themselves into about twenty divisions based on an idea of descent from a common ancestor. These divisions, called clans in English, regulate marriage (a Hmong may not marry some-one with the same clan name) and direct generosity (a clan member is a relative, no matter how distant). Clan names seem not to have been used in ordinary conversation among Hmong in Southeast Asia. Using Hmong practice in Thailand, Tapp (1988) generally separates the clan name from given names (e.g. Suav Yeeb of the Vaj clan), as does Geddes (1976). In America, however, clan names have been pressed into service as last names. This is an innovation in naming, which may explain some in-consistencies. American Hmong names may be arranged clan name first in the Chinese style, as in Dr. *Yang* Dao, or given names first and clan name last, as in Dr. Gary Yia *Lee*. Many of the Hmong in Seattle referred to themselves by their clan name first, for instance *Kue* Koua, but others gave me their clan name last, for instance May *Xiong*. Some switched their clan name from first to last after a few years. One told me that American military personnel had always referred to him clan name first, so that was how he thought Americans did it. In this book I have followed whichever name style my subjects used in conversation with me. For more on Hmong names, see note 2, chapter 1.

CHANGING LIVES
OF
REFUGEE HMONG WOMEN

1

DISCOVERING THE HMONG

The ad said, "Volunteers needed to teach English to Southeast Asian women." It was September 1980, and I was out of school, working nights, so I joined the Indochinese Women's Project,[1] imagining a daytime task both humane and interesting. The project met in a big square auditorium of pale blue concrete block that was also used as a basketball court. The thirty-five Hmong and Mien women who were students in the Indochinese Women's Project were very good-natured and friendly to the six American volunteer teachers. But their behavior was unexpected: they blew their noses in the drinking fountain or wandered away during lessons. Some were intent on learning English, but others approached the classes like play, as if formal school were foreign to them. The subject was "Survival English": letters and numbers, and beginning English grammar and pronunciation, put into practice by memorizing address and phone number, figuring out packages in the grocery store, and getting prescriptions filled on field trips to the pharmacy. These were useful skills, but often the older women sat idly, and always the chatter and screams of little children interfered with the students' concentration.

My class of eleven women was entirely ignorant of English. One day the subject was the difference between singular and plural—which is formed in Hmong and Mien by a helping word such as a number before the noun, in contrast to the English use of -s or -es. It was easier for the class to hear and say the difference between "woman" and "women" ("woo-ma" and "wih-ma" to them) than between "tree" and "trees" (which they heard as "tree" and "tree"). We worked using chairs, tables, hands, eyes, pencils, and pennies.

Using pennies got us off the subject. I discovered they did not understand money and could not add or subtract. For an hour and a half we added and subtracted numbers up to ten, using pennies, nickels, and dimes. They learned that five pennies equal a nickel and ten equal a dime. Some students learned how to use the plural as attached to these coins. Incidentally they learned that our money system is based on tens, matching the number of fingers and toes.

Later I learned that in rural Laos most women didn't handle money. They engaged in gift exchange, and only men traded with cash. But at the

3

time I was surprised at this hole in their information. They were fascinated by this new concept, and quick to learn it. Women who after dozens of repetitions could not turn a statement into a question could whip pennies from pile to pile with hardly any errors. I realized that my mind works through abstractions, molded by years of schooling, while theirs, I thought, were literal, shaped by the actual material world and their experience of it. The best way to teach them would be to tie every concept to something real that could be touched, and to slip abstract ideas like plurality in sideways.

They did not want to end the class. Mai Chia[2] held up a penny. "Dolla?" she said. "One, two, tree dolla? One and fo dolla, fi dolla?" "Yes!" I said. She smiled brightly and nodded with vigor. I hugged her and everybody laughed.

"Fahmah," said Mai Chia, pointing to herself. "Fahmah." She led me by the arm over to the wall and tapped it meaningfully. "Fahmah," she said again. She was, she seemed to be saying, a farmer surrounded by concrete.

It was this particular sequence of events that led me to wonder how the Hmong would adapt to the dominant American society that suddenly surrounded them. They could not continue many of the activities that had comprised daily life in Laos. Like other refugees and most immigrants, they lost their former economic and living arrangements. They found themselves without many of the daily habits and trappings of identity they had taken for granted, that had supported their view of themselves and of reality. No longer farmers, they not only no longer had access to fresh foods, they had lost the sense of self-reliance that came from growing their own rice. Living in apartments built to "foreign" (American) standards made it harder to place the spirit altar opposite the front door, harder to accommodate extended families. Riding American buses and looking for American jobs, they suddenly found Hmong clothes conspicuous, and substituted store-bought clothes for those made by the Hmong women. Since the sense of social identity is affirmed in interaction with the social environment, such radical environmental changes can call self-identity into question.

What is the best way to think about these changes, which appear inevitable and necessary to newcomers' survival? Can the experiences of these particular refugees help improve theories of social change and adaptation? Should policy-makers strive to ameliorate the pain of change for newcomers by programs of retraining or temporary grants, or should they demand that the newcomers fit themselves as well as they can into what they find? Which tactic will produce in the long run better citizens? Should resettlement workers try to speed up or to slow down the impact of the new environment on refugee households? Will former refugees look back with regret at their decision to resettle here? Will refugee children, grown up, understand or care about the challenges their parents faced in trying to navigate the disjunctions between their old and new lives?

Mai Chia tapping the concrete wall exemplifies these questions. Here are disoriented people trying to make over their lives in a bizarre place whose rules and possibilities are locked away in English, which they cannot speak. They are in cities, in a country where land costs money, which they cannot get. A garden, I thought, might help them feel more comfortable.

The P-Patch program[3] in Seattle has converted some park land to gardens that people can rent. I approached Ly Chue Kue, the interpreter for the Indochinese Women's Project about the idea. A vigorous and self-important young man, he had only recently arrived in the United States with his family, joining his uncle Koua Kue. Ly Chue was bossy to the refugee women, but alert and slightly hesitant with Americans, and seemed to be trying hard to get his bearings. In addition to interpreting for this project, he was taking night classes in accounting, which he found very difficult. I outlined the P-Patch program, saying I thought the refugees might like to garden.

"Yes," he said after thinking about it, "You can help us with that. If my uncle says OK."

That seemed curious to me, but I went along with him in the winter evening to Koua Kue's drab rented duplex in a south Seattle housing project. Koua Kue's wife, Yang My, gave me lukewarm instant coffee laced with sugar and I outlined what I had in mind. She was eager to get the gardens going, but he seemed to think this was a very small project indeed. There was something odd—still and watchful—about this short, plump, self-contained man. He turned his head away and slid his eyes sideways to gaze at me in a calculating way from the corner of his eye. Filled with good will, I offered to help families sign up for the program. At last he smiled. He would let me do it, he said. I thought his phrasing was peculiar.

At 7 o'clock on a wet March night I started up the sidewalk into a complex of old apartment buildings surrounded by retaining walls of huge unmortared black rocks, parked cars, slick asphalt paving, small discouraged trees, and packed earth courtyards. A teen-ager carrying a baby on his back in a black-and-red embroidered baby carrier let me into Ly Chue's apartment and led me down the ten foot entry hall. This boy, Ly Chue's cousin, wore a white shirt, vest, and suit pants, and looked very elegant. Ly Chue gave me a Sprite,™ asked me to sit at the Formica™-topped table at the end of the hallway, and sat down himself, all smiles, concentrating on me.

In the living room, chairs and couches formed an L opposite a television sitting on a pile of boxes and chairs. A yellow landscape from a magazine hung on the stained wall above the couch where Ly Chue's mother sat, skinny and bent, with an old wool scarf over her hair, wearing three mismatched print polyester blouses one over the other. Her hand was done up in a rag. Ly Chue said it had been broken but was mending. They had not gone to a doctor. Ly Chue's wife, a small slouching young woman in a shabby dress, took the swaddled baby off the cousin's back and began bouncing her ungently up and down.

The family paid some attention to the game show on the television, but they easily turned to other things. In the tiny kitchen, Ly Chue's young sister was washing dishes. The toddler peed on the kitchen floor, then walked through it. Much later the cousin brought a mop and wiped it up.

Only Ly Chue and his cousin spoke enough English to converse. The cousin was in junior high school, liked shop best, and was dressed up for his school picture. He didn't know how long he had been in the United States; I decided he had not understood my question. I said I'd brought the applications. I had just learned that they should be turned in the very next day, so I hoped people could come over to sign them. We ourselves could fill them in.

"Yes," said Ly Chue. "Who are the people?"

"I thought you knew," I said. So he called Koua Kue, got a list of twelve names, then sat down with his clipboard and began to call them. Then we filled in all the names on the forms. Time passed.

"Is there some reason people are not coming?" I asked at last.

"Well, some don't have a phone, and so I sent some others to talk to them," said Ly Chue. More time passed. Ly Chue called around again. One family was making a cassette tape to send to Thailand and didn't want to come to Ly Chue's. Then it turned out nobody knew anything about the gardening project. The list was possible, not committed, participants.

I asked if anybody was really interested. "Well, I think so," said Ly Chue, "but some say the space is too small, and some say it is too far to go." Ly Chue himself was interested, but what with being in school and working and spending his evenings helping others fill in forms, he had no time, and his wife was busy with the children, who couldn't go outside because of the cold. They never went out. And his sister was in school, and his mother had broken her hand, so his family could not garden.

One by one, small thin men drifted in and sat down or stood around the table. They ranged in age from about twenty-five to about fifty, and most of them were grimly dour and silent. Each wore a dark jacket, a light shirt, and dark trousers. As they came in Ly Chue cracked jokes and had them sign the forms. Eventually nine men signed. A few women came in, too, one loud and merry, the others very retiring, and they all immediately moved into the background with their babies, behind the men, so I could not see them.

It seemed clear that they had no idea what they had signed. I tried to explain the gardening program, telling them about the cost for water, fertilizer, and plowing. I was unable to explain the time they were supposed to spend benefiting the P-Patch program, because they couldn't figure out the program itself. Ly Chue was under the impression that the land belonged to some man who was collecting money for profit. He said they didn't like the local tools and wanted short-handled, heavier hoes. They didn't have much seed. I was about to discuss enriching the soil when the ambience of the room hit me: hard, cold, and emotionally flat. They were not exactly sullen, but conservative, tradition-bound, earth-bound, stolid, and heavy, and seemed to be thinking: "You are a city woman, and we are men, and farmers. You can tell us nothing."

I began to realize how different their values were from mine. Every move we made seemed to be governed by very different assumptions about society and reality itself. Since I had nothing else to say, I said good-night, but nobody noticed. I walked to the door and let myself out, and nobody said good-bye, not even Ly Chue.

Such a leavetaking alarmed me. I didn't think there was any hostility, and I had noticed other people coming and going without ceremony. But I felt entirely dismissed. It was as if suddenly I were no longer there, so I might as well leave. I was bothered, too, because the women stayed invisible behind the men, expressing no opinions, even though Ly Chue had said they would be the ones working in the gardens. In the face of my discomfort I thought, "Either I can drop this, or I can learn more about these Hmong."

IDENTIFICATION OF THE RESEARCH TOPIC

How do Hmong fare in the new location? The Hmong, who brought their silverwork, traditional clothing, knives, and sometimes agricultural tools and seed with them to America, expected a land similar to the one they had left. They found, instead, a land whose people generally had little understanding of them and were often surprised (sometimes even dismayed) at how different Hmong social interactions and values seemed from their own. Although individual Americans may alter, American institutions and their representatives usually cannot or will not change significantly to accommodate refugees. Hmong refugees have generally been expected by Americans to learn how to fit into their new environment, and they themselves have anticipated changes in their lives, welcoming some while fearing or rejecting others.

Coming to America reduces the sense of life as a seamless whole for the Hmong. The dissonance between Hmong ideas of social order and American ideas has caused the Hmong to question specific cultural practices. The questioning stance of the Americans upon whom Hmong depend, a consciousness of having become materially incompetent overnight, a lack of the ingredients of ritual, causing an everpresent need for substitution, and many other factors have led the resettled Hmong in two directions at once: toward preserving the essence of their cultural life in spite of having to give up the exact form or surface that they remember, but also toward questioning and discarding particular cultural practices. Hmong cultural practice as a whole is being reconstructed in a new pattern.

The struggles of Hmong refugees to find a place in American society offer an excellent opportunity to study change, especially social changes: discernible shifts in interactions among Hmong that persisted and could be attributed to the influence of the new society suddenly all around them. I did not try directly to analyze internal feeling states, but looked instead for their manifestations in action. However, persistent new patterns of interaction indicated prior shifts in Hmong attitudes and feelings. Because refugees were attaching new meanings to things and events in their new environment, they began to act differently. New styles of behavior indicated that my Hmong subjects were beginning to interpret their environment in new ways, to believe in new explanations, to construct new meanings for their actions, whether they were consciously aware of doing so or not.

GENDER STUDY

A series of small observations led to my decision to record potential change in Hmong men's and women's attitudes toward gender roles. Here is one such event: In April 1982 I went to accompany my friends May and Xao to a doctor's appointment for their sick child. When I arrived at their apartment, May had gone ahead with the child while her husband, Xao, was waiting for me. I drove him to the clinic, part of a large and busy public health hospital in Seattle, where we had to park two blocks downhill. We got out of the car. He started walking, and I fell into step beside him. He walked faster. I increased my pace to keep up with him. Faster and faster he walked up the hill, with me panting beside him, until we were practically running.

Why is he going so fast? I wondered. Suddenly it struck me—he wanted to walk ahead of me. I began to slow down. He began to slow down. I slowed down further. He also slowed down further, keeping five paces ahead of me. Every few steps he turned his head slightly to make sure I was there behind him, and so at a leisurely pace we arrived at the hospital. All this happened without conversation.

This incident can be compared with the pattern of walking that Hmong men and women maintained in Southeast Asia. About Hmong in northern Thailand, Robert Cooper comments:

> A typical family met on a forest path will constitute a man in front with his gun, the man's horse, the man's wife and children. When approached from behind the woman will normally step aside and stop, allowing the men to join together in front. It is worth mentioning that the male receives no great benefits from this privilege. There is small chance of meeting bandits but a greater chance of treading on a snake. Where the path is overgrown the man will clear it. In the rainy season the first person collects the most leeches. [But] as in the agricultural cycle so in the order of walking: the man comes first. (Cooper 1984:137–38)

Resettled Hmong have brought this habit of walking from Southeast Asia to America. My assumption that Xao and I would walk together and his that he should precede me reproduced in movement two different cultural understandings of proper relations between men and women in social space.

Visible cues about Hmong social hierarchies such as where people stood in a room, posture and actions—for instance the women ducking their heads and avoiding eye contact—and the tasks women and men did led me early to think that the female is considered inferior in Hmong society. Other Americans would probably reach a similar conclusion from evidence such as the photograph of a young Hmong wife kneeling on the kitchen floor to make *zau ntsuab* (pickled greens, which are chopped and then salted), while her husband and father-in-law sit talking at the kitchen table (see photo section). The men seem relaxed and self-possessed; she is wiping away sweat trickling down the side of her face.

The photographer, Neil Menschel, had first met the family in Panat Nikhom transit camp outside Bangkok. Once the family had resettled in Wisconsin, he visited them and spent two days in their company. Menschel knew little of Hmong culture. His view of Hmong family life is based on his own American cultural understanding of what it means when family members act in certain ways. This image—the wife kneeling at work while the husband talks at leisure—struck him because it summarized his interpretation of the relative standing of men and women among Hmong he met (Menschel, telephone conversation June 1989). Menschel is male and uninfluenced by any anthropological study, yet our opinions of Hmong gender behavior were the same and would probably typify the ordinary American interpretation of Hmong gender relations.

Yet a number of Hmong have maintained to me that although men and women do indeed occupy different spheres and pursue different activities, both male and female spheres are essential: Neither can do without the other, and therefore they are at bottom equivalent. Not only are they equivalent, they belong together, as two halves of a single whole. The romantic ideal, expressed by the following story, is that a particular man and woman will find each other, because they are fated to be together.

The Orphan and the Chinese Princess

Once long ago there was a Chinese elder who lived in a beautiful house with a tiled roof. Under the eaves of this roof lived a pair of doves in the most perfect harmony. One day the husband dove said to his wife, "I am going to gather seeds for you, so wait here until I return." And he flew away. But while he was gone, he met some friends, and they played and drank until the middle of the night. The husband got so drunk he couldn't find his way home, and he slept in a ditch until morning. When he finally made it back to their nest, all rumpled and sick, his wife was furious. "Where have you been? Look at you! I have been waiting and worrying, and what have you been doing?" So they argued and fought, squabbling and hollering all up and down the roof of the Chinese house. Finally the old Chinese came outside and shouted up to them, "I can't stand your arguing! If you are making so much noise, you have to move away! Get out of here!"

So the doves flew off into the fields. In a beautiful meadow they made another nest, and soon their eggs hatched into little helpless babies. Once again they were perfectly happy, glad that they had moved away from the Chinese house. Lovingly they spoke to each other, unceasingly they cared for their babies. The husband dove said to his wife, "If any danger should come, we must stay right here by our nest to defend our babies." The wife agreed. But soon the farmers began burning the fields before planting. As the fire came closer and closer, the husband in panic flew up and away into the trees, while the wife stayed with her babies and was burned to a crisp.

Years later, the wife was reborn as a Chinese princess, while the husband was reborn as a poor orphan. The king's daughter was beautiful and accomplished, but she absolutely refused to get married, and would not even speak to any man. In despair, the king declared, "If anyone can make my daughter answer when he speaks to her, I will give him her hand in marriage!" Many princes and nobles came to try, but she would not say a word.

Finally the poor orphan heard about the offer, and he thought, "That king is very rich. I will go talk to the girl." Everybody was gathered in the king's hall, and the orphan began to tell a story. He said, "Once there was a pair of doves, who lived under the eaves of a tiled roof, but the wife argued and fought so much the old Chinese man told them to fly away. They made a nest in a field and had some babies. The wife said, "If any danger comes, we must stay right here and defend our babies," and the husband dove agreed. But when the farmers were burning the fields, the wife dove was frightened and flew away, while the husband stayed with the babies and was burned to a crisp." Angrily the Chinese princess cried, "You know that's not what happened!" (Folk tale retold orally by Ly Hang 1986)

"The Orphan and the Chinese Princess" is an elaborate joke, but it also has a moral. This husband and wife belong together. Over time, through any vicissitudes, even beyond death into their subsequent lives, their fate is bound together. The husband may be irreverent and careless; the wife may be angry and cold. Still they will end up together. The husband will come out on top: While she is determined and righteous, he knows her character and can fool her. He is a trickster, and she cannot avoid his trickery. This must be all right, because they are drawn together by the essence of their own natures. Thus it is between men and women, in the world of this Hmong folk story.

Perhaps we must, as Cooper does in the passage quoted above, separate the fact that men precede women from any notion that male superiority is being expressed. The man's position ahead of the woman need not be seen as a matter of advantage; it could be merely a habit, a way of getting past the question of who precedes whom without continuously having to decide the matter. Hmong men, in particular, in speaking with me about gender, say over and over that there is no advantage to being a man, because men are burdened with responsibilities that often limit their choices and sometimes trap them in prescribed relationships they might prefer to avoid.

However, this disjunction between American and Hmong interpretations of appropriate behavior for men and for women indicated that gender relations among the Hmong would become problematic in an American setting, since Americans would not hesitate to assign their own cultural values to Hmong social behavior. Would Hmong men and women feel misunderstood? Would they absorb American ideas about gender, and if so which ideas would they accept? Would they question their own behavior in the light of these new hybrid ideas? Would Hmong women embrace American gender ideas and the men reject them—or vice versa? Would a gap in gender concept develop between elite and ordinary Hmong? Would a generation gap appear? And how could I best go about studying gender among Hmong in America?

The study of gender begins with describing how tasks and skills, attitudes, responsibilities, powers, and material possessions are distributed among males and females in a social group, and finding out the symbolic or prestige values assigned to them. From these a model can be constructed of social interactions in terms of gender.

Understanding the meanings and values assigned to the categories *men* and *women* helps to explain how the entire social grouping is organized.[4] The economic system, family and household organization, educational practices, political relations, and the rest of social life are not independent systems coexisting to form a larger entity called a society. Social relations are held together and made meaningful by underlying cultural concepts— ideas about right and wrong, human nature, or the nature of religious experiences. Gender beliefs are one of these. While they can often be stated verbally and succinctly, like the others, they operate through symbolic expressions. Symbols that carry gender meanings may be mundane (skirts vs. pants) or esoteric (the Virgo symbol as feminine icon); behavioral (ways of walking, smiling, speaking); referential ("pink collar" for women-dominated jobs); complementary (soft/hard, weakness/strength); or very complex, reminiscent and associational, as with the symbols surrounding motherhood. Gender concepts, like other cultural convictions, organize and give meaning to daily experience. As an explanatory principle for organizing social interaction, gender beliefs are as basic as ideas about ethical behavior.

Ideas about gender shape life by providing models for behavior. By watching how men and women act, even if they do not make explicit statements, we can begin to understand their ideas. Gender concepts express themselves most often in action, whether symbolic or goal-directed. Although people do make verbal statements about ideal gender relations independent of context or specific events, statements about gender are more frequent, more clear, more complex, and more convincing, when acted out. In fact, pronouncements about gender are much rarer in daily life than actions that presuppose unstated gender assumptions. Gender analysis is a way to see segments of action, whether in domestic life, politics, or another realm of social behavior, as expressing the symbols that group members use to explain life experiences to themselves.[5] Hmong express gender ideas in explicit statements of gender ideals, in myths and stories, in household economic relations, in important rituals, and in ceremonies of social life, among other ways.

Once I had begun to know Hmong families, I decided that the best way to look at change in gender concepts would be to track household inter-actions, especially those regarding income and decisions about money. I assumed that economic relations within households would change quickly as family members became part of the larger economy. In urban America, even subsistence depends on having money. While there were urbanized Hmong in Laos who depended on a money income—and in a few such families women are reported to have worked for money—the great ma-jority of Hmong in Laos were subsistence farmers. For them, subsistence production was essentially outside the money economy until war forced them from their farms. The trading economy was essentially in the hands of men. So in America, as Hmong women began working, going to school, and shopping, it seemed likely that their roles in the household economy would change first, and that statements and beliefs regarding gender would follow.

Therefore, in this inquiry into changing gender ideology, I looked first at women's economic lives, comparing them with women's economic lives in Laos. When this yielded only partial answers, as will be seen, I expanded the study.

A FEW CAVEATS

I present the gender roles of Hmong women in Laos as part of a functional and ritual whole, a necessary complement to men's roles, discussing little of Hmong history, politics, or religion except as these impinge directly on gender relations. My analysis assumes that change is imposed upon the Hmong from outside. Of course, Hmong society is not necessarily trans-formed only from external pressure, but for resettled refugees the slower, more subtle changes springing from the workings of internal cultural logic have been overwhelmed by external circumstance. This study compares the profoundly altered present with what is seen as a relatively static past. This view of the past comes partly from my having studied the Hmong in the United States without firsthand study in Laos against which to compare my observations. I have had to depend on reports in the form of life histories and other statements that I gathered from Hmong women and men, and on research published by writers working in Southeast Asia within the West-ern intellectual tradition. Only a few of these focus on Hmong in Laos, notably Lemoine (1972); the majority concern Hmong in Thailand, and the older material describes Hmong mainly in northern Vietnam. There is also a body of research on the Hmong (or Miao) in southern China which lies outside this study.

Research on Hmong in Thailand or Vietnam is usually treated here as if it described Lao Hmong, as far as the culture of household and family are concerned. Gary Yia Lee (1981) adopts a similar stance. Born a Hmong in Laos, he did his research in Thailand, where he does not hesitate to consider the social structure as representing Hmong in general. The wartime experiences suffered by Hmong in Laos (but not in Thailand) mean that this method has clear limitations when seeking to describe the background of Lao refugee Hmong by looking at research on Thai Hmong.

Although I concentrate on the lives of Hmong women, all the works published about the Hmong in Southeast Asia so far have been written by men, who have had little access to the conversation of Hmong women, even though they have sometimes been interested in it. Hugo Bernatzik (1970) had access to his wife's notes, which he freely consulted for his work on Hmong in northern Thailand, and Lemoine, working in Sayaboury in northwest Laos, presents an empathetic view of women's lives based on incidents that he witnessed. Lee, being Hmong, might be expected to have an inside line on Hmong women's ideas of themselves, but as they are so reticent around men—including Lee—this is not the case (Lee, personal communication: 1986). Cooper has emphasized the structural position of Hmong women, first in his initiation of a controversy about the importance of fathers-in-law to sons-in-law (Cooper 1979) and then in his analysis of the economic impact of the opium trade on Hmong families in Thailand (Cooper 1984).

These works contain some views collected directly from Hmong women, but they hardly depend on them. As representations of the lives of Hmong women in Southeast Asia, they present an external view of women's place in Hmong society rather than conveying the women's own perceptions of their experiences. Other research, such as Geddes's important book (1976), that of his student Chindarsi (1976), work by missionaries (e.g. Barney 1957), and by political historians (e.g. McCoy 1970), may mention women in passing, but their focus is clearly elsewhere—politics, economic adaptation, religion.

The life histories I collected from Hmong women in Seattle, Washington, and Stockton, California,[6] and the anecdotes about women's lives in Laos that have been told to me by various Hmong women, convey a particularistic sense of individual women's lives in Laos. But while these life-history accounts are representations of experience, there remains a sense of distance in the gender model I propose for Hmong in Laos. I have tried to bridge this distance in chapter 2 by looking at Hmong origin myths and folk tales.

My Hmong subjects usually turned each of my visits into a lesson, using me as a representative of American society who could help them succeed in the terms demanded by the new environment. As a native informant to the refugees, I could not simply be an observer, and so I could not avoid altering the very topic I studied.

In the usual sort of field work, with the anthropologist going as an outsider to a society in place, the task is to find out what is involved in a normal life, the codes and rules that produce a sense of wholeness and normality to the members of a group, and the environmental factors that impinge upon them. In the field, one is a visitor, a transient, an unnecessary person. Whether befriended or ignored, the field-worker begins as an outsider to the residents, who are at home and have an ongoing life.

Working among refugees is entirely opposite, a mirror reversal of this situation. Here the person with stable cultural knowledge, the person who is at home and knows the environment, is the field-worker. The marginal people are the incoming refugees, who feel unnecessary and transient, yet who must somehow fit into the new location.

Refugees face singular problems. They want to establish or reestablish ties with one another on the basis of their old cultural and social patterns, which have fragmented during flight. At the same time, they need to figure out the socioeconomy of the new location and find a way to fit themselves in. Since American society is very different from Hmong society, Hmong refugees must also discover the unexpected ways that they conflict with the host culture, and then work their way through legal and social landmines, deciding what of their foreign behaviors to conceal, what to pursue in disregard of American attitudes, and what to discard. They worry very much about how to remain Hmong.

They exist in a state of greater or lesser confusion and respond to the pain of confusion in various ways. Some treat the outside world as crazy. Many refugees find teachers wherever they can. Field-workers, who may have an entirely different agenda, are pressed into the roles of teacher, facilitator, intermediary, and protector. Thus the price of doing research among refugees is to act in a helping capacity. During my five years of active research and recording among Hmong refugees, I spent many hundreds of hours teaching and solving problems. It was satisfying volunteer work, and at the same time opened many situations of cultural confrontation to my view. But to take an active part made me an essential participant in the very subject of study. Difficult questions arose. How might the fear that I would stop helping them affect their efforts to present themselves to me?

What attitudes and behaviors were people concealing because it had be-come important that I like them? When I filled out insurance claims, when I found the head of the household a job, when I was interested in what they served for dinner, when I described with oranges how the earth goes around the sun (to explain why they had arrived in the United States the same day they left Thailand, despite spending a night on the plane), what unstated messages were they getting? If I had not been there, would they have gotten these messages anyway?

Another concern was that my particular attributes probably affected how the Hmong reported gender beliefs to me. I am divorced and childless, a situation that arouses among Hmong a suspicion that there is something wrong with me. I said I was not seeking to change my condition, and this made me seem odd, or perhaps untruthful, to people for whom marriage was a natural condition of maturity, and children the only solace of age. I worried that some Hmong would see me as unpredictable, not really to be trusted, too alien. My job became, in part, to make myself seem ordinary and understandable. I confided to my woman friends that I would have liked children, but sterility had led to my divorce; this confidence con-firmed their opinion that something was wrong with me, but it was not my fault, and excused in Hmong terms my divorce and continuing single-ness. I began to learn the Hmong language, let my friends pick my agenda with them, and emulated details of Hmong behavior as closely as I could. I praised those aspects of Hmong culture that I truly admire, such as the kindness with which they generally treat one another.

But my Hmong friends remained uncertain about my childlessness. Furthermore, I was "not patient," and I was "too strong," behaviors unsuit-able to women. They did not cease to view my own expression of gender as problematic. Toward the end of my research period, a Hmong man learned from a mutual friend that I had started to see a boyfriend. They were talk-ing by telephone. She told me he laughed so hard he dropped the receiver. "Now she'll see," he said, "what it's like to be a woman." Behind his state-ment stands the Hmong conviction that one can only be a woman when in union with a man. The converse is also true. Because Hmong men and women must join together in order to realize their true nature, in this they are equal.

PROCEDURE OF THE RESEARCH

The time period covered by my work is almost eight years, but I did not pursue research with equal intensity all that time. From 1980 through 1983 I was coming to know individual families and exploring the structure of the Seattle Hmong community. I developed deep and lasting relationships with two extended families composed of seven nuclear families, and an acquaintance with a number of others. Throughout this period I kept careful notes on nearly every contact with all these families, describing events, feelings, dress, menus, childcare, complaints, accidents, tax returns, and anything else I could think of. From 1982 to 1985 I participated in Hmong class, an informal weekly gathering of up to six Americans who met with Nhia Doua Hang to study Hmong language and culture.

This was a period of great volunteer activity in Seattle to benefit Southeast Asian refugees. I made friends with Americans who were interested in Hmong and in refugee problems. Along with my cohort of "Hmongees" I concentrated on collecting written materials on Hmong history and experience in the United States and began to pick among the flood of programmatic research on refugees. In the winter of 1981–82 I was a founding board member of the Indochinese Farm Project, and I took an active role in farm work and selling produce, especially during 1982 and 1983.[7] In 1983–84 I participated in the Auxiliary to Hmong Artwork Association. This marketing organization had the appearance of a cooperative, but in fact, membership was determined by relation to the leader, whose personality was integral to the structure of the group. Hmong Artwork fell apart when the leader and most of the members moved away (see chapter 7). Besides these two efforts, I also intermittently attended the King County Refugee Forum.[8]

In the fall of 1983, the Indochina Studies Program of the Joint SSRC/ACLS Committee on Southeast Asia announced a plan to begin funding research projects "to construct accounts of the social and political traditions and institutions, as well as the lives of particular individuals, in the recent history of Vietnam, Cambodia and Laos." The projects specifically excluded research into the North American experience of Indochinese refugees, but it still seemed an opportunity to increase my understanding of Hmong culture. With three other researchers, I proposed to construct a historical picture of the lives of a number of Hmong women from their own perspective, emphasizing activities and concerns that they themselves consider to have been most important to them in Laos, and involving textile design, herbal healing, songs and stories, and the transmission of knowledge among women. I completed life-history interviews of seven women, and an abbreviated family-tree interview of an eighth, and also collected information about weddings and funerals, five hours of stories, several tapes of original songs, and some jokes.[9]

In this book, almost all the direct quotes from Hmong women about life in Laos come from these interviews. My understanding of their experiences was deepened and extended by the project, but I came to realize, through this project and my volunteer work with families and organizations, that economic adaptation had less influence over gender concepts than I had expected. This unexpected outcome impelled me into further study of cultural performance, as more indicative of shifts in underlying cultural convictions.

2

HMONG SOCIETY IN LAOS

Northern Laos was very rural well into this century, with only a few sizeable towns, such as Sayaboury, Luang Prabang, Phuong Saly, and Sam Neua (see figure 1). It is an area in which ethnicity roughly follows landscape and thus ecological adaptation. Ethnic Lao cultivate wet rice in the flat lowlands, while various groupings of tribal people live in the hilly hinterlands where they grow upland dry rice and a variety of vegetable crops using swiddening (slash-and-burn) techniques. The highest mountains most removed from the reach of the Lao state were originally the preferred location for Hmong immigrants, who came from southern China and from Vietnam in the late nineteenth century to pioneer those areas.

How many Hmong lived in Laos before the Second Indochina War[1] is open to guess. Dr. Yang Dao, a Hmong scholar from Laos, estimates that there were 300,000 Hmong in Laos by 1960 (1976: 24). Yang made a survey of 341 Hmong families, including 3,195 people, or an average of 9.4 members per family; he thus surveyed about one percent of the Hmong population in Laos—an amazing feat considering the wartime conditions. Half the Hmong surveyed by Yang were under fifteen years old. The age pyramid he provides, redrawn in figure 2, rises from a wide base in the 0-4 year category, with about 10 percent more male than female children surviving to age twenty. Between twenty and fifty, the adult male population falls significantly below the female, owing to the war, and then evens out past fifty (Yang 1976: 25).

Photographs of northern Laos give an impression of vast stretches of tree-covered hills and valleys patched with clear-cut fields. This jungle is not tropical rain forest. At the high elevations where the Hmong live (above 1,000 meters), it contains not only teak, bamboo, and rattan, but also chestnut, oak, pine, and wild fruit trees. Rainfall in Laos averages 1.6 meters per year; in the mountains this often takes the form of persistent drizzle, according to Yang (1976: 16). Swidden farmers other than Hmong live in Laos, but at lower elevations, and most sources present the Hmong as splendidly isolated in their mountains.

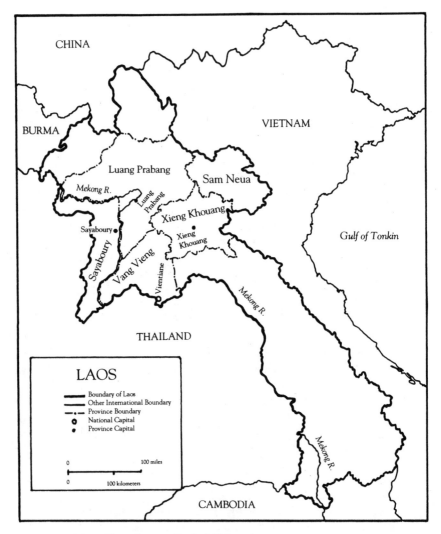

FIGURE 1. Map of Laos (*source:* Dr. Joel Halpern)

HMONG DAILY LIFE IN SOUTHEAST ASIA

Prior to the Second Indochina War and its dislocations, life for the Hmong in Laos was almost exclusively rural and agricultural, with virtually all Hmong scattered in small hamlets high in the hills.[2] Nearly self-sufficient in subsistence production, they grew upland rice, corn, squash, cucum-

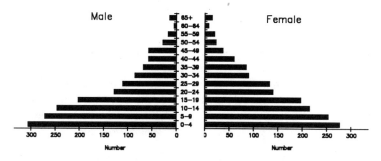

FIGURE 2. Age pyramid of Hmong in Laos, 1972 (*source:* Yang 1976:25)

bers, mustard, and poppies, and raised pigs, chickens, horses, and cattle. According to Lemoine:

> Except for salt, a village produces almost everything that is necessary for daily consumption. It can exist through economic self-sufficiency, however it is sometimes easier to buy that which it can produce itself, but at the price of much work. This is the case with agricultural tools [and] fabric. Another result of prolonged contact with more sophisticated people, Chinese and Thai, has been the borrowing of some things that the Hmong do not know how to make but use constantly: [such as] utensils for cooking and tableware, and more recently small petrol lamps. . . . Hmong have also discovered flashlights [which need] batteries . . . mirrors, combs, [and] Japanese "Zori" sandals. (Lemoine 1972: 138; my translation)

The major cash crop of the Hmong was opium, packed out by horse and traded for silver; most contacts with non-Hmong occurred through trade. The rich silver jewelry for which the Hmong are noted, made from French Indochinese piastres, was one benefit of this trade.

Hmong social organization is built on the patrilineal family. There are about twenty named clans, whose main functions are to regulate marriage by prohibiting unions within the clan and to regulate social reciprocity by prescribing generosity between clan members. Members of a clan are felt to be related to each other more closely than to non-clan members, even when, as often happens, a specific blood tie cannot be traced. In her life history, Mrs. C. Ly says:

> Money was important in some ways in my country, and in other ways, it wasn't important at all. For instance, if I have no rice for my family, I can go to you and you will say, "OK, just come and pick some up!" People just give a couple of bags, a couple hundred pounds, if you need it.

We say, "This time they come to me, and I give it to them. Next time I might have to come to them, and they will give to me." We just trade back and forth like that. If I have something to give, and you have nothing, I don't mind. It doesn't matter if you can give it back or not.

This is not just within the [immediate] family. Our culture is very open. Let's put it this way. Suppose I have a cousin on my husband's side. Like, my children have cousins on my side and on my husband's side. Many cousins, more and more distant. We do the same way for all these cousins, just give food if they need it.[3]

The last name is very important as far as helping is concerned. Like, my mother is a Yang, and my father is a Moua. My husband's mother is also a Yang, but our two mothers never knew each other before my husband and I got married. There are thousands and thousands of Yangs, and our two mothers are not relatives. But the last name Yang is very important, for when they do meet each other, they become just like cousins. That's what we say.

This helps the girls, too. For instance, when I met my husband, he had to be careful of me when I was single,[4] because he knew if he wasn't he would meet some Moua people, the same age as himself, as important as himself, and then if he had done something bad, he would have them to deal with. Things like that.

For instance, in our country, you live in the north and I live in the south, and you come to my area, and we have the same last name. Even if we didn't know each other before, you can come to me and say, "Well, we don't have this or that, we are so poor in these things this year, we don't know what to do. Do you have anything you can give us?" Then we will just give it to you. But what I am talking about is things you get from the farm, it's really food that I'm talking about. People didn't ask for things that you have to buy with money.

Hmong villages in Laos were often located on a ridge crest not too far from a watercourse. House sites were determined by the relative flatness of the ground, by nearness to kin, and by divining the attitude of spirits toward the luckiness of the site. Households tended to cluster together according to common descent in the male line, or by clan group for reasons of political influence. But because Hmong agriculture was not based on land passed from generation to generation but on land worked to exhaustion and then abandoned for freshly cleared land, households and indeed whole villages moved from time to time.

Hmong, according to Geddes, regarded land speculatively, as an exploitable resource. Each family constantly sought better crop land, meaning that the most vigorous families preferred to move as soon as yields fell below optimum, leaving their half-used fields for poorer families to take up. The search for new farm land was not the only reason for migrating. Families also moved if they experienced serious bad luck, unusual hardship, or disease. Then the house site might be thought unlucky, subject to invasion by spirits or ghosts. The afflicted family might build another house nearby, but they might move right out of the village, looking for a more propitious location. Thus even a village in its prime experienced some in-and-out-migration, with kinship connections and various other considerations influencing the exact destination of particular families.

These moves were carefully orchestrated. Household heads would scout an area, looking for gentle slopes with fertile soil appropriate for corn, for rice, or for poppies. If enough land could be found within a few hours' walk of home, the family cleared fields but stayed under the same roof, working both new and old fields. Gradually they came to depend on the new fields, building a field hut at the new site and staying there longer and longer at a stretch, moving more belongings, building a new house, and finally leaving the old house behind.

My subjects' accounts of their childhood include many migrations. Here is one such description, a move in Xieng Khouang province in about 1955.

> I was born in Xieng Khouang Province, in a village called Pha Lai. . . . In that village there were ten or eleven houses. When I was not too big, my parents moved from Pha Lai to Tang Koeui. . . . Tang Koeui was not very far from Pha Lai. If we got up very early, we could walk from Pha Lai to Tang Koeui in time for breakfast. So it was not too far.
>
> The reason my family moved to Tang Koeui was that people had been living at Pha Lai for many years, and the soil was not very good any more. The fields close to Pha Lai did not grow good crops, so every new field had to be farther and farther from home. That means my parents had to walk a long way every day out to the fields and back home. My father had found good land for a big field over at Tang Koeui, so he wanted to move to cut down the time spent walking back and forth.
>
> Tang Koeui was smaller than Pha Lai, with only six or seven households, and there was a lot of good land nearby. My family had a horse that carried some of our things, and we carried a lot on our backs. The path between was very small and narrow, just enough for one person at a time to walk on, and we went up and over a high hill that was between Pha Lai and Tang Koeui. All around there, all trees. Hills, mountains, big hills, small hills, and trees.
>
> It was not difficult to move to Tang Koeui because my father's cousin [my *txiv neeg*] had already moved there, and we just followed his family. He was older than my father, and was the son of my father's father's brother. We

moved into his household and stayed there for one month until we had our own house to live in.[5]

Entire villages could migrate together in this manner. But perhaps not enough fertile lands could be found close together, or disagreement within the existing village might make families want to separate. Then a family's best tactic was to move in with a close relative already living in an area with available land and share the household until new fields could be brought under cultivation and a new house built. Should no relatives be available to live with, a household head would have to apply to some village head for permission to join the village and would have to build a new house before moving.

LIVING IN HOUSEHOLDS

Houses among the Hmong in Southeast Asia essentially followed a single pattern. Despite minor dialect-group differences (e.g., White Hmong built with two doors while Blue Hmong only provided one), the following description by Mee Yang holds for most Hmong homes in rural Laos, as described by my informants from Xieng Khouang, Vang Vieng, and Sayaboury provinces (see figure 3):

> The house that we had in Tang Koeui was like other Hmong houses, and just like the house of my father's cousin. It was pretty good sized, perhaps 25 by 40 feet. The way my father and mother built this house, was that they found everything, all the wood and everything else they needed for the posts and the walls and the roof, and when they had everything, when they were ready to construct it, then everybody came to help them. In just only one day, they finished the basic structure of the house. Then whatever was left to do, my mother and father just did themselves later.
>
> At each of the four corners they had big trees going up, and another one in the middle. Smaller logs went across between them to make the outline of the peaked roof. The post in the center was taller than the others. It was very tall and high. Hmong houses are different from houses in [the United States]. They have no windows, but the gables are open to let in the light and to let out the smoke. In our country it's never very hot and never very cold, so it didn't matter that the gables were open. The roof was made of wood.
>
> Our house in Tang Koeui had three rooms. The wooden entry door, just tall enough for someone to come in, located in the middle of the long wall, opened into the main room. To the left of the door were the two bedrooms, one for my mother and father, one for the children.

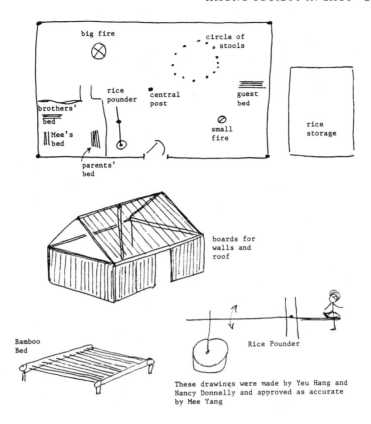

FIGURE 3. The house of Mee Yang's parents in Laos (*source*: Mee Yang)

Also in the main room we had a bed for someone to sleep if they came to visit. My family slept in the bedrooms, where we had a bed for my parents, a bed for my brothers, and a bed for me. All the Yang families with the same grandfather had the same arrangement inside their houses. We can't do that here in America—the apartments are too different! Our beds had short wooden legs and two long pieces of wood at the sides, and then large pieces of bamboo set between the sides to form the body of the bed. . . .

Next to the bedroom wall by the door was the rice pounder. It was used for taking off the brown shell and leaving only the white part of the rice. The rice pounder [*cug tuaj rau noj,* lit.? beat rice to eat] was about nine feet long. The woman would stand at one end. She would push her foot down on [the end of] a heavy wooden bar. This bar was balanced at the middle of the framework. By pushing her foot down she could lift the other end of the bar. The other end had a head like a big mallet. Under it was a strong wooden bowl to hold the rice. When the woman let her foot off the bar, the mallet would fall into the rice and the brown husks were scraped off by this pressure.

Usually we just cleaned enough rice for only one day, but then if some was left over, we put it in a sack to use the next day. For rice that we stored for the whole year, we had a little house, like a shed, close to the house. It's not too far, it's not too near. If it's very near the house, if there was a fire, it would be a big problem.

There were two [cooking] fires, one toward the back and one to the right of the door. The large fire in the back was for cooking the rice and cooking for the animals, and the other fire was for cooking meat and green vegetables for the people in the family. We would usually cook some corn or other food for the pigs and the chickens, and to steam the rice we used a great big shallow round pan, a wok. It was about four feet across.

For places to sit in our house, we used little stools that were woven out of bamboo. We had twenty or thirty[6] of them, of several different sizes, in a circle between the two fireplaces.

For dishes we used tin plates and tin soup spoons. Also we had sections of bamboo, split lengthwise from joint to joint, for the rice. This bamboo was not too big, not too small, and we put the rice inside and put it in the middle of the table for everybody to take some.

For the table we used a round tray made out of woven bamboo, about four feet across, and we put it on the floor and used it to put the food on. Then when we were done eating we could just clean off the tray and put it away out of the way.

All of these things we could make except for the tin plates and spoons. Those we bought in Xieng Khouang city. Also in Xieng Khouang we bought cloth. It took three days to get to Xieng Khouang. And then three more days to come back.

A Hmong household was organized around a married couple and their sons. Daughters married out. As the sons brought in wives, an extended family formed, consisting of the older couple, their unmarried children, and their married sons with their wives and children. Thus Hmong households included one or more nuclear families closely related through the men, sometimes with other relatives as dependents. Families were bound to each other by requirements for joint ancestor worship in the male line. Particularly close relationships between brothers and male cousins were strongly valued. These ritual and emotional ties tended to keep brothers within a single household, within which each nuclear family occupied a separate bedroom, for as long as their father was alive. After he died, sons were likely to split apart into separate households, and the cycle began again. The widowed mother usually lived with her youngest married son, and unmarried siblings lived with their married brothers. This was the ideal pattern, although not all families passed through this years-long process.

Each household was an entrepreneurial enterprise. Within the house-hold, nuclear families formed economic units that shared subsistence prod-ucts such as rice and vegetables, but kept profits from their cash crops separate. The following quotation depicts idyllically the age and gender hierarchy that ordered tasks:

> After we came [to live with my father's uncles], the household included Nyia Yi and Tse Ling [elder and younger uncles], their wives and five chil-dren, and their mother, along with Ntxong [the son of the dead eldest brother], my father and mother with me and my sister, my father's mother and second mother, and the second mother's little girl. So eighteen people were living together, but only three men and one teen-age boy to do the heaviest work, like clearing fields.
>
> I took care of all the little children. Va [Nyia Yi's son] had an older brother named Thao . . . and a little brother about one year old, who could just walk. Tse Ling had two little sons, too. I was eleven, or ten, and when we all went to the fields, we had a little house for the children, and I was the one to take care of all those children in that little house.
>
> Everybody worked together every day. In the morning everybody ate break-fast together, went to the fields together, and at four o'clock came back home together to do the housework together, everything got done together. We made some of the fields bigger. The family had many rice fields and corn fields in different directions, each with a little house. Some were so far from Nyia Yi's house we had to walk three hours to get there.
>
> The fields belonged to Nyia Yi, no matter who worked in them, but he didn't have to tell people what to do, because everybody already knew how to farm.
>
> There were six women living in the house: Va's grandmother, my two grandmothers,[7] my mother, Nyia Yi's wife, and Tse Ling's wife. Nyia Yi's wife was in charge, because her mother-in-law was too old to do anything, she only took care of the children. She didn't have to cook, because Nyia Yi's wife cooked for her. My grandmother didn't have to cook, either, be-cause my mother cooked for her. But my second grandmother didn't have a daughter-in-law to cook for her, so she had to do her own part.
>
> Every morning one woman got up to cook the rice. Nobody had to say whose turn it was, they had to remember by themselves. We had no

problems in that house; the women never argued. I learned about working together with other people because that's how we lived. (Xiong and Donnelly 1986: 210)

Farm technology was very simple. With most land at a fifteen to thirty degree slope, machinery, plows, and even wheeled vehicles were impractical. The main tools were knives, short-handled hoes, and digging sticks:

[After burning the slash] we can plant rice. The man has a stick, he has to do the little hole. One hole here, one hole here, one hole here. All the women, we can put the seed. Little seed in here, little seed in here, little seed in here.

Harvests had to be carried on the backs of people or horses. Farm production was difficult and productivity was rather low. If many children were born their number quickly exceeded their parents' capacity to feed them. But if several nuclear families remained under one roof, household tasks in particular could be handled more efficiently, freeing most adults for farm work.

GENDER HIERARCHY

Household chores and subsistence agricultural labor were done under the supervision of the senior couple, with the senior man ultimately in control of all the farmwork and his wife in charge of the domestic work. Cooper, who was seeking to describe sexual inequality among Hmong in Thailand, nonetheless comments:

There is . . . no obvious pattern of exploitation of the female in the organization and division of labour. Within the household a man may be seen cooking and doing other household tasks probably as frequently as any European male. There is no loss of face involved in such activity. Many of the woman's daily tasks are actually delegated by her to the children, especially collecting firewood and water, preparing food for animals and pounding rice. Younger children are cared for by older children. Clearing underbrush, carrying, . . . child care and preparing ground for opium are dual activities but women contribute more labour. If there is one basket to carry, the woman will automatically pick it up, if there are two, the man will take the second. On the other hand, no job is taboo for a man and he will sometimes lend a hand to weed the opium fields. (Cooper 1984: 117)

Still, the most immediately striking aspect of gender roles in Hmong society, described time and again by researchers, is the apparent hierarchical relation between men and women. Egalitarianism and freedom of choice by the head of each family regarding where to live and whom to live with had been important social values in traditional Hmong society. Hmong men in the early twentieth century have been described as hospitable, proud, energetic, and purposeful, with a fine knack for animal husbandry and great dexterity in blacksmithing, and both Lemoine (1972) and Cooper (1984) say that it was the imperative need to organize farm production around men that gave men control over many decisions and choices affecting the lives of all family members. Access to choice, and therefore training and experience in decision making, was accorded to men and boys, but not to women and girls, they maintain, because men constituted the economic core of the household, and the unit of decision was actually the household, not the individual. All family members were expected to submit to what was perceived as the overall welfare of the group; what that welfare was, was decided by the men.

> My grandfather married his second wife after my grandmother had two or three children. The reason was that my grandmother needed to stay home and take care of the children, while my grandfather needed someone to go with him to help with the farming. My father, who was the first child, was still young at that time. My grandmother was not very happy about the second marriage, because she wanted to go to the farm herself, not stay home all the time to take care of the little children. But my grandfather was a shaman, he was a strong man, and he thought he would have a lot of children, so he thought he would need another wife in any case.

The basic economic unit in Laotian Hmong society was the household. The main way to add to its labor force was by exploiting kinship bonds, which could be done by marrying another worker, persuading other relatives to join the household, or bearing children. Since Hmong reckon kinship through the male line, male kinship ties were those that they sought to expand. Situations like those in the quote above, in which the woman would have made one choice, the man another, and the man prevailed, were common when the topic of decision was one where both men and women felt an investment. This anecdote shows the man citing the benefit of the economic unit to justify his choice, while the woman refers to what she sees as her own good. This accords with Lemoine's and Cooper's assertion that men take a broader view. Since only boys are trained to phrase their goals in these terms, this is not surprising. The benefit of the economic unit is not separable from the man's personal benefit; there is complete structural congruence between adding another worker to the economic unit and adding to the man's strength. This is not so for the woman. Adding to the economic unit may weaken her position in the household by introducing competition. So she opposes it, but her argument is weak because it opposes what is seen as the overall benefit. In some situations, a woman could see a benefit to herself in such an expansion,[8] but in others there were disincentives for her in what men defended as the benefit of the whole. Woman's positional weakness was thus embedded in Hmong social structure as it was constituted in Laos.

Lemoine takes an idealized and poetic view of the relations between men and women:

> In Hmong thought, mankind, like the spirits and ghosts that people the world and the heavens, [and] like all the animals, always lives in pairs, that is to say: *ob tug nam txwv,* or *yog txwj yog nkawm,* which designates the pairs, the couple, husband and wife. No idea expresses better that duality immanent in human nature, [than] the fundamental complementarity of the couple. At this simple level the division of labor between man and wife is practically absent; they face together the thousand travails of daily life and the education of their children. . . . The relations between husband and wife, left to themselves, are generally marked by gentleness and sensitivity. . . . [They] live in constant collaboration with good mutual understanding. (Lemoine 1972: 166; my translation)

Cooper is cooler and more explicit about his view of the relations between men and women:

> There is *something* of a master-servant relationship between men and women.
> It has already been noted that sexual division of labour within the productive process is not unduly weighted against women (although this weighting has increased as the Hmong have become reliant on opium cultivation). A man usually leaves for work in the fields with his wife soon after dawn and returns with her at dusk. There is, however, a distinction in household routine that does not contradict a "master-servant" interpretation of the marital relationship. The wife, and the women of the house, will rise much earlier than the men at about 4:00 a.m. Pounding (dehusking) sufficient rice to feed an average family of eight for one day takes one person an hour. The fire is made up, water is fetched, and, if necessary, firewood is chopped, and a full meal is prepared before the men are called to eat. When guests are present in the house the women must wait until the men have finished eating before

sitting down at the table. In the evening the women again do most of the household chores and retire earlier than the men at about 9:00 p.m. whilst the men sit around the fire smoking, drinking tea and talking for another hour or so. . . .

[There is] in Hmong society . . . a major psychological distinction between the sexes. . . . It is on the basis of this psychological distinction that man controls woman. (Cooper 1984: 136–37)

Cooper argues that this psychological distinction is based on the men's control of felling trees to clear the land, which constitutes producing land as a resource—even though women participate in clearing land by clearing all the undergrowth, and even though now early reuse of fallow land means that trees may not need to be felled at all on some plots. It is still because men are seen by men and women both as generating the economic resource of land, upon which the entire swidden economy is based, that men take their place of priority before women. Cooper quickly qualifies this position, saying that one cannot attribute "universal qualities of determinism" to the economic base of swiddening societies, because not all swiddening societies have the same social structure, and that the "original reasons for sexual inequality among the Hmong may never be known" (Cooper 1984: 138). But he stands by his overall perception that men rule women among the Hmong.

That these two outlooks on the hierarchy of Hmong gender in Southeast Asia are totally opposed in their tone is owing to the different theoretical positions of the writers. Lemoine comes from French structuralism, Cooper from British Marxism. Both writers spent long periods of research in Hmong villages, both speak Hmong, and both also have in common the fact that their principal informants were men.

How do women view the gender question from within the context of Hmong society?

[The husband and father] is the head of the family, he's the one that works hard for the family. He is the one that makes decisions first. And the wife will be the one that says, "Well, this is a good idea. Why don't we do that?" The one that comes after, right? Mostly, it is the man who is doing things for our Hmong people, and the woman supports his idea. [Women] don't come up with a strong feeling. She can ask a question. "Do we need to do that, or not?" That is [only] a question. The father is the part that is very strong, he may say "Are you going to help me with this and this?" And she says, "Why, yes!" The man is the one who thinks harder about doing whatever he likes.

If the husband is good, then the wife is good with him, if he is a professional, she comes into professional [status] with him. Without him, she cannot be that good, because he's always stronger in everything. If he's lazy, the family cannot become strong. In our culture, why don't we ever say [that a woman can do better than a man]? The woman's working hard, too. When you are working very hard to support your husband to be a good person, people will say, "Well, his wife is a very good wife, that family's good, he's a good person." But the woman cannot be stronger than her husband. When people watch your family doing things, they say, "Well, the husband and wife are strong." But the way they are feeling is, the man's stronger. Always, he's coming first.

People always say, "Hmong lady cannot do anything." But that's not true, she's doing a lot. But they mean the man is doing it, the man is getting her to do it. Men and women both feel that way. It's the man who is building the family. When someone says to my husband, "You are working very hard to build your family, and are you that strong?" they are including me in that statement, but the idea comes to me indirectly. They don't mean just one person is building the family, but they never mention my name.

This perception of gender roles in family decision making is a deeply felt part of shared Hmong culture.

Hmong women are often described as productive and an essential half of the household team in Southeast Asia. Hmong usually married for the first time in adolescence when they did not yet have the skills to maintain a separate household, and moved in with the new husband's family. Good temper and work skills were the characteristics most valued in young women. Custom brought the young wife into her in-laws' household with few rights at first; she was expected willingly to obey her husband and his parents. Mothers-in-law trained daughters-in-law, and in fact marrying was called "becoming a daughter-in-law" (ua nyab). Sons followed their fathers' decisions, and after the first flush of married life frequently spent more time with their brothers than with their wives. Generally after marriage a new wife kept in close touch with her own family, who retained moral rights in her welfare, but over time she gradually saw less and less of them. Taboos of avoidance prevented direct communication between a new wife and her father-in-law or elder brothers-in-law.

Ultimately each woman worked under the command of the men of her own household—under her husband if married, under her father and brothers if unmarried, under her son if aged. A woman's primary loyalty was to her father, husband, or brother as the embodiment of the family. Taboos on communication within households, preventing close contact between fathers-in-law and daughters-in-law and between brothers-in-law and sisters-in-law helped to ensure that even young husbands were in control of their wives. Within this family-based (male-based) system of social position existed another, woman-based system of authority and loyalties. The division of labor within households required women to follow and obey other women—wives their mothers-in-law, daughters their mothers, younger co-wives their elder co-wives, younger sisters their elder sisters. Across both these systems of authority cut the hierarchy of age, with old men at the top followed by old women, and young women at the bottom below young men. These three structures of social control could conflict in particular instances. Lemoine, for instance, mentions a man who married as his second wife the older sister of his first wife, so that the hierarchy of co-wives was contradicted by the hierarchy of age:

> The conjugal disappointment of the poor man was the joke of the neighborhood since the two wives never left off disputing the right of each to command the other and the poor husband was continually calling in the shaman in an attempt to pacify his household. (1972: 181; my translation)[9]

Living in busy and crowded households, deferring to the wishes of many people, and seeing their own benefit in whatever was of advantage to their nuclear family, wives often came to favor moving away from the extended family into their own nuclear household. Thus sisters-in-law might become increasingly competitive as their own nuclear families grew. Women's quarrels were often blamed for splitting up large extended households. There was room in complicated multifamily households for jockeying and leverage on the basis of ability and emotional connections as well as on position. Especially for women, whose keynotes were hard work and obedience, it was important to play one kind of hierarchy against another in search of personal advantage. A woman's most effective argument was that she wanted to promote the welfare of the family; personal pleasure seems not to have been a valid goal among the diligent Hmong of Southeast Asia.

CHILD REARING

A major reason to marry was to provide the context for bearing and raising children. Until Hmong marry and produce offspring, they are not considered adults. The natural state of a mature Hmong is as part of a married couple with children. Childbirth at home was considered a normal event, with a healthy mother squatting next to the bed and a strong infant pushing its own way out of the womb. The father helped by holding up his wife and cutting the umbilical cord; usually his mother also participated, instructing the laboring woman, turning the infant if necessary, catching the new-born. But sometimes circumstances were not ideal. Of my eight life-history subjects, three had borne their children without help. One young wife, too shy to let anyone into the room, had had no instruction at all. Years later, a middle-aged mother with eight living children, she pantomimed for me her first childbirth: half-squatting, legs far apart, she staggered across the room gasping, looking over her shoulder in comic astonishment to see the bloody infant where it had fallen on the ground, umbilicus still attached; the placenta following after was a total surprise to her. That particular baby died. Children often died, and the average life span was fairly short even without the effects of war. Disease was common, effective medicine rare. One Hmong recalls:

The next spring that little girl [daughter of the second grandmother, who had moved away], Kai Ying, died. She had a lot of diarrhea. She got thinner and thinner, and everything she put into her mouth just went straight out the other end. If she ate a little rice, then a little rice came out, same thing. I think if we'd had a hospital we could have helped her, but we didn't. It made me very sad. I was twelve then.

We moved during January. About two or three months after we moved out of Va's house, his little brother got a fever. He was sick for four days, and then he died. Va's mother had a new baby girl born in the summer, and after three days, that baby died. My mother was pregnant. My sister Ka Jua got very, very sick with a fever, until between being alive and being dead, I think she was closer to dead. My father called the shaman to help my sister, and she was like that for three months, but she lived. When the fever was gone, she was very, very thin, just bones. Her arm was like my finger.

My grandmother and I stayed out on the farm to work while my mother stayed at home with my sister, and my father went back and forth every day, two hours each way. One day, when the baby was almost born, my mother went outside, and as she squatted down, a goat butted her in the back. My mother began to bleed from the place where the baby is born. The bleeding wouldn't stop. My father didn't know how to help her, but in that village was an old women who we called "grandmother"; she was not really our grandmother, only you call every old woman by that name.

This old lady said, "Just throw mung beans all over the floor and tell her to get down on her knees and pick them up one at a time, putting each one back in the sack. When you pick up the beans," she said, "the baby inside is picking up the edges of the rip, and as you put them into the sack, the thing that is broken inside is being mended."

My mother did that, which took half a day, and when she was done, the bleeding had stopped. After fifteen days passed, my brother Pao was born safely. (Xiong and Donnelly 1986: 211–12)

I did family trees going back three generations for eight Hmong families from different parts of Laos, and found that approximately half of all children reported born to these families died before reaching five years of age, from disease, accident, or war. While I could not usually discover the exact diseases, dysentery and fever seemed common; accidents with knives and fire were relatively frequent (see also Tapp 1988: 207).

Vulnerability to such events focused Hmongs' attention on home remedies, including massage and plant decoctions. Nearly everyone knew some techniques of healing, and there was great respect for herbal healers, both male and female. Women's healing knowledge was concentrated on internal ailments, while men's was more extensive for traumatic injury. Shamanism, that is, dealing with disease and bad luck by curing soul loss and reconciling human difficulties with the spirit world, was open to both men and women who discovered they had a gift, generally after themselves surviving a life-threatening disease.

Shamanism provided a field of power for women as well as men. Strong practices made strong medicine. In one complex case, Ntxai Vue (a pseudonym) saved Thao, a boy of ten afflicted with a ghost (*dlaab puj ntxoog* according to Ntxai Vue, who is Blue Hmong, although Heimbach 1979 has *dab poj ntxoog*) that had previously been driven out of his sister, only to lodge within the father, causing him to talk in his sleep and demand enough opium to kill himself. Next night the infuriated father sat up with his gun, and when the ghost tried to weasel its way through the holes in the wall, he shot it. He followed the trail of blood to a neighbor's house, roused the neighbor, found the ghost behind a storage locker, and beat it to death without changing the position of his hands on the board (so it couldn't escape during the gap as he shifted his grip). This particular ghost looked like a little furry animal, but its face was a humanoid face. It later returned to the son, causing him to giggle and whistle uncontrollably. Morning and night, even in his sleep, he laughed and whistled. Ntxai Vue's cure involved two dogs and a pig. The pig was sacrificed to cut off the ghost's road, and one dog was kept alive to protect the boy by distracting and fighting the ghost should it return. The other dog was stunned with a blow and its ears cut to release blood which Ntxai Vue in her trance sucked, spitting and spraying the blood three times around Thao, and all around the house, especially Thao's bed, while turning three times around Thao, carrying the dog and smearing its blood on him. Then she threw the dog out the door, where it landed head turned away from the house, indicating that the house had been cleaned of the ghost.[10]

When training for adulthood began among the Hmong, at the age of five or six, boys practiced hunting, followed their fathers to trading expeditions and political meetings, and learned how to choose land and clear fields, how to raise a house and perform the household rituals, and how to exercise judgment. Bernatzik, writing in the 1930s about the training of boys, says, "I never met a single incompetent man among the Meau [Hmong]. The stern laws of nature would soon cause him to disappear from this society" (Bernatzik 1970: 136). He is referring to the physical difficulty of life in the mountains, and what he sees as an absolute need to be intelligent and strong in order to survive. Meanwhile, as they grew, girls more and more frequently carried water, pounded rice, cooked and served food, looked after smaller children, learned weaving, dyeing, sewing and embroidery, and with their mothers weeded in the fields.

Children learned ideas of gender not only from daily tasks, but especially from stories their elders told them, both religious stories and folk tales. In analyzing the content of the mythic supports for social behavior, Sanday says:

> Gender symbolism in origin stories provides ancient and hence reliable metaphors for sexual identities. Such metaphors provide emotional guidance in times of stress when institutionalized guides for behavior are absent or do not seem to work. As Clifford Geertz says about symbolic templates, "it is in country unfamiliar emotionally or topographically that one needs poems and road maps." Because they give guidance in times of need, metaphors for sexual identities persist long after the circumstances giving rise to them have changed. (Sanday 1981: 56–57)

This is true not only of origin stories, but of all the many different folk tales children hear. Often learned in relaxed circumstances and an atmosphere of generosity and love, parents' stories teach children how to understand and predict human nature. This does not mean that folk tales form a coherent oral literature inculcating consistent values. Rather, traditional Hmong stories often contradict each other, presenting conflicting views of behavior.

There are two Hmong origin stories, "The Beginning of the World" and

"The Flood and Hmong Clan Names: The World's Second Beginning." In the first, the Hmong universe is people-centered. Only the earth and the low, dark sky exist before Lou Tou and his wife Ntsee Tyee are born out of a vein in a rock. It is a universe filled with human power. Lou Tou brings all the different grains with him. When his wife wants meat, he permits animals to be born out of the rock, and he rules their reproduction. His son Teng Cheu is even stronger than he, having the power to kill and to heal. Teng Cheu raises the sky with four corner posts and a center post (like a Hmong house) and creates sun and moon, day and night. He becomes ruler of the universe, superior to his younger brother who rules all living things, and by ruling his younger brother, he creates Hmong social structure. Only after this cosmic structure is in place is the world ready for the birth of the little "people seeds" that become all the peoples of earth, gestated by Ntsee Tyee, then differentiated and given eyes by Lou Tou.

The active principles in the story are male. Lou Tou brings grain and meat, and later makes baskets and containers and handles the animals. When Ntsee Tyee has a desire, Lou Tou fulfills it. She conceives, but he is the one who invents the ritual of divining; when it comes to producing gods and rulers, Ntsee Tyee is strictly speaking a vessel. Her two ruler sons are not born of woman, but come out of her side, and do not need mothering. Like the earth, she bears offspring; being the only woman in the story, she has no feminized social structures. Meanwhile, Lou Tou and his sons cooperate to develop the sky and the overarching society. The first god son sets up the vastness of the universe in the image of a lamplit Hmong house and then retreats out of reach beyond a now-distant sky that is clearly identified with males. The males create the social order in terms of males. When Nstee Tyee actually delivers (after her third pregnancy) it is as if she has delivered her entire womb, which Lou Tou must open, and the little people seeds are incomplete until he gives them eyes to comprehend the world. They are born into a male-created cultural world constructed on a passive female base.

In the second origin story, the world is flooded and everything is drowned excepting only a Hmong brother and sister, who float in a large wooden funeral drum. When the drum strikes the sky, sky people come out to pierce the earth with stiff metal lances. The waters recede, leaving nothing else alive. The brother wants to recreate the Hmong by marrying his sister, but she objects to such incest. However, she says, if two rocks which they roll down either side of a mountain join together overnight at the top, she will yield. That night, her brother brings the rocks together, and in the morning she acquiesces. From their union, a round mass of tissue is born which they cut in pieces and throw away. The pieces land here and there in places that sound like clan names. From each a clan is constituted, and so Hmong society survives.

Hmong social forms, seen in the sister's unwillingness to break the incest taboo and her brother's unwillingness to force her, survive the flood. The sister, intending to follow custom, sets an apparently impossible condition, so her pragmatic brother tricks her. In his ability to solve problems the brother resembles the sky people. Reluctant to change, and linked with stones, the sister is like the earth. Just as the sky people could act upon the earth with their stiff metal lances, her brother can act upon her; she must obey his wishes. New aspects of gender are embedded in this story. The male is smart and pragmatic. The female is conservative but obedient. The brother is longsighted, the sister shortsighted. She follows a narrow interpretation of propriety, while he thinks of the good of all. With his larger vision it is appropriate that he should rule her; in fact it is essential to human survival.

Gender concepts derived from these stories about the origin of Hmong people might shape other Hmong stories, like "The Orphan and the Chinese Princess," told in chapter 1. However, in that story the dove-princess can hardly be called passive. She argues spiritedly with her irresponsible husband, reveals a loyal and romantic nature, gives her life for her babies, and in her next life resolutely follows her own bent until defeated by her clever former husband. There are many folk tales in which women take active roles—the women in Hmong stories often are not silent, obedient, and pregnant. Hmong stories abound with gracious and generous daughters of the king of heaven, evil stepmothers, girls who set out to look for husbands, sisters-in-law smarter than the family they live with, women who foil evil-doers or earn the praise of powerful personages to bring wealth and happiness to their families. Actually, then, Hmong folk tales also propose an alternative model of attributes for female behavior. No one has investigated the extent to which Hmong children learned stories in Laos, but we can suppose that they formed a cultural fund available to many Hmong, especially since Hmong refugees have encouraged their transmission in written form.

One of the best known stories is "The Woman and the Tiger," frequently depicted on embroidered story-cloths. The following version comes from Johnson (1981a). A young unmarried woman is staying with her sister and brother-in-law and their family. A tiger (an evil spirit) kills her brother-in-law and, donning his clothes, presents himself to the dead man's wife as her husband. The wife does not notice any difference, but her sister is suspicious—something is not right, she thinks, and she decides to sleep up in the loft. In the middle of the night she hears dreadful noises, *nkiib nkos, nkiib nkos,* as the tiger chews the bones of the wife and children. In the morning he tells her, "Come down, little sister, come down, I want to marry you," but she refuses. Whenever he tries to come up, she throws salt or pepper in his eyes and he runs to the river to wash out his eyes. She sends a bird from the rooftop over to her family, and her male relatives come to save her. She calls the tiger back from the river: "My family is coming, I will marry you!" The tiger returns to the house just before her brothers arrive. They dig a pit in the path, covering it with branches and dirt. Politely they offer to guide the tiger back to the river to wash out his smarting and blinded eyes, but guide him instead onto the trap. The tiger falls into the pit and the men kill him. The sister goes home with them.

Another story in which a woman faces moral dilemmas is "The Woodcutter, His Rooster and His Wife." A poor woodcutter is very fond of his pet rooster. Every morning before going to work he gazes fondly upon his rooster, and every evening after coming home he does the same. His wife stays home and keeps house. One day as she is sweeping, a king steps into the house to visit. They are so poor the wife has nothing to feed him, but finally she kills the rooster and prepares a meal which the king enjoys. When the woodcutter returns home, he misses his pet rooster, realizes his wife must have killed it, and strikes her so that she cries out. The king, hearing her sobs, comes into the kitchen and asks what is the matter. "My husband is angry because I cooked a small dinner. You are a king. I didn't cook a pig for you. I only cooked a chicken." The king, pleased with this answer, gives great riches to the couple. A specific moral concludes this story: "A man needs a good wife. She can help him very much" (Johnson 1981b).

In the first story, a smart woman saves her own life by disobeying a spirit's orders; but the actual trapping and killing is done by men, her brothers, and she places herself under their protection. In the second, a moral woman violates a lesser rule in favor of a greater (she destroys her husband's property in order to be hospitable to the king), and then does it again in reverse (she lies to the king in order to shield her husband). In both instances she produces honor for her family; she is morally correct throughout. The husband is ignorant and impatient; his wife helps him to wisdom as she does to wealth.

There are many more stories in this vein, for example of the poor orphan who marries a king's daughter who brings him riches and happiness. But even where the female is quicker, richer, more long sighted, or whatever else seems to give her an advantage over the males in the story, when she is presented as the heroine she uses these qualities to advance the fortunes of the males. When she uses her skills in opposition to males, when she does not subordinate her own good to theirs, she is considered evil or stupid, and commonly she is the tricked rather than trickster. A common thread even in this type of Hmong folk stories, then, is the lesson of gender hierarchy.[11]

Hmong girls in Southeast Asia were raised to be hard workers, preparing for a life in which they could "work all day hoeing the opium fields in the hot sun, carry a heavy pack for nine hours up a mountain, and chop down thick undergrowth with a machete" (Cooper 1984: 137). As one woman recalls:

> The heavy part of the cooking was steaming the rice, because the pan was so big and we always made so much. When I was small my mother always cooked the rice and I helped with cooking the meat and vegetables. It's easy to just boil vegetables in a small pan. When I got bigger and my mother was older and not so strong, then I could help her with the rice and she would do the lighter cooking. Once I knew how to make the rice, it wasn't too hard, but actually, cooking rice was very hard and heavy work, and very hot, too.
>
> When I was fourteen or fifteen, then I was doing all the cooking for my mother. If she was tired, I got up very, very early, about four in the morning, to start the rice for breakfast. The rooster crowing waked me up, even before the daylight came. I made the rice, then everybody else got up, and we ate, then we just went to the farm to work.

Girls learned from elder relatives, as recounted by another woman:

> My mother had younger children to take care of, and she had to go to the farm and take care of the house and everything. She had no time for me. But my grandmother took care of me and taught me many things, and I slept next to her until I got married.
>
> I learned a lot of cooking from my grandmother, and everything I knew about embroidery, making thread from hemp, and making cloth. The easy one we learn first. They have the easy one, and the little-hard, and go up step by step. My grandmother told me how to choose good words to say to others, how to talk nicely about other people, and to do the right thing. My grandmother was the one to teach me good from bad. My mother couldn't tell me things like that, because she was too busy. She thought old people should do it, because they know more than young people. (Xiong and Donnelly 1986: 207)

I heard many stories about learning from grandmother, such as this one from Mai Hang:

I liked my step-grandmother. She was the mother of my father's second wife. I remember when I was still young, I saw someone wearing batiked clothes, and I really wanted to wear the same kind of thing. . . . My grandmother said, "Come here, put the batik pan in the fire, make it warm, and I will show you."

She said, "The boxes are like this," and she used her fingernail to make a gridwork of creases across the plain white cloth. She showed us one pattern, and then said, "After you do this, you do the same kind of thing to the whole dress and after you've done it well enough, I'll show you another, so you'll know how to do different ones," but she only showed us how to make three in the long run, and I didn't learn how to make any others.

WOMEN AND NEEDLEWORK

All thread, cloth, and finished textiles produced at home were manufactured by women; men did not sew. Men provided the tools of needlework: a loom, spinning apparatus, batik pen, cauldrons for dyeing. But they were not even supposed to be in sight of major textile processes such as warping the loom.

Learning needlework was part of a larger range of connections between women. It was an activity that made attachments between them easier. Doing needlework together stood as a symbol of connectedness, a way of expressing social relationships. In the following description, a woman describes herself as a young bride coming into a strange household:

We walked to his village. My mother-in-law and father-in-law had not finished breakfast yet. Maybe it was eight o'clock or nine o'clock. Nobody knew we were coming. My mother-in-law had been crying and missing her son. She went outside and saw me and my husband from a distance. She said, "Oh! My son has gotten married. He's come home!" It made her very happy. My husband said, "Mother, you didn't have to worry, I know how to find my way home. You didn't have to help me find someone to marry. I could find her all by myself."

We sat down to eat, but I was very shy, I didn't want to eat. I just ate a little bit. After eating we didn't have to go to the fields to work, because they had finished the harvest and everything. It was still New Year time. About a week after the New Year, then we would go back again to make the new fields.

So during that week, my mother-in-law and I could sit together and sew. She gave me something to sew, but I didn't know how. My husband said,

"Mother, she doesn't know how, she only knows a little bit. Because you don't have a daughter, you have only three sons, [I hope] you can help my wife learn to sew." My mother-in-law said, "OK, I'm very happy to do that." So we sewed together, and talked to each other a lot.

Mallinson gives training in needlework a high place in girls' lives:

> While the men transmitted a wide range of material knowledge, textile technique was the only part of a woman's knowledge which was expressed in durable materials. . . . Performance as a farmworker was evidence of a girl's health and strength; from her earliest childhood she cared for her younger siblings, but a girl's performance as a needlewoman was visible evidence that she had been brought up to respect and follow the traditions of H'mong life.
>
> There was perhaps another incentive for learning. In her mother's daily activities—tending animals, working in the fields, caring for children (with particular concentration on the male children)—there was little opportunity for a small daughter to get the concentrated attention of her mother (or of any adult woman) and to create a bond. One of the few opportunities came while learning textile skills. (Mallinson et al. 1988: 41–43)

All my life history subjects except one,[12] in talking about learning, emphasized learning to sew. Each remembered with fondness her teacher or teachers, whether mother, grandmother, or mother-in-law. Writers on the Hmong in Southeast Asia all mention girls and women sewing and talking, spinning while walking to the fields, sewing as they sat in the shade during the day or around the fire in the evening. Cotton cloth and embroidery floss were significant items of trade for itinerant merchants. My informants had vivid memories of learning needlework:

> The *paj ndau* [lit. flower cloth, meaning embroidered fabric] that I did as a child, the very first one I began with, I have kept it even until now. It looks new, though it used to be very, very dirty, but I washed it. It's just the beginning pattern, and it's made with a kind of material that was very cheap at that time. We used only cotton, and the nylon we use now was very expensive, so nobody could buy it. All around the edge it had little yellow and green stripes, that we dyed ourselves. The yellow color came from an insect cocoon [*kaab ngug lwg*]. We took the insects inside their cocoons and dropped them into boiling water. Then we stirred and stirred the water with a stick, and the silk thread of the cocoon unwrapped from the insect. We wound the silk around the stick to pull it out of the water. The color went from the silk into the water. If we used a different insect we got white dye.

That edging looked bad after I washed it, so I took it all out and put in white and green.

The pattern is like diamond squares, different colors embroidered next to each other. And the embroidery thread is still very shiny. I bought it from the Lao, and it was white, but I dyed it. I think at the time I made that square I was only about ten years old. When my grandmother taught me to make my first batik skirt pattern, the border patterns were like this pattern. This is the pattern for girls who are beginning. It's not too hard, because it's all diamonds, and you do each diamond with the needle weaving in and out of the cloth.

This sort of pattern, when you die, then this pattern is for the pillows. My grandmother taught me to make pillows for her. Everyone had to make them for their father and mother. I had to make for my grandmother, my father and stepmother, even my older sister, younger sister, older brother, younger brother, I had to make all the pillow covers for them like this one.

Batiked, embroidered, and appliquéd clothes, detachable pockets, and bandeaus were essential for personal adornment, while thread, pillows, and bed covers were made for ritual exchanges and used for religious purposes. All writers on Hmong mention costume as an important element of ethnic identity (see for instance Savina 1930: vii). Among the varied tribes in upland Southeast Asia, Hmong could be identified at a glance by their clothing, with its particular cut and elaborate abstract embroidery, appliqué, or batik. So obvious is the use of costume as a marker of ethnicity, that dialectal subgroups of Hmong are identified by details of clothing (White Hmong, Blue Hmong, Striped Hmong, Flowery Hmong, etc.). The two main divisions of the Hmong in Laos were named for the color of women's skirts, a surface marker that also indicated dialectal differences and, on a deeper level, political divisions. Still we should not make too much of the use of women's skirts as symbols of social cleavages. The skirts are not the source of the divisions, but only a convenient and arbitrary symbol for them, especially as the women have little power in terms of political divisiveness. From women's costumes we cannot learn what the cleavages are, but we may observe where they are to some degree. But even this was not always true in Laos. For a married woman, costume seems to have had two kinds of meanings: loyalty to her husband's family, and recognition of her own family heritage. A White Hmong woman marrying a Blue Hmong man might or might not change her costume; she might or might not learn Blue Hmong textile techniques.[13]

How elaborate each person's costume was depended very much on resources; in poorer areas old photographs show drab indigo-dyed clothes without much embellishment, while in wealthier places the same basic cut could be decorated with highly refined and subtle cut-work, cross-stitchery, and batik. Beautiful examples of costume styles among Thai Hmong can be seen in Lewis and Lewis (1984: 100–133 passim), while Savina's photographs show ordinary clothing worn by Hmong in northern Vietnam early in this century (Savina 1930), and Lemoine (1972) has photographs of Hmong clothing of the 1960s in Sayaboury province, Laos.

White Hmong women wore dark trousers for everyday. Their lovely skirts were reserved for special occasions. A Hmong woman's ceremonial dress in Laos during this century consisted of a heavy pleated skirt of woven home-grown hemp, carefully batiked in tiny designs. It was dyed with homemade indigo if she were Blue Hmong, but white if she were White Hmong. The Blue Hmong indigo-dyed skirt also carried a deep embroidered and appliquéd hem. All skirts wrapped around and tied in the front. To conceal the opening, a woman wore an apron with long embroidered ties that she wound into a bulky sash. Intricate embroidery and appliqué appeared on her sleeves, collar, lapels, and pockets, and she wore a turban or elaborate hat. This costume could easily take a full year to construct, and was further embellished with massive silver jewelry made by men. Clothes made specifically for daily wear were not so fully decorated, though women wore their old ceremonial dresses as ordinary clothing.

Men's clothing was simpler, and daily wear was often plain, but their ceremonial clothes were also bright, with embroidered lapels and sash as well as silver neck rings. Infants' everyday wear included little silver neck rings and pieced and decorated caps which protected them from evil spirits, and they were carried about in decorated baby-carriers whose design frequently included the Hmong cross that also protects children from evil.

Women produced many specifically ritual textiles. Thread itself carried symbolic uses. Spun thread was tied around the wrists of newborns or the sick to keep their souls within their bodies. It was wound around the whole family by the shaman as they stood at the house center post each year to symbolize their spiritual unity. Threads led overhead from the lintel of the front door to the spirit altar so that the movement of spirits from outside could be directed (see e.g. Levine and Waterworth-Levine 1982).[14]

In addition, several textile exchanges reiterated the connection of married women with their family of origin. A bride received elaborate skirts, jackets, sashes, and so on, from her mother at her marriage. A new mother had the right to receive finely decorated baby carriers from her mother and her mother-in-law. Other women could also give her these carriers, and sisters often gave to sisters. A baby carrier is a rectangle of cloth about fifteen by twenty-four inches, with a smaller rectangle like a tail piece at the bottom. At the two top corners long slender ties are attached. A woman wraps the cloth around the baby's back, passing the ties under his armpits. Pulling the ties together around the baby's chest, she swings him onto her own back. The long ties then go over her shoulders, cross between her breasts (or just wrap under her armpits), wrap around over the baby's hips, cross under his bottom, go under each leg on the opposite side, and come forward to tie in a knot over her belly. The baby is safe and comfortable, and its position is well balanced for carrying. Small children ride in these carriers even up to the age of two or three. Men carry babies this way as readily as women do.

Married women also made funeral cloths, pillows, and full costumes for their parents to wear into the grave. Such textiles were used during life as ritual gifts at lifecycle events (notably at parting for long journeys) and then laid away for their ultimate use. Textiles enter the symbolism of the funeral ceremony in several ways: the corpse is well dressed in clothes made by the daughters; it lies on its blanket with its head on a funeral pillow or pillows; it may wear Chinese felt shoes (as at a ceremony I went to) or woven hemp sandals (Lemoine 1983); the mourners may wear red ribbons to keep off bad spirits (Lemoine 1983). I am not aware of special patterns used in these items, except for funeral pillows, which have a symbolic meaning attached to the textile pattern, or rather lack of pattern. Given to parents for use inside their coffin, these pillows were not supposed to have appliqué on them or the parents will have a rocky road into the grave.

Textile exchanges were very meaningful, particularly the skirts that brides were given upon marriage by their mothers. These were important not only for their memories, but also as a textbook of patterns. Some refugee women in America still own the skirts their mothers made them, despite flight, refugee camp, and all their other travails. Others could not keep them.

> When we left Long Tieng I had six Hmong skirts with me. I had the first skirt I ever made. I had the skirt my mother made for my marriage. But I had to throw them all away in the jungle. We couldn't carry them any more. (Xiong and Donnelly 1986:233)

The importance of skirts can be inferred from the tenacity with which women tried to keep them. Clearly intense emotions surrounded needlework for Hmong women. It was a domain entirely belonging to women; men did not participate in it at all. Finished textiles had no place in trade. Women are said not to have engaged in trade with money. Particularly with outsiders, this was men's domain, and its products accrued to men. But trade in purchased materials used in producing needlework increased during the twentieth century. Besides their handmade hemp fabric, Hmong women increasingly had available Chinese silk floss and French calico, hawked by itinerant Chinese traders, though these items were quite expensive. Sources are ambiguous about whether Hmong women were consumers within a money economy prior to the social changes brought by warfare in Laos. I have searched without success for explicit statements of whether Hmong women were buying the floss and cotton that they used, or whether they depended on their men to do the buying. Geddes (1976) describes Chinese shops in Hmong villages as places where Hmong men can sell opium and arrange credit against future sales, and where unspecified things are sold at retail, but he does not describe the retail customers or the trade. Lemoine (1972), also, in discussing the types of things that Hmong buy in northern Laos, such as tinware, batteries, mirrors, and fabric (but not skirt fabric, which was always made at home), says nothing about the actual purchases.

Earlier, Bernatzik (1970: 568–71) in northern Thailand described barter in the 1930s between Hmong and Haw Chinese traders, who brought wares to trade for opium, stag and rhinocerous horn, elephant tusks, rattan, and baskets (all products controlled by men), or for a variety of different kinds of silver money. He quotes Lumet de Lajonquiere, writing in 1904: "They [the Hmong of Haut Tonkin] procure from the outside only the colored silk for the embroideries and the colorful bands which fops are beginning to add to their attire. . . . The custom of buying cotton goods on the market or among the natives who produce it is spreading more and more, for the weaving of hemp is difficult and laborious." It could be that the weavers are doing the buying, meaning Hmong women were buying fabric in 1904 in northern Vietnam, but it is equally possible that men are doing the buying. All discussions of fabric buying contain the same ambiguity.

If women were doing no purchasing, researchers might have thought this odd, and they would probably have mentioned it; so when they say "women do not engage in trade" they probably mean that women do not buy and sell for profit. This fits the commonsense understanding of my informant's statement quoted earlier that "I bought [the thread] from the Lao." But we must be cautious in translating the word kuv as "I" because it also means "me" and "my." Hmong commonly abbreviate sentences in ordinary conversation, so the sentence could easily mean, "My [family] bought from the Lao."[15] If she bought it, then over fifty years ago in the mountains of Sam Neua, at the age of ten this highland child was handling money in a commercial transaction with a Lao. This is a little hard to believe, but it cannot be checked, as my informant is unfortunately no longer available.

Trade was said to be the province essentially of men even into the 1970s. However, as the economic and political situation of the Hmong changed in the second half of this century, especially as Hmong became refugees within Laos and began living in towns, women routinely shopped for food-stuffs and textile materials. Increased wealth and access to foreign goods changed some elements of style in the textiles; for instance brighter colors and more elaborate embellishments were introduced. Soldiers' wives living in towns on their husbands' salaries had the leisure to create large ward-robes if they were so inclined. However, educated and elite women during the 1960s tended to adopt Lao or even Western styles if they lived in cities.

3

CHANGING TIMES

Changes in women's lives accompanied the changes coming with colonial expansion and the Second Indochina War. Men's public roles expanded in the twentieth century owing to growing trade and to political involvement in French-controlled Laos. In the 1940s, as new French-built roads reached into the hill areas, new economic opportunities arose for hill farm families. Farmers were able to sell potatoes and other crops in Hanoi, notably from the area of Nong Het on the Vietnam-Lao border. The variety of goods brought by traders to some villages increased markedly; women added new colors and materials to their needlework repertoire, using French cotton and Chinese silk floss. The jewelry women and men wore was made from French coinage—Indochinese piastres either pierced and hung in great jingling arrays, or melted and formed into hollow tubular neck rings and incredibly intricate chainmail-like breast coverings.

Hmong were able to accumulate more and more of these expensive decorations as the century progressed, and also to increase the amount of silver used in bride wealth exchanges and in ritual, because with the encouragement of Chinese and French buyers they became increasingly involved in the opium trade. As this developing trade increased the Hmongs' wealth it also reduced their isolation, as did their rapid population increase and consequent spread, and the ever more effective means of transportation and communications through roads and telegraph. With the ejection of the French and the formation of the Royal Lao Government, rural development continued, for instance in the increasing number of schools that were founded in rural towns. Previously I described how girls learned domestic tasks in traditional Hmong villages in the Lao mountains. For girls in rural towns, different opportunities were available:

> When my family moved out to the country, we built another little house in town for our children who wanted to stay in school. There were eight of us, six girls and two boys, all Blue Hmong children of the Xiong clan. My grandfather's cousin's son, who was about 15, was the oldest. It's OK for girls and boys to stay together if they have the same last name, because then they are like brother and sister, and the boys will not do anything bad to the girls.

In that house everybody took care of themselves. Each of us had to know what to wear and how to be clean. For school we had uniforms. Boys wore white shirts and short blue pants. I had three white blouses and three blue skirts with three white stripes around the bottom, and each one I had to wear two days, and then wash it by hand, as my parents told me. I did all my own cooking. In my country, children learn to wash and cook by the time we are seven, and gather wood and do all sorts of things. I think if you tell children how to do things when they are young, it's easier to teach them everything when they grow older.

On the weekend we went back home, all walking together because we all lived close together in the village for Blue Hmong that my grandfather started. We arrived Friday nights. Saturdays we would go to the farm and get everything we needed for the next week at school. Sunday afternoons we went back to Phu Khao Quoy. We had a vacation in June, July, and August, so the Lao teachers, who came from the lowlands, had time to plant irrigated rice in their farms. We also had three days off at Hmong New Year.

In my school, we learned to read and write Lao. We learned arithmetic, we learned the school song. In the third year we began French. We studied Lao history, and how the body works, and how to use a special stone to make dye, heating the stone in a fire until it crumbled, and soaking those bits of stone in water.

I think I was a good student, too. Every month I was the student of the month. Every month I got the prize, one writing book and one pencil. Only once I came in second, and only got a pencil. Even today I can remember what they taught us about planting vegetables in a garden in different seasons. They said, "In the wintertime, you make the soil very smooth, very even, but in the fall, there's a lot of rain, so you have to pile the soil up in mounds so the plants are above the water; in the summertime it's very hot, and then you plant the seeds deeper." They said, "when you plant corn, you have to weed it until it's 30 inches high, and then you can let the weeds go." I really liked school.

Between 1950 and 1960, American fundamentalist missionaries converted thousands of Hmong in Xieng Khouang Province. Even the missionaries were astonished to see how fast Christianity caught on. Often they would enter an area only to find that entire villages had already heard of them from other Hmong, had burned their spirit paraphernalia, and were waiting for Christian instruction. Initially this was evidently owing to the open approval of Touby Lyfoung, a leading Hmong whose second wife (with her children) became Christian (Ruth Andrianoff, personal communication 1985). These lightning conversions probably signified effec-tive provincewide political structures rather than religious zeal.[1] Eventually about 5 percent of the Hmong in Laos became Christian; these later formed a disproportionately large segment of the refugee Hmong.

If Hmong did show provincewide political structures by the 1950s, this was a recent development. The Hmong are considered tribal because their political structure is not different from the relationships produced by kin-ship and clan membership, with political loyalties prescribed by family membership. The ties that provided reasons to form villages with fellow clan members and that justified generosity were still invoked as long-distance communications improved and the Hmong were drawn into the larger political events of the time. Government and military leaders broad-ened their base of support via the preexisting kin and clan structures. Divisions created by family quarrels deepened into political enmities as the struggle for control of territory turned into civil war and the Vietnam War next door spilled into Laos with the aid of the United States.[2]

My topic is ideas about gender, so I shall concentrate, not on political or military history, but on the personal experiences of women in wartime. As the war continued to expand, with the American government supporting the Royal Lao government and the C.I.A. underwriting anticommunist military activities in which Hmong men were leading fighters, for some Hmong families the focus of ambition changed, affecting the opportunities of such Hmong girls as my subject Mrs. Ly:

> Soon after my family moved from the north of Laos into Long Tieng, my cousin who was working for General Vang Pao told us about the new hospi-tal they just built in Sam Thong, where they were starting training programs for nurses, pharmacists, people like that. Usually they called it the *Aas Kiv* ["ang key", i.e. Yankee] hospital. My cousin told me that they said, we only have this many nurses from Vientiane, so we need to train some more for about two or three years. Everybody knew about it. So my cousin brought me an application and I filled it out and he took it in. Then I had to wait about three or four months, and then I got a letter saying I could go to that class. So I got into the first group. My mother had never been to school or held a job, and she had always stayed home sewing and taking care of all my brothers and sisters. She was happy to see me go to school, and the first time I went, she went with me in the taxi.[3]   .
>
> Sam Thong was an old village, and a few people had been living there all their lives. It started to be built up about 1964–65, two years after we moved to Long Tieng. So in that sense it was a new town, full of soldiers, and refu-

gees from the north, and people who came up from the south to work, when I went there in 1966. The population of Sam Thong was not that much, but it was a very large town, because it was very spread out. It was very different from Long Tieng. In Long Tieng, people lived very crowded together. The mountains were all around the sides of the town, very steep, and everybody lived packed together at the feet of the hills. But Sam Thong was flat and spread out. There were lots of gardens, and Lao-style farms with rice growing in water.

In Long Tieng the majority of people were Lao. In Sam Thong most of the people were Hmong. Hmong people living in Sam Thong used the Lao farming technique, growing wet rice. There was a group of houses here, and a group there, and another over there, depending on where the people wanted to put their houses and their farms and gardens. I guess there were between five hundred and one thousand houses in Sam Thong when I lived there. We had a big airport there too, and one of the big offices that the C.I.A. used, that delivered all the things like rice, blankets, hundreds of things to help the refugees who had come crowding into the little village. And there was a big hospital there, and a pharmacy, and the hospital had its own little airport so the helicopters could bring down the soldiers right into the inside of the hospital. The hospital was big, the school was big—everything was big in Sam Thong, compared with the north of Laos.

At the hospital there was a building just like a school, and then one apartment building for girls and another for boys to stay, like a college. We had big rooms where seven or eight girls slept together, and one living room for everybody, and a kitchen where meals were prepared for us to come and eat at set times. A lot of girls lived there, because there were a lot of classes.

I don't remember exactly, but I think there were about twenty-six or twenty-seven students in my class. There were many different classes, not only nursing, but they didn't train doctors there. The doctors came from Vientiane. Two of the Lao doctors had been to France to study. The person who planned what to teach the nurses was an American lady named Betty. The other teachers were Lao, and one of them was a man. The training was not the same for all the classes, and one class was only for male nurses, who got sent to the military to be with the soldiers.

We had five very big buildings for the patients, one for the people from the town of Sam Thong or whoever came in from the area, just normal patients, and four of the buildings were for soldiers. The nurses came from many different places, Vientiane, Long Tieng, some from the south of Laos, too, and also Sayaboury. We had several teachers.

For the first two years I had six hours of classes every day, and then two hours of practice work doing easy things like taking temperatures and things like that. Then the third year I just went ahead to do whatever a nurse would do.

For me it was not really like living in a town of strangers. I had three cousins in my class, and two of the nurses who had gotten their training in Vientiane and then come back to work in that hospital were people I had met in the north of Laos when I was growing up there. We had a Laotian girlfriend who was in our class who had come from a different town. So when we had the chance, in our time off, when we had finished our classes for the day, we could say, "I'm going somewhere, do you want to go?" And then we'd all go together. We did many different things. Sometimes we played games like volleyball or also checkers, we had a game where you jump, or we would just run around, or go up into the hills and walk around. Sometimes, on a Saturday, I would go with a group of girls and we would take a picnic and go up in the hills. I had a very happy life at that time.

Wartime is above all a time of rapid change. It is not only a time of loss. While there is pain, destruction and fear, opportunities also arise for many people. Like other times of ferment, wartime can provide chances for women to step out of tradition-bound roles into suddenly invented and still fluid activities, specifically because war produces upheaval, cracks in the social fabric. Several of my subjects took advantage of new possibilities. May Xiong deliberately married a soldier to get away from farming and then increased her husband's income by trading chickens, fabric, and household goods between her parents' village, the city of Long Tieng, and the front (Xiong and Donnelly 1986). Mai, a shaman, used the skill she had already developed in a new setting:

> The communists came to our village in Xieng Khouang Province, so the whole village moved to Kam Hong, closer to Xieng Kouang City. When the communists came to Kam Hong we all ran out in the jungle, and everything was back and forth. Some people went to Pha Leung, close to Phu Lom. The communists fought us again, and we moved to Pak Qha, which is close to Meung Ah in Sam Neua Province. Then we had to take the plane to Na Khang, also in Sam Neua. We didn't have to buy tickets on that plane, we just took it. It was an army plane.

> Then we took another plane and we moved to Long Tieng, and I was helping people there too, only privately, just close friends and relatives. We stayed in Long Tieng about one year, and then moved to Sam Thong for three or four years, and I kept my medicine secret, just in the family. Sam

Thong was a big city in Xieng Khouang Province, close to Xieng Khouang. Then after that we moved to Na Su, in Vientiane Province.

When we moved to Na Su, close to Long Tieng, I had thirteen children. The youngest one was three years old when we moved. There was a big hospital there. Even very sick people, they took out of Long Tieng to Na Su. I began to help in that hospital, but the doctors said, "The Hmong, they don't know anything about medicine, they just take any leaf in the jungle and give it to the patient." They said if any patient died, they would put me in jail. So at first I could not do anything. But there were some people who were so sick, the doctors didn't want to take care of them, because they were sure those patients would die. They let the family take them home, and I could help those dying people at their house. So they did not die, but got better again, and presently one doctor saw that and began to trust me. If there was a patient who was very, very sick, he told the family how to get to my house. Then before the doctor gave any medicine to that patient, I would give some herbs to help him.

After a while I began to go into the hospital again. I would put the medicine in a bottle, cover up the bottle, take it into the hospital and give it to the patient to drink secretly before the doctor gave any medicine. Then I would take the bottle home very quickly. We moved to Na Su in 1971 and I helped people like that until 1973. In 1973 the doctor invited me to come into the hospital, too, so until 1975 I was working with the hospital. In all I helped more than a thousand people in that hospital, I think, and the government said the doctor was a very good doctor. They promoted him! The family of the sick person paid me, and as I saved my money I ended with almost a million kip before we left Laos.

As war increased, the proportion of men to women declined because of the men's death and absence. Living in larger and larger concentrations as refugees even within Laos, women met more strangers and learned more about the world outside their own extended family. Soldiers' wives sometimes lived apart from their husband's family and made daily decisions about their own activities and conduct (see Xiong and Donnelly 1986). Women living in provinces relatively untouched by combat, such as Sayaboury in the far west of Laos, continued living traditional lives, but some women in more compromised areas, such as Xieng Khouang Province where the Plain of Jars is located, found themselves leading new lives.

Women whose husbands were fighting were told not to sew; if a wife pierced the cloth with her needle, her husband would be pierced with a bullet. Other female activities also were held to affect the luck of soldier husbands. A woman carrying water in a bucket usually floated her dipper upside-down on the water to reduce sloshing and spillage as she walked. But setting the dipper upside-down would supposedly trap her husband so he could be killed. A wife was not supposed to handle a knife lest her husband be stabbed, a serious inconvenience if she had no one else to slice meat for cooking (Xiong and Donnelly 1986). Thus women's traditional tasks were disrupted even if they did not have to flee their homes.

A surprising number of the women I interviewed lived in combat zones. I was particularly surprised to learn that the army encouraged families to remain directly behind the lines. Men and women agreed: Hmong soldiers were more willing to fight when their families were threatened—exposing families to harm was good policy.

> Not far from our village was a high mountain, and my husband was with the army on that mountain. It was close to Phu Lai, and sometimes when my husband missed me a lot, he came to get me and I went to the mountain to stay with him at night. Then in the daytime I came back to work on the farm. It was only about thirty minutes walk. The name of the mountain was Pha Lai.
>
> The soldiers lived on the mountain and slept under the ground. They had dug holes in the ground and let big trees fall over the holes. Then they covered the trees and branches with dirt, so they would be safe at night. They could put their beds in there, and curtains between the beds.
>
> We [she and her parents-in-law] lived in Phu Lai for more than one full year from New Year to New Year, and we had planted the new rice for the next year. The rice was as high as my knee. But there was a lot of fighting at Pha Lai, so we could not go on living there. The army had two thousand soldiers on that mountain, and all the soldiers and their families in that whole area moved to Long Tieng. Nobody lived in Phu Lai any more.
>
> We had to wait for Koua to come get us, and soldiers were shooting, they were fighting all around us. We took some rice and some clothes, and left everything that was heavy. People went in small groups, just households together. We were too frightened! We were moving and the enemy was coming and all around was fighting and running. We were all trying to get away. If soldiers got killed, they just had to leave them there.
>
> Koua stopped fighting to help lead us into Long Tieng. We had to go around the fighting. Walking straight to Long Tieng took only six days normally, but we went in the daytime and in the nighttime for one month before we were able to get there. We didn't have any way to carry food with us, or pots to cook in. When we came to a village, we stopped and waited for the airplane to drop rice to us. Hundreds of people were trying to get to safety.

Koua's father's brother and his younger cousin and their families were all killed, and also his father's older cousin, and also Koua's older brother who was a soldier. The rest of us all lived. Of the four families in our part of Phu Lai, only two got to Long Tieng.

Such incidents were repeated over and over from family to family. Wives, children, and older people lived near the soldiers, moving when necessary, fed by air drops from CIA/USAID planes, until their temporary villages were overrun by fighting and they had to fall back, with losses.

The American plane dropped rice for the soldiers and the women. They had to drop the rice, we couldn't grow any. The men put a piece of white cloth on the ground in a clearing, the airplane circled around all the towns so people knew, then the airplane dropped the rice bags, black plastic, about 150 pounds. They broke on the ground. There were soldiers who watched it, there were a lot of people, Lao people too. They called my name on a paper, I don't know how they got my name. They dropped canned fish, too. We had a little squash, a little cucumber, but no rice. The plane came every month. Every family got the same. I had no children, so I got too much rice and I could sell some. My husband earned three hundred kip every month, so I had that. We stayed in Kha Hong one year and a half. I had a little house. Then we moved to Phu Viang and my husband stayed with me there. Usually in those towns, the young men were all soldiers and only old men lived in the town. Maybe there was one old man for ten houses of women. All that time I couldn't sew anything, because my husband was fighting. In Phu Viang, my husband finally taught me to shoot, but in Kha Hong I didn't know, so I was scared. One time when we got rice, big guns came, shot at the plane, right over me. Too scared!

This woman began having babies about 1963. The following discussion includes the important contributions of her oldest daughter, Pheng:

MOTHER: The first baby came in Pu Kung, the second, Ah, in Phoua San, the third, Sue, in Pu Kung. I moved to Long Tieng one year, then I lived at Seng Le five months, moved again to Na Ndau, lived there four or three months, then back to Seng Le, where I had my Mang. Na Ndau was very small. From Seng Le to Mong Peng, then by airplane to Som Lai. I lived in Som Lai six years with my husband, and I had May, Tong, and Kong, three children. Then from Som Lai we walked to Phu Kong and I had my Yeu in the road. Really, it was too hard!

PHENG: We stayed at Phu Kong only nine days, then moved to Ma Hong, then walked toward Thailand. When we started to walk, it was 1978, when we got there it was 1979, almost 1980. It took so long, and we were so skinny, only our bones! A lot of people were dying in the street. You keep moving and people keep dying, you just walk across them. I was eight or nine years old. People just sit like that, then they die and when you see them, they're still sitting.

MOTHER: We had no food. We ate food in the mountain, bamboo shoots and weeds. Nobody could help each other. If you didn't find food for the children, they would just die. Nobody helped each other. We had so many children, nobody wanted to be with us, we had to go alone. I would pray to God every day, "God help me, oh please," and I would be looking for food for my kids, I never closed my eyes![4]

People said a lot of things to me, they said too much. I got so mad, I said, "You hate my babies? Maybe you want to kill them? Here, I'll kill the little one, we can cook her, everybody eats!"

PHENG: So then they didn't say anything to her any more. But we were too slow and we got behind everybody, and the soldiers were shooting at us. They shot my daddy, and we stopped because we couldn't leave him. My mommy tried to carry him but he was too heavy, and then he died. The soldiers caught us and they dug a hole and put my daddy in it. So then we couldn't go anywhere and we stayed there about six months.

MOTHER: They kept us in a house at *Tha Nbos* [sp?], and watched us very closely. We couldn't do anything. It was right at the river, we could see Thailand. A lot of Hmong people had to stop there with us, and there wasn't much food so some people died there too. The soldiers poisoned the food, poisoned the water. They gave us rice, but it was poisoned. They said, "The little baby has a fever," and they gave medicine, but it was poison. Then they said, "Oh, did the little baby die?"[5]

PHENG: But her older brother gave some money to four men, who found us in the night. Then we moved in a Vietnamese taxi to *Phu Nyaws* [sp?] with about fifteen families, where we lived for about three months. The taxi was like a van. We pretended we would live there, and kept our plan a secret. But then my mom decided to stay in Laos because my daddy had died, but some older people said, let's wait and see. We weren't close to Thailand. And we asked people for money so my mom could buy food for us, and nobody would give us any, and we asked people for money for the boat, and nobody would give us any, and my mom had to promise my uncle would pay later, because it cost a lot, 3900 baht[6] and later he did. And one night those men came and we walked five nights. The babies couldn't cry because maybe someone could hear.

MOTHER: I carried two babies on my back. My back hurt so I thought I would die. People were giving the babies a little medicine to keep them quiet, but if you gave too much, the baby died.

PHENG: They gave us some for my little sister but my mom gave her too much, they said to give her too much. If it hadn't been cold and raining she would have died. She couldn't eat or drink, it was like she was dead, but my mom didn't leave her, that's why she didn't die, but now she's too skinny. Then suddenly we saw the river, and those men brought a fishing boat, and the people with no daddy had to go first, then the people with a daddy had to go last, and they went back and forth. We were lucky because at the end the boat burned and I think some people got killed.

Not all Hmong who left Laos had such dreadful passages. Some in Saya-boury simply walked across the border in whole villages. Hmong living in Vientiane were among the earliest to depart, and if they left within days of the fall of the coalition government, they could cross by boat a river whose commercial traffic had not yet been closed off. But many did experience severe deprivation. Thousands of Hmong fled into the jungle mountain of Boua Mu, and for them, nothing was easy. They had had to abandon house-hold goods, animals, tools and spare clothes, along with much else. The account in Xiong and Donnelly (1986) of the experiences that followed has been confirmed by other women who gave me life histories. Domestic life collapsed. Men organized desperately for mutual defense, but eventu-ally there was no salt, no soap, no medicine, no food; starving families ate chopped and boiled clothes. Corpses had to be buried without funeral clothes, and ritual, if any, was abbreviated. Hmong who went through that terrible time arrived in Thailand in rags:

Our clothes got dirtier and dirtier, and full of holes, and we had no new ones to put on. Just one or two pieces of clothing was all we had. We just had to patch and patch the same clothes to wear, but some families didn't even have a needle because they broke their own. (Xiong and Donnelly 1986.233)

Believing their political and military leaders would return and lead them in battle against the communists, some of these resisters survived up to two years in this way, patrolling their own borders, making harvest expeditions to lowland rice fields in the dead of night, digging for roots, not daring to light fires, constantly damp in the rainy season, threatening with death those who would flee. At last, however, their failure became obvious, so many were dying. The survivors tramped to the Mekong, stole or hired boats, bamboo rafts, even inner tubes, and braving night patrols that shot on sight, floated across to Thailand.

The earliest Hmong to cross to Thailand were well organized and not destitute. Some had the honor of helping to build the camps themselves, and within months were on their way to the United States.[7] Later escapees arrived sick and ragged. Some of my informants who arrived in 1977, 1978, and later were greeted with great kindness by Thai peasants who fed and clothed them before delivering them to camps. Others experienced threats, shakedowns, and extortion from Thai military patrols or others. One group of families was turned back to Laos by Thai soldiers, only to escape again. Eventually the women I talked to in Seattle found themselves in Nong Khai, Ban Vinai, Chiang Kham, or another camp, where some of them stayed as long as three years before resettlement. The difficulties and necessities of refugee life at Ban Vinai camp, Thailand, have been described by Long (1988); for other perspectives on camps, see also Cerquone (1986), Hurlich et al. (1986), Mason and Brown (1983), Robinson (in press), and the United States Committee for Refugees (1983).

In the safety of the camps in Thailand, the women began sewing again; indeed one informant (who had worn Lao clothing in Laos) made her first Hmong skirt. Relief workers came to see needlework as a marketable resource for the Hmong. Both missionary and secular agencies provided thread and fabric and encouraged the development of salable goods. As refugees accepted resettlement in third countries, they took with them not only their traditional garments and the cultural knowledge of how to make and use them, but also these new commercialized pieces and some rather tentative and uncertain notions of what constituted salability.

4

THE HMONG IN SEATTLE

My name is Mai Hang. My father's name was Shoua Chai [Suas Ntshai] and my grandfather was Shoua Lu [Suas Lw]. I came to the United States in 1980, and now it's 1984. I have some American friends who want me to sing some Hmong songs. When we have lived in America a long time, the young people will want to know how Hmong songs go, and from this tape recording, they will know. The young people will forget Hmong songs, so I will sing some Hmong songs for the young people to keep. Now I will sing.

> The year is through, twelve months are over.
> The weather will change from summer to winter.
> Winter will come, winter will go away, and summer will return.
> Leaves will come out and grow green on whole branches,
> Insects will sing. Pairs of insects will sing,
> That the old year is past and the new year has come.
> New Year is come. Everyone is killing boars, the relatives
> All join together, every brother, every cousin
> Join together to make parties. Once parties are done,
> They support their leader and praise his name.
> Now we have come over here and the New Year has come.
> But we don't kill the pig, and we don't have a party.
> We have no boars, for we have no land,
> Nowhere to plant our rice and corn.
> Because we have no animals, we cannot have a New Year,
> We cannot invite anybody to come.
> We live on rock. We have no spirit money or incense to burn.
> Religion is different here.
> We came to this country, and saw nothing but crows.
> The birds fly up to catch hold of the branch.
> The birds fly up and sit on the tree.
> We have food, we have clothes, but we don't have our country.
> We have clothes, we have food, but our family is homesick.
> We came and saw only those birds,
> Flying up to catch the tip of the branch.
> Even though we have come to live in this country,

59

Even though we have clothes, we have food,
Still our family is homesick, missing our country.
Why did I come? I have my papers and passport,
But still I am lonely, still I am homesick.
The insect flies to the treetop,
The singing insects fly to the tops of the trees.
I can go outside and see them singing and flying up,
Catching the tips of the treetops.
Why did I come here to be so lonely?
I have clothes, I have food, but I think about my country.
I remember my farm in the valley.
Though here I have three meals a day, still I remember my country.
I live here with plenty of clothes, but still I recall
My country, the trees, the grasses, my own farm, the town.
I think my birth was unlucky.
My parents could bear me, but they could not raise me.
They could not find a good spot for me.
My parents could bear me, but they could not raise me.
They could not help me be adult in this country.
I worry about my future.[1]

In this chapter and the next two, I will describe how the Hmong have lived in the United States, especially in Seattle, from their arrival to the present, concentrating on the period 1980–85. Into this account I weave stories about Hmong women, particularly my friend Ker. My Hmong friends and research subjects now live in Michigan, California, and Wisconsin as well as in Washington state. Some of my information comes from them in their new homes, but in describing their American milieu I emphasize Seattle, where most of my work has been done, and with which I am most familiar.

In 1980–81 the few Hmong already in the city were joined by many newcomers; the population exploded from fewer than a hundred to somewhere around two thousand. These years were marked by intense community organization, much attention from sponsoring and helping agencies and individuals, and energetic efforts by the Hmong to settle in and make a place for themselves while retaining political and social forms from Laos. Some converted to Christianity, mainly by joining the flourishing Christian Missionary Alliance Church; others resolutely maintained the old ways. Many Hmong made unwise purchases, were robbed or suffered other crimes, or acted in other ways that betrayed naiveté in urban settings.

In 1982 cuts in federal benefits cost many families in Seattle their income; Seattle lost about a third of its Hmong population during 1982 and 1983 as families searched elsewhere for jobs and support. These years saw dismay and greater impoverishment, but also efforts at entrepreneurship and holding jobs, and a growing sense of determination to learn how to prosper while explicitly remaining Hmong. There was a continuing and increasing level of attention from sponsors and volunteers, and high public awareness of the Hmong as a definable group. Out of the public eye, the community's financial problems caused the Hmong political leadership to lose credibility with its people, and new leaders came forward, struggling openly for power, with the Hmong church as battleground.

By 1984–85, there seemed to be less of a siege mentality as Hmong families began to cope with their economic situation, but Seattle continued to lose families to California and the Midwest. Those who remained were adapting to American jobs and schools. Sponsor and agency interest was declining. Most Hmong households turned to the new leaders; the former leader moved away. These were the years of our research project.

By 1986–87, numerous Hmong, many with permanent jobs and a strong community organized around the church congregation, appeared to consider Seattle their permanent home. They became United States citizens and some sponsored relatives coming from Thai camps; thus the Hmong population grew slightly. The Hmong became less visible, less written about. They bought homes and consumer goods, and held a public Hmong New Year in Seattle Center each year and a community Hmong New Year for themselves in a high school gym. It seemed they were becoming a permanent ethnic minority.

SEATTLE BETWEEN 1980 AND 1986

In 1980, when the Hmong were arriving in great numbers, Seattle was a city of half a million people, with neighbor cities adding a quarter million more (Bureau of the Census 1981).[2] The city, bounded east and west by bodies of water, is laid out on a north-south axis, with freeways and the railroad cutting around the business core in the middle. Seattle's Asian business area, the International District, sits just south of the financial core, adjacent to a sports palace whose construction displaced Asian households eastward to the affluent suburbs or southward to the nearby neighborhood of Beacon Hill. Industrial neighborhoods sprawl southward around a brewery and toward various Boeing installations. On the near south side, dingy business streets run the long way through valleys folded by ancient glaciers— Rainier Avenue South, Martin Luther King Way South (in 1980 called Empire Way South). On the ridges above these valleys, on the water side, sit expensive homes with views; in the valleys live the poor. Farther south, jets glide in toward SeaTac airport every few minutes. In the houses under the flyway, people stop talking when the jets pass overhead. The tarmac streets are cracked; there are no sidewalks. On the far south side, Seattle fades into the towns of White Center, Burien, Kent, and Renton, where formerly rich farm land has been covered with huge warehouses, factories, and malls. Boeing has a massive factory in Renton.

In 1980, 87 percent of King County's population was white, and about 80,000 people were of Asian descent (Office of Financial Management 1981). Most Asian Americans and Asians in King County in 1980 were Chinese, Japanese, Filipino, or Vietnamese, and mainly white collar or professional workers. The median income for Chinese families was $21,754, for Filipino families $22,637, and for Japanese families $28,705. Nearly all the Vietnamese were recent arrivals (89 percent had come in 1975–79). They were similar to the Chinese and Filipinos in education (77 percent had finished high school, compared to 74 percent of Chinese and 77 percent of Filipinos), but were comparatively financially disadvantaged, with a median family income of $10,238, and 37 percent living below the poverty line.[3] The International District and Beacon Hill were centers for Asian residents, although many Asians did not live in easily defined ethnic neighborhoods. Seattle's other visible ethnic groups—African Americans, Pacific Islanders, and Native Americans, tended to cluster in the Central District (southeast of the main business district), and in Rainier Valley.

THE HMONG COMMUNITY IN SEATTLE

How many Hmong lived in Seattle? In early published reports of the decennial census completed in April 1, 1980, the Bureau of the Census lumped the Hmong with "Other Southeast Asians,"[4] preventing any clear idea of actual numbers. Eventually, in 1988, the bureau reported that eighty-nine Hmong were living within Washington State during 1980, but this figure is an estimate.[5] By mid-1981 Kue Koua, the community leader, was estimating that two thousand Hmong lived in Seattle (personal communication, 1981). Other published estimates such as Yang et al. (1985) and the Office of Refugee Resettlement (ORR 1984), which match Kue Koua's estimate, based themselves on reports of community leaders, in this case Kue Koua himself. But perhaps we can find slightly firmer ground. By October 1980 there were actually 106 Hmong-speaking children in Seattle schools. In the two age pyramids (figs. 2, p. 21, and 4), about one third of the Hmong are of school age. If one third of the Seattle Hmong in 1981 were of school age, and if nearly all school-age Hmong children were actually in

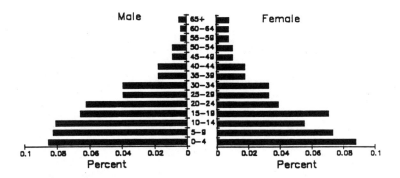

Male   65+   Female
                   60—64
                   55—59
                   50—54
                   45—49
                   40—44
                   35—39
                   30—34
                   25—29
                   20—24
                   15—19
                   10—14
                    5—9
                    0—4

0.1   0.08 0.06 0.04 0.02   0   0   0.02 0.04 0.06 0.08   0.1
        Percent   Percent

FIGURE 4. Age pyramid for Hmong in the United States, 1980 (*source:* Bureau of the Census 1988)

school,[6] we can suppose that about 325 Hmong were living in Seattle by October 1980. Since census estimates were collected before April 1, and the school statistics were collected in October, the period between presumably saw a dramatic increase in the number of Hmong living in Seattle. A year later, the number of Hmong-speaking children enrolled in public school had increased to 143 (a 32 percent increase), implying a community size of about 430. Thus although Kue Koua's estimate of two thousand Hmong in Seattle in 1981 certainly seems high, yet it is understandable, since at the time no one was making actual counts, and even community leaders were only estimating.

The Hmong community did grow fast in 1980 and 1981, not only because many Hmong were being resettled to Seattle, but also because Hmong were coming to Seattle from initial resettlement sites elsewhere. The presence of a national-level Hmong leader, Kue Koua, drew adherents who remembered his power in Laos. The Hmong in Seattle were always divided into factions based on ethnic and political experiences in Laos, but Kue Koua was nevertheless able to place himself in a position of preeminence. In the role of middleman, he brokered benefits from the mainstream society to the Hmong community. Hmong household heads told me that as far as they were concerned, ultimately all resettlement benefits came to them because their leaders were persuasive with the Americans. Therefore community disputes were repressed and a strong front of unity was put forward, symbolized by the densely packed New Year's celebrations of those years.

Despite the song that begins this chapter, some sort of New Year celebration has taken place each year. My first Hmong New Year, in 1980, took place in a November downpour at an old wooden hall near Mount Baker Apartments, the building complex that was becoming the principal

Hmong enclave. A friend and I paid two dollars at the door and pinned small handmade paper flowers on our lapels. Mount Baker Community Club could comfortably hold several hundred people, but that night it was hard to edge onto the main floor, hard to hear over the din, impossible to find a chair. Dignified and slow-moving women in tall turbans, men with bright embroidered sashes, children chattering loudly, teen-agers in elaborate finery, amazed American sponsors and volunteers like me all crammed together inside. Somehow we managed to line up for a buffet dinner of chicken and rice, to step back and clear a space for speeches and singing and *qeej* playing,[7] and to survive screeching microphone feedback and the press of overheated human bodies. Performers were all properly dressed in Hmong clothes. The announcements were long in both Hmong and English, the songs and *qeej* went on and on, and there was no printed program. It all seemed highly successful and well planned to me, except for the place being too small.

Scott (1982) has described the Hmong New Year in San Diego and its shifts of symbolic emphasis. With the old Hmong life torn apart, and the survivors forced into this new urban environment, the play and rituals of renewal connected with the New Year were rendered obsolete and their performance became artificial, self-conscious, alienated. They became "cultural displays" rather than lived rituals, icons of a remembered past rather than natural expressions of an understood reality.

Such falseness was not visible in the 1980 Seattle New Year, thus it was all the more apparent in the New Year of 1981, which took place in the windowed auditorium of a new high school. This place was much larger and more modern than the old community club, with a raised stage and an extensive carpeted foyer where the food was set out. Perhaps over a thousand people attended, yet the place was not crowded. The program took longer, and departed from the schedule (printed in Hmong and fractured English) because of long delays between what can best be called presentations. There was a fashion show put on by teen-agers dressed in different Hmong dialect and regional styles from Laos, their costumes tricked out with flocked velvet, fluorescent threads, and plastic bangles. They kept glancing sideways to position themselves relative to each other, flicking their sashes into position, the boys abruptly flashing big smiles, the girls with downcast eyes and scared faces. A female announcer in spike heels talked them onstage with bright patter in English. The *qeej* performance was short, the political speeches long and exhortatory. There was a brief effort at a New Year ritual, with an old man stating the auguries of a ritually sacrificed chicken, but since many in the audience were Christian and had given up reading auguries, this seemed to have been put on the program to signify the Hmong past, a deliberately conceived "old culture from Laos." For the first time I saw what were called "Hmong dances," a bevy of little girls making something like the hand movements of Lao dance, and acting out the broadcasting of seed, the harvesting and winnowing of rice. Girls' line dances as expressions of cultural traditions are innovations among refugee Hmong, not present in Laos. A short performance of the courting ball game, *pov pob* [toss ball], was given by giggling boys and girls. Outside a soccer tournament drew many onlookers. In contrast to the previous year, family groups sat at separate tables, and some people looked bored or sad. The 1981 New Year seemed a transitional event put together by people who were trying out various experiments. The 1980 flush of success at simply having arrived had given way to the dismaying recognition that life was not at all easy in the new land.

THE UNITED STATES HMONG POPULATION IN 1980

Searching for adequate objective or statistical descriptions of Hmong refugee households and household economics in Seattle and in the United States as a whole usually turns up statistical summaries for the larger categories "Hmong/Mien," "Highland Lao," "Lao," "Indochinese," or even "Southeast Asian." On the local level, Seattle is not always the unit of analysis, which is likely to be King County, or Washington State, or the Seattle-Everett Standard Metropolitan Statistical Area. Some kinds of statistics, such as age pyramids, have apparently never been constructed for Hmong anywhere in the U.S. Different sources disagree about number and distribution of Hmong. Most figures are estimates.

Hmong are most often grouped with other tribal refugees from the Lao mountains—the Iu Mien and the Lao Theung—into a group called "Lao Highland refugees." Approximately 90 percent of all Lao Highland refugees are Hmong (Yang et al. 1985: 5). The first Lao Highlanders came to the United States in 1975, and from 1976 to 1980 their numbers doubled each year, so that by the end of 1980, 46,700 Lao Highlanders had arrived (ORR 1985:1: 36). In 1981, however, paralleling the decline in all refugee admissions, fewer than 4,000 were admitted, in 1982 about 2,500, and small numbers each year until 1986, when 3,670 admissions reversed the downward trend. In 1987 admissions grew to 8,300 (ORR 1988: 26). Though admissions peaked in 1980, the Hmong population has continued growing apace, owing to the famous Hmong fertility rate.[8] Estimates vary as to current Hmong population. In 1983 the Hmong population in the United States was estimated at 60,000–65,000 (ORR 1985: 1), and later estimates varied from that number to about 100,000 American Hmong, depending on how birth rates were estimated. The 1990 census counted 90,042 Hmong in the United States (Bureau of the Census 1991).

Information about the economic and social characteristics of Hmong in the United States as a whole can help describe the Seattle Hmong, though the Seattle Hmong would not exactly match the profile provided by national census data. The census estimated 5,204 Hmong in the whole United States by April 1, 1980, nearly all in cities. More than 25 percent lived in Minnesota, 14 percent in California, and most of the rest in Illinois, Wisconsin, Iowa, Utah, and Oregon; Washington was estimated to have 89 Hmong.

The median age of resettled Hmong in 1980 was 16.5 years. Table 1 presents the census data. Comparing percentages by three age groups (0–14, 15–64, 65+) with the percentages for Hmong in Laos in 1972 (Yang 1975, see chapter 2), yields a slightly smaller percentage of children under 15, a larger percentage 15–64, and a smaller percentage again for 65+ (47 percent, 52 percent, and 1 percent in 1980 compared with 49.7 percent, 48.8 percent, and 1.5 percent in 1972). In table 1 the age groups under 25 are arranged by five-year intervals, while ages 25 and above are arranged by ten-year intervals. I have constructed an age pyramid using the census data in figure 4. The age pyramid for 1980 uses five-year intervals throughout, dividing the ten-year figures in half, so the pyramid is more readable and will compare with Yang's pyramid. Thus the upper age groups in figure 5 are presented schematically.

TABLE 1

Sex and age of Hmong in the United States, 1980

Age	Male	Female	Total
0–4	446	458	904
5–9	431	383	814
10–14	422	289	711
15–19	343	370	713
20–24	325	205	530
25–34	412	348	760
35–44	187	191	378
45–54	90	113	203
55–64	39	83	122
65+	25	44	69
Total	2,720	2,484	5,204

Source: Bureau of the Census (1988).

The differences between this age pyramid (fig. 4) and Yang's (fig. 2, p .00) based on data collected in 1968, are most noticeable. In his pyramid, boys outnumber girls by about 10 percent in every age group up to age 20. From 20 to 39, women outnumber men by 13 percent: the shortage of men can be attributed to warfare. Above age 40 men outnumber women by 8 percent, but the numbers are very small. The 1980 age pyramid is twelve years later, so the 20–39-year-olds are now 32–51. If the distribution by sex were the same as in 1968, one would expect an excess of males below 30 and an excess of females above 30. This is the case, even though the figures are obscured because the age categories are 25–34 and 35–44, instead of 20–30 and 30–40. But the percentage of difference is much greater in 1980. Males outnumber females by 17 percent in the group 5–35, and females outnumber males by 21 percent above age 35. An exception is the 0–4 category where the proportions are about equal (these represent births since 1975 and would seem to indicate that little girls are now surviving as often as little boys, which was not the case in 1972). The greater percentage of young men and boys suggests that migrating households attracted young male relatives to them, and the greater number of older women means that widows migrated more readily than older men (being either mothers attached to migrating families, widowed heads of household, or second, levirate wives of migrating men).

The interesting anomaly in the number of 15- to 19-year-old females makes it appear that many young women also were attaching themselves to migrating households. In chapter 6, I will describe a wedding that took place in Seattle. The young couple had eloped in the refugee camp, so in traditional Hmong thinking they were already married, but the bride had not gone to live with the groom's family, nor had the final wedding parties taken place. Each had remained in their parental household until after migration. Her family had feared that if one family were resettled to the United States and the other to France, and she were with her new husband's family, they would lose touch with her. They had persuaded her to wait and see where each family went. The implication was that if the families were separated, the marriage could be canceled (and indeed I knew a young Hmong man in Seattle whose incomplete marriage to a girl resettled to France was canceled in 1987).

There would also have been practical considerations for the boy's family keeping their new daughter-in-law with her parents. The United States was a more attractive resettlement site than France. If her family were resettled to the United States and she accompanied them, then the young husband could join his wife, and his parents could accompany him, taking advantage of the resettlement principle of family reunification. His family could use the children's marriage tie to ensure resettlement to the United States.

Perhaps many betrothed or married girls thus migrated with their own parents if their husband's family remained in camp. Meanwhile, married boys going for resettlement would bring their wives, whose parents could then join them for family reunification. Daughters plus young wives would thus outnumber sons, and the excess of girls 15 to 19 years old would be explained. This interpretation depends on the Hmong structural principle that a young wife should join her husband's family, but a young husband should not live with his wife's. The boy would not accompany his wife's parents, even if they were migrating, because he is only and forever part of his father's descent group.[9]

The Hmong in the United States in 1980 look like a very young and family-oriented population. Ninety-eight percent had married by the age of 25; virtually all were living within families.[10] Most families (88 percent) included both members of a couple, and nearly all (96 percent) had children. The average size of households was 5.8 persons, this number often including relatives other than parents and children. The high percentage of two-parent families indicates quick remarriage for those refugees who lost spouses in war or flight. As the average education in 1980 for Hmong males over 15 was 8.3 years and for females 6.9 years, these Hmong constitute a relatively urbanized first wave. The average education of resettled Hmong after 1980 is 1.8 years.

The figures show that at the beginning of 1980 these recently arrived Hmong were an economically unstable population, mainly very poor and probably working at parttime and temporary jobs. Of 862 Hmong families, 388 had no working members during 1980, 290 had one worker, 121 had two workers, and 63 had three or more. About 32 percent of men over 16 years old were working during 1979, but only one-quarter of these worked all year;[11] working men averaged 15 weeks of unemployment. During the same year, 18 percent of women worked, with about a third of them working all year; working women averaged 19 weeks of unemployment. Half of all Hmong families had incomes from work of less than $5,000 for the year, and 66 percent of families were below the poverty line. The census also estimated that nine Hmong families had incomes above $50,000 per year, but there is no information about the size or composition of these affluent families.

No mention is made in the census statistics of federal Refugee Cash Assistance (RCA), but clearly many Hmong families were receiving such payments, available for the first thirty-six months after arrival. The Office of Refugee Resettlement's *Report to the Congress* (ORR 1981: 29–33) does not break Hmong out of the category "Lao" and does not provide the explicit amount given to refugees. Eligibility criteria were left in the hands of the states and generally were the same as those for welfare eligibility. ORR's total cash assistance budget for all refugees in 1980 was $177,951,000, and its total number of cash assistance cases was 60,907, yielding an annual average payment per case of $2,922. Since cases averaged 2.89 persons, cash assistance averaged just over $1,000 a year per person, plus Medicaid and food stamps. We may guess that the average Hmong household of 5.8 persons received about $5,860 in RCA, plus Medicaid and food stamps.

HMONG FAMILIES

I began to visit Hmong families, using the garden projects as a reason to get to know them better. Helping them find tools and seed, Rototilling with them, driving them from home to garden, and working alongside them, I found my access to their lives improving, though often at first our communication was poor because of language difficulties. My early notes often report this kind of interaction:

> Xee's is a household of women—herself, her mother, her sister, and all their children. There is no husband, but still she has had a baby who is now 20 months old.[12] Last Saturday I picked her up, along with her mother, See Ya, for whom we were preparing a garden at Thistle P-Patch. Laura B., a medical intern who wants to serve in a refugee community but thinks there will be no jobs in this era of cutbacks, came with me.
>
> The work consisted of clearing grass roots from the space Xee had earlier broken with the *hlau* [short-handled hoe], then reducing the clods to friable soil, and the two Hmong women beat us at speed and efficiency. Xee and Laura on opposite sides of the strip on their knees beamed at one another across the language barrier, their grubby hands full of weeds. See Ya tried the American hoe with its long handle and narrow neck, weighing it against her experience of the more substantial *hlau*, accepted the (to her) foreign tool with a smile. We traded vocabulary regarding rocks, weeds, planting, flowers, seeds; we made long furrows and planted beans, radish, mustard. I made mounds for summer squashes and was rewarded by a very dubious look from Xee, which made me wonder if she will undo them later and make rows.
>
> Mr. Gransberry arrived to work his plot (which we'd had our eye on in case he abandoned it). He's a trim fellow in his middle years, dressed in clean sports clothes and clean sneakers, with a jolly smile and a friendly manner, an avid flower gardener. He has devoted his entire plot to dahlias and gladioli, double digging it and removing *every* grass root, making elaborate

mounds and then spading a trench which he practically paved with sprouting bulbs. We looked at his hundreds of bulbs, all dusted with an antibacterial agent and *so* carefully handled. He means to show the flowers at the Flower Festival and the Dahlia Show. Gransberry offered a double handful of bulbs to Xee, who ducked her head and gazed wordlessly up at him from under her eyebrows, standing like a peasant with feet wide apart, her Laotian skirt muddy around the bottom, *hlau* in hand, hair escaping from its knot, staring silently and somehow darkly. She couldn't figure out a polite refusal, but seemed disdainful of his project, for to her wasting time on flowers seemed unbelievable and maybe immoral, and she doubted his common sense or maybe sanity.[13] I diverted him with a laugh and we agreed food plants are more important to her family. (June 1981)

Soon, by expanding contacts and following social networks, I was well enough acquainted to visit with eight or nine families. Their living situation was depressing. They lived in rough neighborhoods, in apartments that invariably had roaches and various signs of decay, fallen tile in the bathroom, balcony doors that had come off their tracks, leaky taps, and broken kitchen exhaust fans. Since steaming rice the Hmong way involves an elaborate process of half-cooking, then rinsing, then re-steaming, kitchen walls grew dank with mildew. People who had grown up with dirt floors found it hard to keep shag carpets clean. Sudden accumulations of clothes and household goods were tumbled in corners, and in each room a single overhead light bulb cast harsh shadows. Practical old Formica kitchen tables and plastic covered kitchen chairs were popular furnishings, as were big old television sets. Usually the whole family slept in one bedroom on wall-to-wall beds, using second and third bedrooms for storage. Living room furniture showed some variety, being usually donated, and fell rapidly into incredible disrepair.

I came to the conclusion that sleeping arrangements were more important to Hmong families than any other element of the apartment. It was very comforting and important for them to sleep all together and was thought unkind to the children to shove them off to another room. A second very important element of most apartments was a line of eight by ten inch photographs, hung high on the living room wall, of family members in Hmong costume and old images from Laos and from the camps. Parents and grandparents, enlarged from old snapshots, looked out over their descendants. One family (composed of two brothers, their wives and children, and the husbands' aged mother) had a poster-sized enlargement of the husbands' father from a snapshot taken years before, surrounded by four of his five sons each touching him, and the family told me often how the father had died, how this brother had disappeared in Laos, that brother now lived in Santa Ana, that one in Wisconsin, and the youngest brother had been absent when the picture was taken. The history and unity of the family were summarized in this poster; each living brother, I was told, had one on his wall.

Many of the families I visited were nuclear. Others included aged parents. One included the husband's two brothers, another the husband's sister and cousin, and two families were headed by widows. Household form was deceiving, however, because apartments and houses were the wrong size and shape for Hmong families. Limits of responsibility and duty were not defined by apartment walls. One widow was actually the levirate second wife of a youth who lived down the hall with his young wife and son. Another couple could tell the husband's younger brother (who lived nearby with his wife) whether and when to have children. Groups of brothers pooled all their money, except immediate household expenses, for buying such items as cars in rotation.

Almost the first thing many people told me was of their tragedies:

[Ker said,] "We walk thirty-two days from Laos to the river. All is trees. I carry one boy and one boy walk. Chue Neng carry rice. We carry one pan and knife and clothes. We carry silver, also seeds. Little Neng have four years that time, and Ly more than two years. Food is not too much."

I looked at Ker squinting into the warm spring sun, Chue Neng beside her, walking from the garden through the neighborhood of small neat houses. There was a wall of unmortared rocks beside us, well grown with cascades of alyssum. Ker pulled off a bit of green, glancing up at me.

"We eat like this. How you call this?"

"Leaves."

"We eat leaves. Everybody eat leaves. There is one leaves, I give it to the younger boy and he die. Many people die from that leaves, maybe more than two hundred. We just keep going." (February 1981)

The first thing people wanted to know about me was social context:

"You are married?"

"No, not married."

She looks at me. "Your husband die?"

"No, we do not want to be married. He lives far away, married again. I do not want to be married."

"Hmong everybody married." Clearly she does not believe my preference for the single state.

"In America no husband is OK. Husband, too much time. Too much cooking, too much cleaning. I like no husband."

Ker stares at me. She and Chue Neng talk together very seriously. "You have children?"

"No, too bad, no children. But now I have more time, I can take my time to help some people." I smile, but though they smile they seem uncertain, unconvinced. (February 1981)

What Ker and Chue Neng have learned here is my marginality, in Hmong terms, to social life. If I were Hmong, I would be thought crazy to prefer this state. Indeed, the situation of being a divorced and childless woman was so devalued by Hmong as to be associated with utter failure, so it was hard for them to put me together with financial success and educational attainments, nor did they understand my independence as a virtue. I represented an aspect of American society that puzzled and alarmed them. Only after either I let them know it pained me to be childless, or we could develop a joking relationship around my despised American feminism, could particular Hmong feel comfortable around me.

Once they began to open up to me, my women friends complained endlessly. They were often feeling sick, and did not like the climate or the food. Often their sicknesses were explained by long-ago hardships in Laos— carrying burdens that were too heavy, being persistently cold, or having to work when ill. I heard about the tough parts of life in Laos and about terrific feats of endurance. They described life as a round of suffering in which they were defined by their labor and their generosity. I noticed a rhetorical component in these stories: describing a current problem was how women asked for advice or reached out for sympathy; describing the terrible past helped create empathy and friendship. Their many complaints seemed a form of social glue, contributing to the reestablishment of community cohesion, so fractured in migration.

Also, I felt, my Hmong friends were really bewildered and dismayed by aspects of American society they found after resettlement. Easy promises ("See you later" or "We'll do it next week") they took literally. Casual speculations ("Maybe you could do practical nursing") they interpreted as firm plans. Hopeful reassurances ("Things will get better") they saw as indicating foreknowledge. Americans are full of such easy phrases, which trip off the tongue in social situations without necessarily implying commitment. My Hmong friends came from a harsher school, in which a promise was a vow and a statement was a fact. Words were not used idly, which might have to do with nonliteracy and the binding nature of verbal contracts. As my Hmong friends became aware of the extent to which Americans ignore our promises and the literal implications of our words in daily life, they began to apply this knowledge to American military promises of the wartime past, where to their newly opened eyes there seemed to be a chasm of dishonesty and false speaking. (I draw this interpretation from comments of various Hmong men.) This was shocking to them because, while Hmong might not always tell the exact truth to non-Hmong, many of the life decisions of their recent past had been predicated on their trust in Americans' essential reliability. So I tried to judge my words more carefully before speaking, and as I became very close to some families, I tried to assess my perception of their own basic honesty within close-knit groups by asking to know things (especially attitudes) that they might not volunteer. What I found was how I was placed in the Hmong hierarchy, sometimes outside and sometimes inside it, above most women depending usually on age but below the men. The degree of truth one received had to do with one's social place and respectability, with how well one was trusted. And so if Americans habitually were careless with communications, my Hmong friends were distressed because they read in this contempt for themselves. This became very pointed when funding cuts occurred, as described below.

Out their windows, the Hmong saw the economic bottom of Seattle. Though Seattle's poorest neighborhoods are not like the slums of larger, older cities, still they are depressed and demoralized areas. Hmong men and women both were shocked by theft and especially by armed robbery; they could not believe that American society at large so easily tolerated such offenses.[14] The women generally felt unsafe outside their apartments, not without cause. In Laos women were commonly entrusted with the family's wealth, acting as banks and hiding the money and silver at home. Because they knew their apartments were vulnerable to burglars, these same women now were too nervous to leave money at home, so at first they carried it with them in their purses. Considerable sums were lost to purse snatchers before families figured out they needed bank accounts for their money[15] and safety deposit boxes for their gold and silver jewelry. Experiences of theft, personal violence, or threats contributed to the desire to shut out this new world and create a private world where Hmong values and manners would prevail and children could be raised with the Hmong values of hard work, family loyalty, and self-reliance.

SOCIAL CHANGES

Many of the American sponsors, volunteers, and agency personnel interacting with resettled Hmong were women. They did not treat husbands as the sole channel to families and dealt readily with Hmong women.

Although the Hmong ideal was to make decisions within family-based social groups, which were always headed by men, in the United States both men and women were being asked to make decisions as individuals.[16] Women were expected to learn to work away from home, to spend money, to drive a car, to speak English with non-Hmong, to have ideas of their own. Most were in contact with American women who did such things outside families, even with some who did not live in nuclear families at all. Most Hmong could not see the structural hierarchies of American society that frame our lives, so they perceived American society as disorderly in terms of Hmong society. This perceived chaos was compounded for Hmong by the trouble they had setting up again their own economic and social lives.

One most notable barrier to reconstituting Hmong society in America was that many mature Hmong men, heads of families and responsible for the welfare of their household, found themselves economically dependent, unable to comprehend the job market, find or keep a job, or (if working) earn enough to support their families. The biggest problem was English, a problem well shown in the film *Becoming American* (Iris Films 1981). In this film, Hmong hold their 1981 Fourth of July celebration in a Seattle park. Hundreds of people attend, sharing a meal of rice with chicken, fruit, and soda. While children run about, the women sit gossiping on the grass in the sunshine and the male heads of household hold a "town meeting." They stand in a circle with Kue Koua in the middle, talking about their problems. Kue Koua listens, and the men speak out. Meanwhile, I was sitting with some women as Kue Koua's wife explained that this is how Hmong communities air grievances and reach decisions, and that this circle of men could be standing in the Lao mountains. At the end, Kue Koua will say what they all have said; he will summarize and express the consensus of the whole group. Because he can do that, he is the leader, she says proudly. In the film one man says, "I was a soldier; now I wash dishes. I can't understand what anybody says. The only English I know is 'OK.' If they say 'how you doing,' I say 'OK.' If they say, 'do this,' I say 'OK.' Whatever they say, I say 'OK.' They could say, 'eat shit,' and I'd say 'OK!' "[17] At the end, Kue Koua can only say what everybody already knows. "Just keep trying. We have to try harder, there's nothing else to do."

Tension grew in Hmong households because men felt they were losing their basis of command. This can be seen in the following joke: "When we get on the plane to go back to Laos, the first thing we will do is beat up the women!" This joke, told at a family picnic at the end of July 1981, appeared to be thought very funny, with both men and women laughing heartily. The joke has a complicated ironic underlay of male unhappiness and helplessness, a combination of the men's unemployability, the sudden economic value placed on women's work, and men's fear of losing power in their families. The state could circumscribe the authority of a man even within his own household, for instance by forbidding him to beat his wife. When T in terrible anger beat his wife, in 1981, she called her friend who called me to ask what T's wife should do. She should leave him, I said immediately. But instead they called Kue Koua, who convened the men of T's family and told them T could be put in jail. Later T's wife told me he wasn't hitting her anymore, which I took as being true. The women laughed at the joke above because when a Hmong man makes a joke, a Hmong woman laughs. But in addition, they could laugh easily because they did not expect a plane back to Laos. No Hmong woman has ever told me she wanted to live in Laos again.

In 1982 the California brother (cousin, we would say) of a Seattle man named Chou died in the night of Sudden Death Syndrome. Chou went to California to exercise his levirate right [18] over the pretty widow, but she refused, saying she'd rather live on welfare. He piled all his brother's stuff into his brother's car and drove up in one furious dash. When I said I thought the widow inherited the car, Chou's older brother's wife set me straight: the nearest male relative inherited everything; the widow got nothing. Six months after this I visited the widow, who turned out to be young and vivacious. She had bought a little car. She and her two toddlers had an apartment near her parents, and she was taking English classes and intended to become a secretary. I never found out whether she succeeded, but if she and her husband had remained in Laos and her husband had died, she would have needed to marry Chou. In the American economy she could strike out on her own.

The new environment was reaching into the Hmong family in a thousand less dramatic, but equally fragmenting ways. This was particularly visible with the second son of Ker, Pao. The family story about this boy was that he was the mischievous one. He was conceived during a period when his father had been very sick, and the piglet that would have been sacrificed to ensure a good birth for the baby was sacrificed instead for the father's recovery. His birth had almost killed his mother. She viewed him as the one who disobeyed and got into trouble. When he fell off his bike at five, during one of my first visits to their apartment, tearing his ear open and howling helplessly, she gave him little sympathy, berating him roughly as she patched him up. Pao did act wilder than the other children, staying outside and roughhousing, shouting in the house, ignoring orders, hitting his little sisters. But I thought he appeared eager, curious, smart— and frustrated, without approved outlets for his high energy. His teachers liked him. He made friends with the black neighbor children (who were disapproved of), talking their slang, swinging his hips, and mouthing off to his parents—and was kept inside with nothing to do. His older brother was being taught responsibility, and his little sisters were learning obedience, but Pao, while there was never any doubt he was part of the family, was out of step and uncooperative, often being told to "stop that." By the time he was eight his mother was saying she didn't think he was her child and his father was trying to control him with ridicule. When the family moved from Seattle, one reason they gave was removing Pao from the environment of the housing project. This child might have been the family problem in Laos as in Seattle, positioned as he was to be the scapegoat, but in Seattle, additional alienating opportunities were available to him at every turn. In their next location, a small Midwest town, as Pao grew he stayed outside even more often, but at eleven this meant fishing, playing with other Hmong boys, and running errands, all approved activities. He and his family were more cordial to each other and the problem seemed to have abated.

THE JOB MARKET

My entrance to Hmong households was by helping husbands and wives adapt to their new surroundings. Starting with helping them find gardens, I soon found myself teaching English one-on-one, explaining and filling out car and hospital insurance forms, teaching driving, and looking for suitable jobs. Many of the things I did had economic implications, so I was often able to watch individual Hmong encounter the American job market. The Hmong I knew had clear ideas about economics. Any increase in income was worth taking. The female interpreter at the Indochinese Women's Program quit, although she liked the job very well, because she had a better offer ironing shirts in a laundry. This woman was living in West Seattle, a long bus ride from the IWP. She deducted the bus cost from the IWP salary, and balanced that amount against the laundry job minus child care (which had come free at IWP), and figured she would clear three dollars a week more at the laundry.

More than one woman wanted to sew for a living, sewing by machine being an extension of women's hand sewing. I took Ker and Ploa to meet Barbara M., a transplanted New York clothing designer. Ker and Ploa seemed abashed before Barbara, slipping their samples out of their purses with downcast eyes, although Barbara thought their sewing was good. Barbara explained her work designing maternity clothes for a mail-order house. She selected fabrics from swatches and bolts sent from New York, draped her dressmaker's dummy (made pregnant with a wad of paper) and cut the pattern right in the cloth, later drawing it on paper. Cloth and pattern she sent to a specialty seamstress in New York, who made samples. The samples went to a factory in Pennsylvania for cost analysis, and then were made in thousands by a troop of garment workers sewing parts. This kind of complicated arrangement was entirely new to Ker and Ploa, who could not fathom the purpose of such a long-distance operation. Barbara showed us in a catalog a picture of the same soft, draped, printed blouse that we were holding in our hands—and this picture made it all clear to Ker. This blouse cost eight dollars to produce, but sold for eighteen in the catalog.

It was the job of garment worker that Ker and Ploa aspired to, but clearly they were not ready. We talked about producing vests with Hmong embroidery (Barbara's idea of a sideline, piecework at home for Ker and Ploa) and Ker even made a sample later, but this was not cost effective. Already in 1981, without having held a job yet, they both had realized that time is money. Government refugee benefits saved them from having to work for next to nothing.

In the early spring of 1981 I found a job for a young man named Tria washing dishes in a new French restaurant. The job involved scraping dishes, fitting them into a machine, putting in detergent, choosing various settings depending on the load, pulling the clean dishes out and stacking them, as well as the usual pot scouring and garbage hauling. Also there were a lot of people to establish friendly relations with—chefs, sous chefs, a pastry chef and a *patissier* (who made paté), waiters and the *maitre d'hôte*. Tria had hardly any command of English. I got frantic calls about spots on the crystal; Tria couldn't read directions or follow oral instructions. I got an interpreter, and we all kept at it. Tria didn't like washing dishes, but he persisted because he had a wife and two children to support, as well as car payments.

Refugees coming to the United States had been promised cash and medical assistance, English as a second language (ESL) training, job training, employment services, and mental health counseling. Federal grants of up to thirty-six months of income had been promised in support of families making this cultural and economic transition, partly so states would escape the financial burden that might lead them to refuse refugee resettlement. This strategy had worked successfully in resettling the Vietnamese who arrived 1975–76, a group characterized by a mainly urban background and high educational level. However, the Hmong and Mien who came after 1980 had an average of only 1.8 years of education in their homeland. One-third of household heads and two-thirds of spouses reported themselves as

unable to speak any English even after an average of 633 hours of ESL
training:

> Likely to experience long-term hardship are those refugees who have been
> relatively unsuccessful in adapting to the American way of life. One measure
> of adaptation is level of English language proficiency. From this perspective,
> those having the most difficulty are from rural, subsistence farming back-
> grounds in Southeast Asia . . . have little or no formal education, and have
> job skills less transferable to the American labor market. A disproportionate
> number of . . . Hmong and Mien fall into these categories. (Wilson and
> Garrick 1983: 18)

The Hmong, with mostly rural backgrounds and little formal schooling, also arrived just as the American political and economic climate was
changing. High inflation followed by high interest rates precipitated a deep
recession. Jobs became scarce at the same time that a new conservative administration focused on reducing funding for social programs. The refugee
assistance program was politically vulnerable to financial cuts, and in 1982
the federal government suddenly reduced the length of possible refugee
support from thirty-six to eighteen months. Though a temporary restrain-
ing order forced a postponement, this funding cut was finally carried out
in June 1982. Refugee families who had been in the United States longer
than eighteen months but less than thirty-six months, and who were still
dependent on federal assistance, found themselves with no means of support.[19]

In Washington State, almost 4,000 "refugee assistance units" (individuals and households), including about 10,000 people, were affected by the
federal cuts. About 13 percent of them, or 445 cases, were Hmong and
Mien, almost all from King County, where Seattle is located. Since the
average size of the Hmong and Mien assistance unit was 3.8 persons, this
means that almost 1,700 Hmong and Mien were affected. We do not know
exactly how many of these were Hmong, or exactly how many lived in
Seattle, rather than the rest of King County or Spokane County, the only
other county in the state with Hmong. Still, we can guess that most of the
Hmong in Seattle lost support at this time, since refugees arriving in the
United States in 1979 and 1980, the period of the great Hmong influx,
were those affected by the cut.

Four months before and three months after termination of assistance,
the Washington State Bureau of Refugee Assistance (BORA) conducted
surveys of families dependent on federal refugee assistance (Wilson and
Garrick 1983). Included in the BORA study were forty-eight Hmong and

Mien assistance units. Between February and September 1982, 40 percent of the units moved out of state (mainly to California). The thirty households remaining in Washington increased in size from an average of 5.7 persons to an average of 7.0 persons. By September, eleven households had someone working at least part time. For these working families, average household income was $632 a month. Only eight households received cash assistance, leaving eleven households with no apparent money income. Presumably these were among the twenty households getting food stamps.

Washington is considered a "welfare-unattractive" state (ORR 1984, vol. 1), because it does not provide support to unemployed two-parent households, so that intact families with two healthy parents are left without recourse if they cannot find work. Refugee family heads might have been able to find some sort of work, despite low education and few transferable job skills, but in 1982 there was another reason for their unemployment: the recession. The Seattle job market could not absorb the suddenly needy Hmong. "Seattle was hard hit in 1981 and 1982. Timber, construction, and the aerospace industry all suffered" (Caplan et al. 1985: 29). The consequence was not only high unemployment but also downward mobility for mainstream workers, who took low-end jobs refugees might otherwise have had. At the same time, "services—language, social, and vocational . . . were cut back considerably in 1981–1982 due to the problems of the recession and state and federal budget reductions" (ibid.). Families that turned to state welfare found a highly bureaucratized system:

> In Seattle, the application for assistance requires a refugee service worker to interview all adults in the household, with the result being a Personal Employment Plan. Once they receive cash assistance they must report monthly to the EOC employment program. . . . In mid-1982, the Federal government began to require everyone on [Assistance to Families with Dependent Children and Refugee Cash Assistance] to submit monthly reports on their eligibility. Only Washington had implemented this requirement by the time of [Caplan's] survey. The complexity of the form resulted in a good deal of confusion among the refugees, and some 150 families lost their eligibility that fall because they did not submit the proper forms. (ibid., 38)

In spring 1982 I was away, and when I came back in June, the cut had just taken place. I remember going to visit one household and being politely served Kool-Aid and pickles, that being all they had except rice to feed their family of four children. After the cuts, American friends of Hmong plunged into job finding. My notes from that time detail searches at various employment centers and job-training programs in the following areas: delivery companies using Mopeds, bicycles, vans, or the worker's own car; grounds maintenance, janitorial, or food service work at large corporations, churches, hospitals, or schools; newspaper delivery; supermarket work; home childcare; restaurant work; stocking shelves; construction; landscaping; green plant maintenance companies; slaughterhouses; jewelry making; hair cutting; truck driving; gas station work; general day labor; and luggage sewing. Nearly all these notes are labeled "Washout."

In July I arranged an honorarium for Ker to talk about Hmong women's health-care needs to a two-day conference sponsored by Federal Region X. We passed a picket line of Hmong and Lao, arranged by Employment Opportunities Commission, protesting the federal cuts. The picketers looked as if they were on holiday, joking for the TV cameras; only the Americans looked grim. Funding was not restored. A few temporary jobs came along— playing Hmong music; delivering newspapers; dishwashing; pick-up day labor for an odd-job man. Later in the summer there were out-of-town jobs harvesting. Many women seriously tried to sell needlework at fairs and in shops as discussed in the next chapter.

By May 1983 the Office of Refugee Resettlement estimated that Seattle had lost many refugees to secondary migration, retaining only about 700 Hmong, 550 Iu Mien, 150 Lao Lue, and 230 Lao Theung, for a total of 1,630 persons in the general category Lao Highland (Yang et al. 1985: 8). However this estimate, based like the figures at the beginning of the chapter on M.A.A. reports, is doubtless incorrect, since only 98 Hmong students were in public school in October 1983. This should indicate approximately 300 Hmong remaining in Seattle.

A QUARREL ABOUT MONEY

Meanwhile, Ker had begun working full time, as had her husband, Chou Neng, she at housekeeping, he stocking shelves in a grocery. They had joined the Missionary Alliance Church right after arriving in the United States, because when their child was born, they could not find a live chicken to sacrifice. This meant the infant had no spirit protection; their first view of Christianity was as a way of subverting malicious spirits. But if they found safety in Christianity, they had little knowledge of its tenets. She could go to church, but he worked on Sundays. As time passed, she learned more about the Bible than he.

The couple shared cooking and childcare on an equal basis. As Ker's English improved and she began reading and writing, her comprehension of American society at large also increased faster than that of her husband, who had little skill with English. With my help, she began communicating with her children's teachers, with the doctor, and medical and auto insurance companies. They opened a bank account; she paid the bills. She got a raise so that she earned slightly more than he per hour, although since he worked longer hours, he still made more money. He had two car accidents, both owing to slow responses, and seemed increasingly timid.

He said he didn't know what to think anymore, and increasingly stayed home. He began experiencing serious headaches for which his sympathetic doctor could find no remedy. Presently he expressed a strong desire to go to church, to learn how to think. In a time of recession, however, taking Sunday off would have meant giving up his job. In this family, the wife was becoming stronger and more capable, while the husband was trapped in a situation more and more out of his control.

Besides themselves and their four young children, Ker and Chou Neng's household included Chou Neng's younger brother, Bee, and a young male cousin, Va. Both youths were in high school and working part time. They paid a little toward household expenses, but covered only about one third of their own consumption, spending their money mainly on cars and clothing.

Over time, Ker became increasingly irritated at spending on these youths money she and Chou Neng had earned. In the fall of 1983, when they had been in the United States for three years, she demanded that they pay more toward the rent. They refused, arguing that the real family consisted of the three Ly brothers (Chou Neng, Bee, and Va) along with the children, who carried the name Ly. Because Ker was not a Ly but an outsider (being a Lor), she could not ask them for money. Only Chou Neng could do that. After much discussion, arbitrated by the harassed and discomfited husband, this argument prevailed.

Family finances continued as before, but Ker found her respect within the household diminished, and strove to reestablish herself by sending cash and presents to her husband's father in Thailand. It appeared that she had no comeback to the claim that she was an outsider in a family of Ly men. Though she handled the money, managed the bank account, and made such decisions as what vehicle to buy, these were explicitly defined as services to the Ly family, and not as the acts of a spouse in a nuclear family.

Ker's assumption that the nuclear family formed of herself and her husband and children was the core of the household was partly a consequence of resettlement in the United States. It is not that in Laos the Hmong did not establish nuclear families, but this kind of family unit was secondary to the more important family of related men who worked together and stuck together throughout life. In the United States, however, apartments were generally too small for more than one nuclear family, and incomes were pooled within the nuclear family. While related men tried to live near each other and continued to cooperate in many aspects of life, day-to-day life in the Seattle Hmong community was conducted within a nuclear framework, which is why Ker supposed it was more important. Lines of respect and obedience are clearly visible in this episode: Ker accepted her lesser status and strove to placate the elder male head of the Ly family by sending presents, for though he lived far outside the household his power as family head was expressed through his male descendants. Ker's husband did not have a strong or decisive nature, but tradition gave a weight to his decisions that hers did not carry, although hers was the stronger personality. Even teen-age boys proved more influential than she, because they, being male, were essential to the paternal line, while she, being female, was not. In Laos, Hmong women left their homes at marriage to move into their husband's families, while men stayed near their kinsmen throughout life if they could. Thus women existed on the periphery of Hmong families, in terms of domestic power, their security coming from their sons, while men were central and commanded obedience.[20] The survival of this social structure is visible in this incident.

Clearly Ker yielded to the men's conceptions of family. She had an alternative model for behavior, however, that of another Hmong woman who did not yield to the patrilineal model. Not long before, this woman, who had several small children, had been mistreated by her husband, and with the help of her American sponsors had divorced him. Ker told me about this in an agitated fashion one evening when I happened to visit just as the ex-husband was leaving after a visit to Chou Neng. He had come to express anger that Ker still talked to his ex-wife. Although Ker reported that "all the Hmong" agreed the divorce was entirely the husband's fault, it was not he who ended up excluded from Hmong society, but the ex-wife. She could not visit anyone when her ex-husband complained, and eventually moved away under the care of her sponsors; her divorce cost her her place in Hmong society, bringing her to the necessity of Americanization. Ker, negotiating within herself whether to stand up to the Ly men, had this model before her, and she compromised her own ideas to retain her place in Hmong society.

CLUSTERING TOGETHER

Since accurate estimates of the Hmong population at any particular time are hard to find, it is difficult to find objective support for my subjective observations that as the number of Seattle Hmong became smaller, they clustered together in fewer neighborhoods, chosen not only by economic level, but through the search for safety and the vicinity of other Asians. To support these observations we must look for new ways to discover how residence patterns changed during the short period (1980–88) for which survey statistics are not available.[21] One way to track changes in the distribution of the Asian population in Seattle over short periods of time is through information collected on schoolchildren by the Seattle public schools. Every child when first entering the school system is asked what language the family speaks at home, and every October the child's current address is recorded by census tract.[22] The primary reason is to estimate the demand for bilingual education classes, but the answers also provide a secondary benefit as an indicator of children's ethnicity.

From these data, however, we learn nothing about the number of households per se, we learn only about children, because we do not know the number of siblings. Obviously this is not a perfect locator for communities. Not all households have children in school: singles and families with no children in public school were missed. Even so, the outcome of this method is striking. In 1980 there were 4,999 children in the Seattle public schools who used one of the 30 Asian home languages. There are 121 census tracts within Seattle; all (except the naval base tract) had at least one Asian schoolchild. Distribution was relatively sparse across most of the city. The greatest concentration was on Beacon Hill, with three census tracts and 20.9 percent of the Asian children. (For a series of maps for different language groups over time, see Donnelly 1989b.) From 1980 through 1988, the distribution of Chinese, Filipino, Japanese, Korean, and Asian Indian language speakers changed very little and did not affect overall Asian residence patterns. The residence patterns of Southeast Asian refugee children, however, shifted dramatically. Vietnamese children increased 38 percent and Laotians (including Hmong and Mien) increased 100 percent, while Cambodians increased the most of any group, nearly 500 percent, from 161 students in 1980 to 803 in 1988. At the same time these groups shifted within the city, concentrating in the far southside census tracts by 1988.

What of Hmong children in particular? In 1980 there were 104 Hmong children in school, representing 63 or 65 households in 24 census tracts.[23] The total movement of Hmong children (table 2) paralleled the larger group's movement. The number of Hmong schoolchildren peaked by 1981 and has dropped steadily ever since, except for a temporary shift in 1987, a year of increased migration from Thailand. After being spread throughout the city in 25 census tracts, by 1988 they lived in 6. While the number of

TABLE 2
Location of Hmong Schoolchildren by Year

Year	Number of Children	Number of Tracts
1980	103	24
1981	143	25
1982	124	18
1983	98	17
1984	84	16
1985	80	18
1986	67	13
1987	73	10
1988	63	6

Hmong schoolchildren had fallen 56 percent, the number of tracts of residence had fallen 76 percent. In 1988, 83 percent of the children in school (23 families) lived within a quarter mile of one another.

RETAINING HMONG IDENTITY

Within Seattle there was clearly a clustering of Hmong households in the same vicinity. This was part of an effort to maintain community, and through community to permit Hmong identity to endure. So many aspects of the new environment challenge cultural continuity that first-generation Hmong were moved to think carefully about what constitutes "being Hmong." When, in 1983, Dr. M. Hurlich and I began asking what was necessary to an identity as a Hmong, we found it was not a new question, but one that was already being debated among the Hmong in Seattle (Hurlich and Donnelly 1984).

We asked: Do you think your grandchildren will still be Hmong? and What does it take to be considered Hmong? Compared with the number of identity markers mentioned in chapter 2, the Hmong required fewer elements. Wearing a particular costume was never mentioned, nor was living in a particular area, nor engaging in any particular work. Physical characteristics like race were always dismissed, and it was not necessary to be born to Hmong parents. When we mentioned any of these, they were always rejected as sources of Hmong identity; but those criteria were straw men, since the Hmong in Southeast Asia adopted children from outside their communities, and the other criteria are elements of life that the Hmong had to give up in moving to an urban society.

Specific ritual practices were invariably denied by all as intrinsic to being Hmong. Several men explicitly mentioned that unity of belief was impossible since so many Hmong had become Christian. While expression of belief was very important, the contents of belief could not be relied on as an indicator of ethnicity. This position, that ritual could not define the Hmong any longer, is particularly noteworthy in view of the great importance assigned to ritual by Hmong in Southeast Asia (see Tapp 1988). However, many specific practices are difficult to maintain in urban America. Sacrificing pigs or cattle is awkward (although possible) and expensive; shamanic performances are noisy; *feng shui* divining rituals for siting graves are irrelevant where graves must be placed in cooperation with cemetery staff. A continuing crisis of believability floods the old religion in America, leaving agnostics in its wake. Yet not all Hmong who lose their old convictions convert to Christianity. For instance, in 1985 and 1986 one young wife in Seattle was afflicted with terrible abdominal pains for months, eating a special diet and enduring rough Hmong massages as her husband sponsored sacrifice after sacrifice. His aged mother (he was the youngest of 13), deeply experienced in shamanic performance, did everything within her power to persuade her spirit helper to aid her. The patient was perhaps not pure enough in her loyalty to her husband, so at one ritual I attended they wore twin cut-paper people pinned to their backs and had their souls tied to each other with strings; nothing worked. Finally, as his wife seemed to be dying, the young husband won his mother's permission to call a doctor. Gray and unconscious, she lay in the hospital when I visited. It was kidney problems, the nurses whispered, brought on by bearing five children in four years, and wouldn't I speak to them about birth control? She lived to bear two more children, but this couple will now have nothing to do with any unseen universe, although the husband's mother is still a shaman.

In Laos this young mother would have died, but her husband might not have responded with unbelief. While Seattle medical personnel are not perfectly sensitive to Hmong culture, their treatments are sufficiently effective to threaten the traditional beliefs attached to curing rituals.[24] Hmong need not interpret this as insulting to the old ways. They can (and often do) say that in Laos spirit-based treatments would have worked, but life is different here. This opens the possibility of a secular Hmong perspective, which no researcher nor any Hmong whom I have asked has mentioned as part of life in Laos. However, Hmong women's lives in Southeast Asia generally, and in Laos particularly, may have been inadvertently secular, as few of the women I spoke with seemed to have any systematic knowledge of traditional cosmology or ritual practices. In describing their lives, only the two who had been shamans and the Christians mentioned holding or being guided by religious convictions. Most of my subjects were afraid of spirits but drew a blank when asked about how beliefs fit together. The extensive spiritual understanding and practice described by Chindarsi (1976), Tapp (1988), and others was the province mainly of Hmong men.

Unified political loyalties appeared in people's recollections of Laos, but not in their ideas about Hmong society in the United States. Hmong political arrangements could not be binding within the American polity because Hmong leaders had no legal means of enforcing their will. They might try to enforce their will outside of legal channels, but if their will were not consistent with American legal forms, ultimately their position would be weak. This was what Hmong said, but since this was our own opinion, there remains the possibility that respondents were merely trying to please us in the conversations. But I had heard so many bitter complaints about American law, and so many expressions of fear—especially about the dread potential of deportation—that I believe our Hmong respondents really held this opinion about their own political activities above the level of the extended family. (For further discussion, see the accounts of quarrelling within organizations in chapter 5).

Although large areas of life were no longer included in Hmong identity by the Hmong we talked to, all of whom had come to the United States within the previous five years, two major areas were still often cited as intrinsic to being Hmong. Almost everyone thought it was necessary to speak Hmong at home, which meant the same thing as having Hmong as the native tongue. One exception was a woman who felt her children were perfectly Hmong although they preferred English, but several people felt that if their grandchildren did not speak Hmong at home, this meant they were losing an intrinsic portion of Hmongness, because they would not be thinking in Hmong.[25]

Everyone thought that for someone to remain Hmong, the roles within the family, that is, the division of tasks and the lines of authority and obedience, must be organized as they were remembered from Laos. There was total agreement that families had to be structured around lines of patrilineal descent, and that men were in charge. All informants, regardless of sex, social position, or religion, volunteered without being pressed that a woman adopts the social identity of her husband, while a man born of Hmong parents is always and invariably Hmong. A Hmong man in Detroit who had married an American woman was still completely Hmong, but a Hmong woman in Seattle who (being widowed) had remarried a Lao should follow Lao ways, though if she should ever divorce him, since she had sons by her Hmong husband, she could become fully Hmong again. In 1983 a Hmong woman who had left her husband and six children in California to follow the crops with an itinerant Chicano farm worker (a story that was widely known) was not received by Hmong in Seattle, although she brought gifts—boxes of peaches newly picked.

Thus Hmong identity appeared to have a more inborn character for men than for women, and to depend more on social links for women, who got their identities from men. A wonderful example of the continuing strength of this concept is Doua Hang's descent tree, which he constructed in 1985, after several different efforts, in the form of a circle. In the center is the most distant remembered ancestor. In the next circle are his two sons, in the next their sons, and so on to the current generation of children, who are at the periphery of the wheel. Women are omitted from this chart, because:

> The important part of a Hmong family from one generation to the next is the men. This is because the clan name is handed down through men, and the sons carry the family traditions from their fathers to their own sons from each generation down to the next. A man depends on his sons to do this. Women are important, but women change. When they grow up they leave their family and go to their husband's family. Even as wives, if their husband dies, they can marry again into still another family. Wives and daughters are like the leaves and flowers, but men are the branches and trunk of the tree, always strong and never changing. That is why in recording the descent of my family I have only put in the men. (Hang 1986: 33–34)

5

SELLING HMONG TEXTILES

With commercial development, the types of needlework items produced by the Hmong resettled in the United States changed dramatically, as it had in Thai refugee camps. Flat funeral cloths evolved to wall hangings, pillow covers, and bedspreads; appliquéd works sold so well that batik was eclipsed; patterns got larger and coarser; colors changed to suit Western taste. Representational embroidery became possible as women learned new stitches, and story cloths blossomed with scenes of Laos, warfare, Hmong legends and rituals, and animals and birds in fantasy woodlands. Some men living in refugee camps took up embroidery to make political statements, selling their story cloths in the quickly developing American market (Kohler 1986; Symonds, personal communication 1985).

I had decided to investigate the economic adaptations being made by Hmong households in order to see how gender relations would be changed by new relations brought about by production. My attention was first drawn to the economic relations between Americans and Hmong in the arena of needlework marketing. For Americans, small commercial ventures (especially having to do with fabric) are not confined to men's domains. Resettlement workers, sponsors, and volunteers have expected the women who make commercialized pieces also to engage in selling them. That Hmong women expected this, too, is obvious, because in Seattle, as around the country (Fass 1986), it was Hmong women who first approached American women volunteers asking them to buy. Fass comments that most Hmong needlework ventures

> began as social and cultural service undertakings, but many subsequently shifted priorities towards promoting self-reliance. This rearrangement of priorities resulted largely from pressure for change put on Americans by the refugees, either directly by the women or indirectly by [male] mutual assistance association representatives and Hmong community leaders. (Ibid., 361–62)

This was the case with needlework projects in Seattle. There were two needlework cooperatives in Seattle, one an offshoot of the other. When the first, composed of American volunteers working with Mien and Hmong, did not adjust quickly to a profit orientation, twenty-five Hmong women split off, forming their own cooperative with an auxiliary of American volunteers (Donnelly 1986). However, in neither of these organizations did worker control emerge, so they cannot be considered true cooperatives.[1]

ASIAN NEEDLECRAFTERS

In 1980,[2] Hmong and Mien refugee women in Seattle who attended classes at the Indochinese Women's Project in the YMCA asked their American teachers to help them sell their needlework. The American women began to arrange entry into street fairs and other markets, eventually organizing a nonprofit cooperative with themselves as officers, the many refugee women as members, and other American volunteers as an auxiliary. In the fall of 1981 they incorporated as Asian Needlecrafters (AN). Soon they moved into a small shop in the Pike Place Public Market (Harris 1982). By the fall of 1982, more than one hundred women had sold *paj ndau* and other handmade needlework through AN. Sales in 1982 exceeded forty thousand dollars. Though I knew both the American and the refugee women from the beginning of this project, I was not involved in the start of the needlework group and did not begin to collect data in a systematic way until late in the summer of 1982. So my discussion of early events is based on informants' reports, which do not always agree, and on materials such as newspaper articles and brochures.

When the store opened in the spring of 1982, the organizers talked in terms of putting refugee women in charge of sales, and in articles and public statements the refugee members were clearly implied to be running the operation. Officially, AN was under the control of a board which included refugee women. But in fact, AN continued through the summer of 1982 to be run by a core of American volunteers who made such decisions as whether to accept particular pieces made by refugees; how large an inventory to retain undisplayed; which fairs to enter; which pieces to take to what fairs; what materials and thread to order; how to display merchandise; how the shop would be staffed; what hours the shop would be open; what new products to try; whether to attempt selling wholesale; what publicity to seek; how to set up the bookkeeping; what receipts, price tags, and brochures to use; and what nonprofit grant funding to pursue. In making this list I have followed the perception of my Hmong informants, not my American informants, who did not agree about the first, second, fourth and fifth of these items. Certainly by late summer of 1982, the American volunteers appeared to me to be making these decisions.

Furthermore, the American volunteers were the ones who had decided that the general goals of the organization should be "cultural preservation and supplemental income" (Thomas 1982), and that to facilitate these two goals they would engage in "production and sale of handcrafted art and needlework by Indochinese refugees *living in Seattle*" (Hafey 1982; emphasis mine). This position, that all the work was to be done locally, distinguished AN from importers of needlework. It appealed to buyers with charitable interests, permitted higher prices, and furthered the goal of cultural preservation.

The American managers promoted the sense that AN was a cooperative venture, that everyone was helping in her own way to make a success out of it, and that everyone was helping each other. They made home visits and redistributed used clothing. Relationships between the American women and the refugees were warm. Personal income generated by AN's sales accrued only to the refugee women.

Hmong and Mien members of AN made some decisions during the summer of 1982: whether or not to sell through AN; the color and style of the products they made (out of a range of possibilities suggested by the Americans); how many hours to spend sewing at home; when to "donate" two half-days per month in "volunteer" work at the store (this was required); and what price they wanted for their work (the Americans often recommended that they raise their prices). When these overall descriptions are examined, it is clear that there was a discrepancy between the public stance of AN as an enterprise operated by refugees and the actual operational structure. Notably, decisions made by American women affected the overall operation and deeply affected the income levels of individual refugee members, while decisions made by refugee women affected themselves almost exclusively.

Refugees selling through AN were not quite in the position of pieceworkers producing on consignment, because one major decision was jointly made: the amount of the markup (20 percent) was the outcome of negotiation. The refugees would have preferred no markup at all, and various Americans suggested a range of markups between 10 percent and 40 percent. In discussion at group meetings, the compromise figure was eventually reached.

The negotiation over markup, with the Hmong and Mien women wanting to receive all the profit without consideration for shop overhead or taxes, points to compelling reasons for the division of responsibility that existed in AN during 1982. The refugee women had no previous experience selling needlework or anything else in the American market. They did not know ordinary business practices, and they lacked business foresight. Also, they lacked skill in English, as well as in salesmanship and in knowledge of their market. They could not have continued selling their needlework, especially through a retail outlet, without the help of the American women.

In addition, there were reasons on the American women's side for the division of responsibility, stemming from the personal goals of the American volunteers. By the summer of 1982 (although this had not been true at the beginning in 1980), the volunteers consisted almost entirely of committed Christian women. None of them had had prior business experience; they were oriented instead toward service. Besides the novel experience they were gaining in running a business, they developed friendships among themselves by working at AN. They received positive attention from members of the Seattle community working in refugee resettlement and from the press. They were happy to receive the expressed appreciation and good will of the Hmong and Mien women and their families, and they felt that they were demonstrating Christian love and achieving a sense of greater closeness to God. They believed that the forced cooperation through work in the store made AN a nursery of democracy. Since all these goals were accomplished within the status quo of AN, the American volunteers—who remained in control of AN's structure—had little incentive to push actively for greater autonomy among their refugee members.

The relationships outlined above bring to mind the classic patron-client relationships described in anthropological literature. *Patrons* possess material resources or favors that they distribute to others in return for loyalty and praise (and ultimately for profit, since a sizeable following generally facilitates the aggregation of resources in various ways). *Clients,* who have fewer material resources, nevertheless can offer the patron an intangible good—loyalty—needed by the patron to continue in the superordinate position. Clients gain directly from the patron through the patron's disbursement of goods or favors, while patrons look for an indirect gain (having clients puts them in a position to realize gains from third parties).

These are in fact relations of exchange, although friendship (or at least cordiality) is an important element of patron-client relationships. It is easy to distinguish them from true friendship, and also to identify the patron in contrast to the client: the decision on which goods are transferred, and when, is in the hands of the patron. The patron takes a position of leadership, while the client accepts the position of a follower. In Lande's (1977) view, the counters of loyalty have less value than the counters of material benefit, so that clients are at a disadvantage, and have to even the score by giving an added increment of obedience when necessary to the patron.

Much has been written about patronage structures (see Eisenstadt and Roniger 1980 for a thorough review). Most anthropological work has concentrated on Mediterranean and Latin American societies, but patron-client relations can be said to be commonplace, a worldwide phenomenon. Clientelism has been recognized as part of formal governmental structures in Southeast Asian societies (Hanks 1977). Informal patronage networks have been described within Euro-American societies, too, for instance inside corporate structures (Lande 1977). Patron-client relationships have also been noticed growing up between people from different societies who have economic interaction and great disparities in wealth (Hendricksen 1971).

Refugees enter the United States in a condition of dependency. Clientelism is a fact in the heart and essence of refugee resettlement. Clearly the largest patron is the federal government, and there are many other clientelistic networks. Clientelism cannot be negatively viewed in this setting, as there is evidently no other way to pursue resettlement. How to bring these relationships to a close, however, may not be readily apparent, especially to the patron, whose social power depends on the presence of a clientele.

AN looked like a classic example of a patron-client relationship. Money rewards moved downward while needlecrafts and "volunteer" time moved upward. No material profit accrued to the American volunteers, who received praise and loyalty instead. Vertical associations between the American volunteers and the refugee members were characterized by friendship, but horizontal ties between refugee members were much weaker (another characteristic of patron-client arrangements), and were charged with competition and hostility, especially across ethnic boundaries. American volunteers arranging for fairs needed to call a dozen or more Hmong and Mien women, each of whom would then contact her own small network, usually of relatives. Once at a fair, certain refugee women were likely to bury other work beneath their own, and hostile scenes occasionally occurred.

AN might have continued unchanged, except for the crisis precipitated by the federal funding cuts of May 1982. Hmong families began to leave for states with more generous welfare programs, or for states where they could get work. The remaining Hmong women found themselves having to take farm labor and house-cleaning jobs. Suddenly they noticed the value of their time. Before the funding cut, an embroidered panel that took two months to complete might sell for fifty dollars (Harris 1982). Afterward, women saw that they could not retrieve the value of their labor in this way. They solved this problem by importing the time-consuming centers of appliqués and embroideries from their relatives in refugee camps; they expected to remit part of the profit from the sale of a piece to the needle-worker in the camp. But AN would not accept these imports, for AN was differentiating itself in the local market by selling only locally produced needlework. The American women felt that they could not accept foreign-made work because of their previously announced goal of cultural preservation. One Hmong woman commented to me that these women didn't see that cultural preservation was dependent on making more money.

Faced with this dilemma, some Hmong women quit. Others began to present the imported work as their own, perhaps adding a border first. Thus a conspiracy grew to deceive the American women. But the volunteers were evidently not deceived, they merely closed their eyes to the deception and kept going, thus continuing to occupy their market niche. They thought they had to continue to claim that the work was local. However, out of this dispute or misunderstanding about the origin of pieces, the Hmong women became convinced that in spite of appearances and rhetoric, the Americans "owned" AN and were ignoring the needs of the Hmong women in favor of themselves.

Some became quite assertive, even offering right in the shop to meet customers later at home to avoid charging them the 20 percent markup. Disputes arose as various Hmong and Mien women accused the Americans of favoritism. Nobody could get enough money to live on, it seemed. Everyone appeared desperate. It was at this juncture, in the middle of 1982, that I began taking notes. AN members began inviting me to their board meetings, and I openly took notes at the meetings. I visited the shop often, and talked with American volunteers, some of whom I also visited at home. I talked at length with Hmong members of AN (I could not talk with the Mien members because of the hostile relations between Hmong and Mien; I was identified with the Hmong). At that time my focus was not on gender relations, but on economic interactions between Hmong and Americans.

When Federal Impact Aid funds became available in August of 1982, AN successfully applied for a training grant that provided funds for twelve part-time clerk-trainees to staff the store and two part-time translator-organizers, one Hmong and one Mien. The Mien choice was a needle-worker who had been involved with AN from the beginning. The primary candidate for the Hmong position, however, was a woman who had never been a member of AN and who did not produce needlework. Vang My (a pseudonym) had good business skills and experience, but her main qualification for the job was her political position as the wife of the Seattle Hmong leader, Kue Koua.

In October 1982, in a meeting attended by about sixty people, Kue Koua—who had never come to a AN meeting before—announced that the Hmong women had formed a new organization, the Hmong Artwork Association (HAA). Its members included nearly all the Hmong women currently in AN; the president was his own wife. Presenting himself as spokesman for the Hmong women (who he said were "too shy" to speak for themselves), he said that the women all demanded that his wife should be hired as AN's Hmong translator-organizer.

The American women of AN felt that Vang My would try to sabotage the success of any other candidate, so they hired her. But after this meeting they were angry and alarmed. They were convinced that Kue Koua, through his wife, intended to take control of AN, eject the Mien, and convert it into a vehicle for reinforcing his own increasingly shaky position in the Hmong community.

In this assessment they were correct. By November 1982, he was indeed cheerfully and excitedly speculating to me on tactics for taking over AN. The American women of AN saw him as an independent force bearing down from above on the hapless and bedeviled Hmong women, but they saw his wife only as an agent of her husband. They were unaware of the Hmong women's anger over the policy on imported pieces and the perceived favoritism toward the Mien, because in their position as clients, the Hmong women had felt unable to express this openly (they were indeed "too shy"). So the American women did not see that Kue Koua's actions were permitted and invited by the Hmong women themselves, who were hoping in this way to increase their own earning power.

The winter of 1982–83 was a struggle between the American women and their new Hmong translator-organizer, full of jockeying and distrust. This middle-aged woman had spent her married life in a position of real power and influence, and while unschooled, had a deep understanding of political process. The grant specified that classes should be conducted in math; soon the teacher realized that Vang My, in her position as translator, was answering the questions herself. When queried, she said she knew the answers, so the Hmong women members didn't need to know them. She could not be shaken from this position. She called herself a "management trainee" while the Americans called her an "employee." She asserted that she should be taught to operate the store and should take it over. It was one of the grant's goals to turn operations over to the refugee members. But the American women did little to facilitate this goal, and the point was not discussed at AN meetings. They refused to give her any but the most rudimentary financial information about the operation of the store, and they would not let her distribute fabric, which was supposed to be sold to members, in case she gave it away. Hostility between the Hmong and Mien members increased during this period. Hmong complaints, directed through the translator-organizer, did not reach the AN management. Attempts at reconciliation by the American women, expressed to the translator-organizer, did not reach the Hmong women.

By February 1983, the rift between factions had become unbridgeable. The catalyst for action was very trivial, a Hmong baby hat that the Americans would not hang in the store because it had not been made locally. Vang My loudly interpreted this as clear evidence that the Americans of AN had contempt for the Hmong, since there was a Mien baby hat displayed right in the window of the shop. Early in March, amid acrimonious debate, almost all of the twenty-six actively selling Hmong women followed their translator-organizer out of AN into the independent Hmong Artwork Association.

After the split, the American managers of AN declared they had no objection to the creation of the opposing organization—helping the growth of a refugee-controlled organization was what they had had in mind all along, although they regretted the hostility marking the split in their own group. They said their main goal in the conflict was to prevent the aggressive Hmong from overpowering the more passive Mien members of AN and depriving them of an outlet for Mien needlework. One of their early acts was to support HAA's application for a table in the Pike Place Market to sell needlework on a daily basis; the site was located within fifty feet of their own shop and thus was in direct competition with it. This was an act of generosity, as there is no doubt that their business was deeply hurt by the split that so shook AN.

HMONG ARTWORK ASSOCIATION

The Hmong Artwork Association was born from the conflicts in Asian Needlecrafters, as young Christian women tried to maintain the status quo, Hmong women tried to gain more control over their economic lives, and a strong Hmong woman, Vang My, tried to maintain her family's political importance. Vang My took conciliatory gestures from AN as signs that AN was seeking to overthrow her leadership and win back her flock of members. Hostility to AN appeared to be an important factor in persuading Hmong women to draw together into this new group.

Vang My had been aided in her revolt from AN by Corinne, a volunteer for AN, who (along with some other volunteers) had been distressed at what they considered the patronizing attitude toward refugee women of AN's management. Vang My engaged Corinne's help to create a durable organization. Their personalities were important to the success of the enterprise. Vang My had been the manager of a wealthy and extensive household in Laos and a shopkeeper and entrepreneur in her own right; she was used to command. Corinne, a nurse with six years of experience in Vietnam and Nepal, had a strong helping ethic. They shared a deep friendship, with

Vang My in the position of decision-maker and Corinne in the position of support liaison and facilitator.

HAA took the form of a marketing cooperative of Hmong women, with an attached auxiliary of Americans called Hmong Women's Assistance Project Association (HWAPA). The reasons for this structure were external to the Hmong community. Americans working with Hmong refugees not only at the local level but also at state and national levels had observed close cooperation between Hmong and assumed that this indicated democratic ideas, socially validated concepts of generosity, and affective loyalties. They concluded that the egalitarian ideology of cooperatives was similar to Hmong social ideals, and that Hmong refugees would feel at home with cooperative principles. Also, there were tax advantages to cooperative organization in Washington State, and cooperatives were eligible for seed money from private foundations and public agencies and for inexpensive federal loans; they could also attract consultant funding (a point of particular interest to some volunteers who were seeking support for themselves). Professional services given freely (for instance by a lawyer or an accountant) were tax deductible as charitable donations. For these reasons and perhaps others, American helping personnel had for several years encouraged Hmong leaders to consider cooperative organization. The previous year while working at AN, Vang My, along with her husband, had attended a workshop in cooperative organization sponsored by the Overseas Education Fund so she was familiar with the language of cooperatives. The particular Americans who helped to form HWAPA, including academics like M. Hurlich and me, professional people (a lawyer, an accountant), and nurses, but only one businesswoman (who wanted to be a paid consultant), also felt comfortable with the idea of cooperatives, despite little practical experience.

HAA intended to be a profit-making organization whose product was Hmong needlework, while HWAPA considered itself a nonprofit association providing volunteer assistance to HAA. HAA and HWAPA sought a number of outlets: a table in the Pike Place Market; various fairs from May through early December; retail stores; shows in galleries, restaurants or other locations; demonstrations at colleges or elsewhere; and mail order. Not all of these succeeded. Mail order was never pursued; wholesaling to stores did not materialize; participating in a fashion show did not result in sales; and at several fairs HAA lost money. However, the market table, most fairs, and several special shows were quite successful, so that sales during the first nine months of HAA's existence (about $42,000) were encouraging.

During 1983 HWAPA volunteers helped HAA members by arranging entry to fairs, transporting them and their goods, providing two portable booths to sell in, writing up sales slips and figuring the tax on a calculator, and staffing the booths next to Hmong counterparts in order to do much of the talking to American buyers. As time passed the Hmong women learned more and more of these tasks. Volunteers also did HAA's legal work and bookkeeping, which Vang My gradually took over. HWAPA also sponsored a wine-and-cheese benefit at the Chateau Ste. Michelle winery. These activities were the same sort of thing that AN had done earlier.

At a more sophisticated level, HWAPA provided liaison with the Overseas Education Fund of Washington, D.C., whose Refugee Women in Development (RefWID) project sponsored a two-part nationwide teleconference on marketing needlework in June and September of 1983. RefWID sent a marketing expert to Seattle to help HAA develop retail outlets. HWAPA tried to find grant funds to support Vang My (who gained little material benefit from her many hours of work), and solicited donations of fabric and sewing machines. These projects generally did not succeed. No grants were received, and the businesswoman whose primary interest was generating support for herself as a consultant dropped out of HWAPA. The RefWID marketing expert talked over the heads of the Hmong women, alarmed Vang My and all of us with various psychological problems, and could not persuade retailers to carry Hmong products. The teleconference was well attended by both refugees and Americans, generating favorable interest in the press, and subsequently HWAPA received a large donation of fabric from a Seattle dress designer, but it had no longterm effect at the local level. The marketing expert left in her wake a lot of fence-mending for us.

As the summer of 1983 progressed, I kept the financial records of HAA and set up booths at fairs. Each women member gave Vang My as many paj ndau as she liked, which were listed on a page under her name, along with a code number and the price she set. The code number, along with the person's name and the item's price, was written on masking tape fixed to the back of the piece. When it sold, the tape went on the carbon of the sales receipt. This was basically AN's method. The time-consuming matter of making lists took place at Vang My's house. She had piles of paj ndau from which she selected what to take to fairs.

All members' pieces were supposed to be displayed equally, but this concept depended first on Vang My's selection process, and second on how the women staffing fair booths set out the pieces. Vang My selected fairly, but booth displays certainly favored whoever was staffing the booth. For instance, at the Langley Arts and Crafts Festival in July 1983, Chao brought numerous paj ndau—including pillows, small embroidered squares, coasters, and three baby carriers—that she had not listed with Vang My. She displayed these conspicuously and the coasters were sold for twenty dollars (four dollars each). Because a receipt was written out, Vang My could trace these unlisted sales, list the item, and collect HAA's markup of 20 percent, plus sales tax, after the fact. Chao said that Vang My had so many *paj ndau* that her own got buried. She had the list of the forty or so items she had given Vang My for HAA's inventory, and if any sold she would give her a replacement, but she did not make her own list of the ones she brought daily, because she "could remember them."

Women trying to bring unlisted items on a daily basis and then take them back at the end of the day had caused many arguments between Hmong and Americans at HAA's predecessor, Asian Needlecrafters. The Americans sometimes found the inventory short and attributed the shortage to Hmong women taking home more than they came with. The Hmong said their missing pieces must have been sold or stolen and insisted on being paid. Eventually the Americans refused to let them bring unlisted things. Since the bitterness caused by these quarrels was exploited by Vang My in setting up HAA, she could not now insist that everything was to be listed. But if there were no receipt Chao could make a sale free of tax or mark-up. Vang My had to trust her to make out a receipt.[3]

During the first four months, sales per member varied from a high of $2,013 (15 percent of all sales) to a low of $12.60 (.1 percent), with the average money earned per woman on the low side ($254) and the median even lower ($103)—that is, as many women earned under $103 as earned over $103.[4] Four women made 46 percent of the sales. Several of the low sellers had dropped out by the end of July, and one went back to AN.

By the beginning of August 1983, forty-six women had sold needlework. Thirteen of them (30 percent) were White Hmong, the rest Blue Hmong. Twenty-four lived in Seattle, eight in California, four in Providence, Rhode Island, and nine in camps in Thailand (one I have no information on). Twenty-six women called themselves members. Thirty-three had a kin tie to Vang My's husband, six to Vang My, and seven were unrelated (although of those unrelated sellers, three had the clan name Kue and one the clan name Vang).

Of the kin ties on the Vang side, two were wives of male relatives (brother's wife and father's brother's son's wife), and one was brother's wife's sister. The other three were also kin through Kue (being related through the marriage of one of them to a Kue cousin), but Vang My considered the Vang link to be the significant one. Two of them seemed to have a very tenuous connection, because while the name on the pieces was Vang, the names of the women who actually made them were unknown to Vang

My; they were the wife and mother of a Vang who was the brother of the other woman of these three, who had married a cousin of Kue Koua. To us this may be confusing. Looking at kin ties as the Hmong figure them, it is significant that Vang My did not say the two women were related through the woman (their daughter and sister) who had married a Kue. Instead she said the two women were related through a man (their son and brother) whose sister had married a Kue. This was not an idiosyncratic usage peculiar to Vang My. Hmong seek out and invoke ties that run through male relationships.

Of the kin ties on the Kue side, four were women closely related through a Kue male (Kue Koua's brother's wife, brother's daughter, and father's brother's son's two sons' wives), and four more were women more distantly linked through a female who was either Kue or married to closely related Kue (son's wife's mother, sister's daughter's husband's mother, daughter's husband's grandmother and classificatory sister[5]). The other twenty-five were wives, ex-wife, widow, sisters, mothers, or in-laws of male "cousins." (See the discussion of cousin in note 3, chapter 1. It is impossible to say how many of the cousin relationships in the HAA membership would be literal descent relationships. These cousin-statuses in the member list may have been stated as cousin to permit kin-type relations.)

In July 1983 I was trying to find out how decisions were made in the group and how members viewed the organization. One of the earliest discoveries was that the decision of whether or not to sell needlework at all appeared to be decided by men in the case of married women; if a husband was opposed, the wife did not participate. Within HAA, when something needed to be done, all the women characteristically refused for one reason or another: they had to cook, their children needed them. Vang My listened to all the complaints and objections and then assigned someone to do whatever it was, and the woman never seemed put out or dismayed. Corinne speculated that this was how they put Vang My in their debt, so that she would owe them hundreds of small favors. Then when a woman really needed to get something done, she could go to Vang My and on the basis of past favors get her to act on her behalf. I saw this process in action, while setting up for the fair at Langley. Chao had put up tremendous resistance to going, because she was nursing an infant, but when on the morning of the fair I picked her up, she said very cheerfully that she was going "because Vang My asked me to go." It seemed that social cohesion might be strengthened by a concept of indebtedness.[6]

However, certain clues went contrary to this model. For instance, at the end of August 1983 I visited the HAA booth at the Monroe county fair. It stood in a row of mini storage buildings between candles and epoxied coffee tables. The crafts section stood among the horse barn, the stock car speedway, the carnival, and numerous junk-food booths. The fair was aesthetically crude. The most successful seller in the row of booths made Raggedy Ann dolls; other sellers reported poor or no sales.

Va, Yia, and Yee were sitting disconsolately on the three chairs in the HAA booth. Chao was asleep in the corner, her little boy suckling in a litter of plastic bags, coat hangers, blanket, bits of food. The booth was dark, its lights not having been turned on. On the two card tables at the front of the booth, piles of *paj ndau* concealed each other. They were so densely stacked and arranged that trying to pick one out would have seemed an affront to their careful placement. On the walls were hung a careless array of wares. It appeared to me that a customer would have had to be very brave to buy; no one had. The women, dressed in shabby, mismatched polyester blouses and pants, their shirttails hanging out one over the other in ill-assorted layers, glared out from the recesses of the booth in silence.

I took Va, who had the best English, out of the booth and tried to convey to her the presentation of a booth, to give her a feel for other booths that were clean, not packed, light, sometimes with the merchandise in front on the walkway, with sellers who were friendly, not to mention nicely dressed. Va seemed to get the idea, and spoke at length with the others, but they were greatly reluctant to change anything about the booth, to spread out some *paj ndau* so their patterns could be seen, or to string a cord across the top of the opening to hang "ginkoes."[7] I did this myself, and as the late sun caught the beads the women seemed to like to see them up there, since they smiled and stopped being so negative. But Yia and Yee started to eat, making a big mess in the back of the booth and ignoring any of the potential customers who now began to stop by. There were no sales.

The women complained about being there. They wanted to shut the booth and go home. This being against the fair contract, I discouraged them and said that after all, they had all asked Vang My to sign up for this fair. They denied this. I pressed them, asking whether they had ever had any meetings with Vang My about HAA. No, they insisted, they had never heard of this fair before last week. "Don't you have meetings?" I asked. "Don't you meet Vang My to say what you want?" They all denied attending HAA meetings and said they had never asked Vang My to send them to this fair. Their bewilderment at my questions was apparently genuine.

However, Vang My had said to me earlier, when we were signing up for this fair and I had wondered aloud whether it was worth it, that she had asked her members and they told her she should sign up for all possible fairs, since winter would be slack. There seemed to be three possible explanations for this contradiction: the four women were not telling the truth; Vang My consulted a core of several women members who were her advisors, but didn't poll all the members all the time; or she consulted no one, but only said she did because she understood the American cooperative requirement of grass-roots participation.

I decided to go home. I left at about eight thirty, getting promises from them that they would stay until at least ten or ten thirty. I stopped to say good-bye to another seller, who told me the contract specified they must stay until eleven, so I turned back to the HAA booth, where I found Chao pulling down ginkoes and Yia folding up *paj ndau,* while Yee was packing up her food. They were extremely surprised and embarrassed to see me again. Chao said the headband she was unfastening from the cord, she wanted to put on "to be an example," but this didn't fool me, and we laughed together at her transparent lie.

Gradually it became clear that day-to-day decisions were made by Vang My after consulting a small coterie of close friends, and that the young women particularly had no share in the direction of the organization, but still were expected to donate their time in selling. They did not seem to have the option of dropping out, as they all were married to Kue men, who needed to maintain cordial relations with Vang My's husband, and their response to this situation seemed to be passive resistance or subversion, with obedience when necessary or when it seemed profitable to them. HAA began to seem to me less like a marketing cooperative, and more like a patron-client organization along the lines of Hanks' entourage model (1977: 161–66; see also Mortland 1988).

In September 1983, $47,000 in federal Lao Highland Initiative (LHI)[8] funding was designated for the Southeast Asian Refugee Federation (SEARF), composed of the heads of various refugee organizations, with Kue Koua as president and James Raddle (a pseudonym) as executive director. The committee in charge, acting on the complaint of a competing Hmong leader that HAA was Vang My's private business, decided that $30,000 would go to a needlework project, but not to HAA. Soon, however, Kue Koua asked Raddle, who knew nothing about sewing, training people to sew, or needlework markets, to write a proposal to SEARF for use of the funds. He "could control" Raddle, he told me, adding that since Raddle would be monitoring the use of the funds, he might as well write the proposal. Thus Kue Koua regained control of the money temporarily lost by the decision of the recalcitrant committee.[9]

Earlier I had seen that issues of control over resources and over people were at the top of Kue Koua and Vang My's agenda. The rewards to them of maintaining control, however, had not been apparent, because financially they never seemed to come out ahead, while both spent hundreds of hours in tasks of direct benefit to others. They expressed a strong sense of responsibility for assisting hapless followers that I felt was genuine, yet it also seemed to me that they wanted to build personal networks to validate their personal power, with resources such as LHI money or HAA used to tie people to them through financial rewards. Kue Koua in particular did not differentiate in conversation between SEARF, Lao Highland Association,[10] HAA, and HWAPA, speaking of all of them in terms of his own control. "Controlling" meant being able to make others do as he told them, it being understood that this served their own advantage as well as his, since he was better placed than they to generate economic improvement for them.

Now it seemed he was tiring in an environment that did not sustain this effort. Both Kue Koua and Vang My were continuing to construct networks in which they garnered resources and distributed them to followers as they had in Laos. But compared with Laos, their efforts in Seattle could produce little and they could retain little, both financially and in terms of power over lives. Without control over sufficient resources, and without means of enforcement, they could not prevent followers with other options from defecting.

The women members were interested in HAA for its potential of generating income, but if their goods did not sell they resorted to other tactics, such as selling through AN on the side. In November, Chee Her (a pseudonym), one of Vang My's core members, and the most dedicated at staffing the table in the Public Market, was found to be cutting prices on her own *paj ndau* and hiding the *paj ndau* belonging to others. She was also accused of putting her own name on other people's work. She had cleared a thousand dollars in the month of October, when the rest made virtually nothing. At a members' meeting early in December she was strongly criticized.

At the same meeting Vang My offered to divide the year's profit among the members if they would staff the market table. Few were interested. Three women said that flatly they only wanted to go to fairs where they knew sales would be good. Vang My said the women who did staff the market table wouldn't accept this, and the three women just shrugged. Her angry comment was, "Let them go then, we have freedom in this country." She would use her own family to staff the table.

Things seemed to be coming apart, as quarrels increased. But Kue Koua had a solution: The men should tell the women how to act. Women, he said, are irresponsible because they have no experience with public matters or cooperation. In Laos only the men had meetings; the women stayed home and kept house, so they knew how to do only what they were told. Here in America it was different, but while women were "free" here, they didn't know what that meant. They could not see beyond their own doorstep. The men had to take the situation in hand.

The members of Lao Highland Association who were husbands of women in HAA formed a committee to oversee the setting of prices, the number of pieces each woman could submit (twenty to the public market, thirty to fairs if they staffed the table), and the work schedule of the women. In this way, by January formal decision-making in HAA had passed to Hmong men. This was seen by both the men and the women I talked to as a desirable way to reduce tension and argument. But it was not an entirely successful tactic.

In February 1984 a serious problem arose over the issue of whether the co-operative should report members' sales to the IRS. Most of the pieces were made in Thailand, and the ostensible owners of the pieces, the individual members of HAA, sent significant portions of their needlework income to relatives in the camps. Thus income to HAA members was much lower than sales, but being in the main illiterate, the women kept poor records. In an ordinary business, the pieces of needlework consigned to HAA would be treated as a business expense and the consignees would be responsible for their own dealings with the IRS. When HAA began operations HWAPA members thought the needlework would be dealt with in this manner. But after the end of the first year, HAA's volunteer accountant thought that members were like employees and HAA should report their income as an employer would do.

When this decision became known to the members, they all immediately quit since they didn't want their sales reported. Ten were receiving welfare (including Chee Her, the high earner and the women who had cut prices in December) and were afraid of losing their support. Vang My lamented that "the Hmong are terrible." She said that Chee Her was her oldest and dearest friend, her trusted advisor. They had known each other for many, many years, and she and Kue Koua had helped Chee in many ways since her soldier husband was killed. But she undersold other women, took money out of the till for food, and put her own name on others' work; some pieces were missing and Vang My was afraid Chee Her had sold them and pocketed the money. Other members wanted her expelled. Apparently Vang My had told the members that if HAA stopped, the assets would be divided. Chee Her wanted to take the nine hundred dollar year-end profit and split it proportionally (meaning she would receive most), leaving nothing to begin signing up for fairs next year. She also wanted part of the fabric donation. Vang My seemed devastated by these developments.

Later that evening Kue Koua called me, upset. He wanted HWAPA to tell members of HAA what to do. He confirmed the problem as outlined above. I suggested dumping Chee Her, but he was reluctant to do this. He said the majority must rule, as members had voted to retain the year-end profits, but that all members should stay in, though the vote to expel Chee Her was 27–1. The problems, he maintained, would fade away since the men had taken over.[11] He wanted HAA to survive, and told me HWAPA must act like a parent. He hated welfare, he said, hated being dependent; members should get off welfare. He wouldn't consider reducing the membership even by one. We should be an example and help all the people, he said.

Eventually the HWAPA lawyer and the accountant concluded that co-operatives need not report the income of their members but could treat the inventory as a business cost. So the tempest ended, but the tensions it had engendered remained.

Three days after the resolution of that issue, Chee Her came down to the public market booth. She pulled pieces off the table onto the dirty concrete floor, stamped on them, and even blew her nose on some of them, damaging and staining a total of twenty-three pieces owned by various women, with a retail value of $1,037. Kue Koua called Chee Her's son. He said she must make restitution or they would take the damaged pieces and demand that welfare pay for them. Then the whole story of Chee Her concealing her income from welfare would be out in the open. Chee Her capitulated and agreed to pay. At a meeting the next night between HAA members, Lao Highland Association, Chee Her, her son, and a man from the Hmong Association (the opposition faction) who acted as Chee Her's spokesman, the eleven member male board of Lao Highland Association decided she should pay 70 percent of the retail value for the pieces she could not repair, or $447. I taped the comments of a member of the board:

> On Saturday we have a meeting, we solve the problem, but I'm not sure if solve or not, if stop or if something happen again. [Chee Her] come too. She going to pay for the pieces she ruin. There are three owners, each one took one back, so not pay for those, then we reduce 30 percent of the price. Twenty percent is the price for the market, but we reduce 10 percent more to apologize for her.[12] One hundred percent she's wrong, but that cost a lot of money, so we bargain a little bit. Based on twenty piece. After we figure out, cost $447. She has no money, but her two sons agree to pay, because they know she's wrong. We give the embroidery to Chou Neng to hold until she pays those three people.

Meanwhile, Chee Her asked to see me, in the presence of an interpreter. She said she had been expelled from the group with no warning and for no cause. She had no idea she was ever in any trouble; no one ever asked her any questions or let her defend herself. She was completely surprised; that was why she came back and trampled the needlework. She was "too angry" because it was all so sudden.

But, I said, hadn't she had trouble last fall when people said she put her things out in front of everyone else's, and hadn't people said she took money out of the till? She leaned forward in her chair, staring at the floor. "Yes," she said, "but I never steal anything. Who said I steal? Who?" I said I didn't know. Chee Her and the interpreter agreed that Vang My had "a big mouth." The meeting ended with a lack of good feeling. I suspected the interpreter had not been aware of the accusations of theft against Chee Her; her last comment to me was that the important thing was to help Chee Her feel good about herself again.

Presently Chee Her said that since Vang My had such "a big mouth" (because she had told me, a non-Hmong, about Hmong arguments), she didn't have to pay the fine. To Chou Neng, the neutral party holding the damaged pieces, Chee Her was adamant that she had never stolen anything.[13] But Ker, his wife, thought Vang My was not compromised by telling me things, since there were two eyewitnesses (the women staffing the market table at the time), and either of them could have told me. That point was not the issue. Chee Her simply didn't want to spend the money. Ker thought Chee Her was crazy; she attributed her craziness to not having a husband. Chee Her had told Ker she was lonely, and Ker thought loneliness was the source of Chee Her's troubles. A few days later, when Chee Her called me, I said there was no connection between the accusation of theft and her responsibility to pay this fine. She had trouble conveying to me, but I eventually understood, that she didn't care whether the connection was logical, the only way she could hurt Vang My was to hold back the money. "Oh, you want to hurt Vang My?" I asked. Yes, she said, she was very angry at Vang My.

According to my traditionalist male informant:

> I say to Kue Koua, "you know in Laos we always solve the problem, money drop on the table, we sign the paper [to say] it is done. But here we sign the paper [just an IOU], you believe it's OK, but I'm not one hundred percent sure." Now I think she will not pay. She call me, say "last Saturday we agree I will pay, but now I will not pay."
>
> From this kind of thing, solving so many problems, we know who is a good person and who is not. You know, last Saturday when we talk about this problem, we have a tape recorder, because many times we solve a problem, later people twist the words around, but we have no tape. This time we

have a tape. In Laos we never have that kind of problem, because we have older people to solve the problem for us. After the problem solve, everybody agree, and it's OK, never happen again. I never saw a problem happen like this, where she turn back and say no! That's the reason that I told you, that some people outside support her to speak like that. Here in America, you talk more, you have more problem. Here, before you talk to somebody, you have to know, what are they going to do [with your words].

As far as I learned, this fine was never paid.

Vang My was deeply shocked by this entire event. She said it was evidence of her husband's decline in power in the larger community. HWAPA volunteers tended to consider the Hmong women members as independent actors, but she always saw them as agents of community attitudes and values. In Laos she would never have had any such problems as she did in HAA, she declared, because everybody would have been afraid to offend her husband. Here, they could not maintain control over people. So in this triple conflict about paying taxes, retaining welfare, and raiding HAA's assets, the issue of freedom versus control was just under the surface.

In various contexts, women were expected to act, not on their own, but in response to the requirements of others, to be patient, to do as they are told. Sullenness and subversion were the only paths of protest open to young married women, since cheerful obedience was required of them, and they were not easily able to express open dissatisfaction.

This process could be seen at work in Chee Her. In the setting of HAA, in return for the opportunity to sell, Vang My required Chee's loyalty. She wanted a trusted advisor, someone who would bend her attention to the good of HAA members and the organization as a whole. But Vang My did not differentiate this from her own personal good and from the good of her husband, the faltering community leader.[14] In short, she wanted Chee Her to devote her time to sustaining the power structure in which Kue Koua stood at the top.

But in acting for the good of HAA, Chee Her would have had to refrain from behavior that other women engaged in (such as putting her pieces in front), from which she was earning a substantial income supplement, and because of which she could pass along income to relatives who provided pieces to her. Chee Her was building her own network of influence, based on her ability to reward her needlework producers. She could not have built a network of her own by helping HAA, but only by using HAA as the other members were doing, to produce personal income for herself. Vang My felt that because of their years of association in Laos, in which she and Kue Koua had acted as patrons, Chee Her should reciprocate with friendship now, when they needed it.

That Chee Her did not share this opinion speaks clearly about her view of their relationship. Bourdieu speaks of the euphemization of purposeful action under a screen of emotional ties and kinship obligations (Bourdieu 1977: 191). The density of relationships among the Hmong means that all interactions bear the weight of numerous threads of meaning. Complex ties constructed in Laos, based on webs of reciprocity, were held together by ritual and economic exchanges mandated by kinship. To some extent in Laos they were held together by force ("They would have been afraid to offend my husband"). Kinship determined the division of labor, based not only on sex and age, but also on hierarchies that sprang from differential access to resources. The bitterness and anxiety accompanying the breakdown of these social structures demonstrates a painful emotional component to them and lets us portray them as far more than merely purposeful in intent.

During 1984, HAA's second year, fewer HWAPA volunteers were available to help, and the Hmong members were thrown very much on their own resources. HAA members had to act more independently at fairs, and were needed to staff the table at the Pike Place Market (something they were frequently unwilling to do). During this period Vang My hired her daughter as well as other HAA members to staff the table, paying minimum wage out of the 20 percent mark-up. Husbands of members, motivated by their membership in the Lao Highland Association as well as by desire for sales, provided much help in transportation to fairs. Bee Vue in particular (he and his wife are referred to by pseudonyms; his mother was a Kue), a close associate of Vang My's husband, spent many hours pricing goods and keeping the extensive lists of pieces. He and his wife, Xai Khong, had been promised control of HAA, and in fact were running the organization by late summer. Vang My continued to do HAA's accounting (along with HWAPA's volunteer accountant) and to arrange participation in fairs, but Bee Vue and Xai Khong began to share these tasks as well. American volunteers still helped somewhat with transportation and staffing at fairs.

On the weekend of July 4, 1984, men of the Kue clan from around the United States held a meeting in the Midwest, resulting in their decision to concentrate the clan in that region. Vang My's husband readily agreed to become their leader. Kue families and other families closely associated with them began to think about moving from Seattle. Several left before the school year began in September. Participation in fairs continued during the fall of 1984, with one show lasting nearly three months in a restaurant/gallery. Sales during HAA's second year fell to about ten thousand dollars, which the remaining American volunteers found quite adequate, considering, but which was unsatisfactory to the Hmong members. Vang My and Kue Koua moved to the Midwest in January.

Neither HAA nor HWAPA survived these changes. Hmong women remaining in Seattle who had been members of HAA continued to sell needlework in fairs but did not think of themselves as members of HAA. Former HWAPA members continued to help them at times, for instance setting up the pre-Christmas restaurant show for two more years, and HWAPA also took on other functions, but it diminished very much and was later abandoned. Thus the active period of HAA and HWAPA lasted about a year and a half.

OTHER NEEDLEWORK MARKETING

Meanwhile, in 1983, AN sold about twelve thousand dollars worth of needlework. Zer, a White Hmong woman selling in fairs only for her own relatives completely apart from either AN or HAA, did well enough to warrant continuing in business, and other private and gallery sales also took place. In 1983 Duongporn Dunning and two friends opened a shop in a Seattle suburb that sold imported needlework and fabrics from Thailand; they handled refugee work in special weekend sales semiannually. In addition, the Asian Elderly organization at Asian Counselling and Referral Service (ACRS) sold needlework at the International District Fair and a few other outlets, and the Fremont Baptist Church entered fairs for refugee parishoners, mainly Mien but a few White Hmong. AN continued to sell through its shop in the market, and some Hmong used it as an outlet. Chee Her also continued selling in fairs on her own. Other individual women sold needlework in fairs; in 1987 I spoke at length with a thriving newcomer whose suppliers were her relatives in Thailand and California and who considered needlework sales a very decent supplement to her regular income as a hospital janitor; her business still continued in 1991.

After the demise of Lao Highland Association (which like HAA did not survive the moving away of its leaders and members), Hmong New Year came under the sponsorship of the Hmong Association. The association produced two different events each year. The first was a public event held at Seattle Center, where craft tables were set up and women offered needlecrafts in conjunction with a raffle of two bedspreads, managed by Zer. Jane Mallinson and I assumed the job of hanging the Christmas sale in a restaurant. In 1985 we recruited work from many women as before, including Zer, but we found that occasionally women came into the restaurant and added or subtracted pieces to the stock hanging on the walls. No matter how carefully we kept records, one or more was sure to believe we had lost her needlework and want reimbursement. This was the same problem Vang My had had, as well as AN. In 1986 we asked Zer to help manage the sale; in 1987 and 1988 she handled it alone.

In Seattle AN alone retained an idea of permanent structure. Even Zer, who consistently sold needlework for years, taking a table at the public market and going to fairs, always spoke of it as a temporary project, and indeed later passed it along to her sister-in-law. Zer had begun needlework sales in 1981 by setting up a cooperative structure through her church group. There were members and an organizational structure, and participation in fairs and table-minding of members' consigned goods. Not all members were related. Zer encountered the identical management problems that I have been describing for AN and HAA—quarrels over inventory and accusations of bad faith—so she had quickly shifted to a family operation, handling financial details completely in the open. She marketed work done by her relatives, and herself made clothing incorporating *paj ndau*. Her early inventory system was similar to HAA's and AN's, taking work on consignment from needleworkers who owned their pieces until sold. Zer imported work from camps in Thailand and from Vientiane, Laos, as well. Slowly the proportion of goods bought wholesale (rather than taken on consignment) increased, until her business was completely self-sustaining; this was her method of overcoming the suspicions and problems of consignment. Zer is cynical about non-family-based business ventures for Hmong.

OLDER MEANINGS ASSOCIATED WITH NEEDLEWORK

Older meanings associated with Hmong needlework—ethnic identity and the ritual connections between social groups—diminished but certainly did not die out during the period of my research. These categories continued, coexisting with commercial uses. Hmong women among my informants continued to create grave garments for their parents, which were given to them at ceremonies occurring particularly when either the woman or her parents were about to move. The cut and decorative style of these garments did not change essentially, although details like the color and type of fabric increased in variety. These clothes are supposed to be sewn by the daughter, not purchased, because the decoration includes family motifs. Many women undertook long-range projects such as making their daughters' wedding clothes, but busy women also bought these costumes, or parts of the costumes, from camp-confined relatives.

Hmong women generally ceased to produce clothing for day-to-day wear. Initially, refugees continued to wear their handmade traditional clothing, but quickly the men and then the women took to less conspicuous clothes. The main ceremonial occasions for which traditional garments were still worn were weddings and New Year. Trading in textiles by Hmong women led to an unforeseen change: the costumes still associated with ethnic identity could also now be bought and sold among Hmong women. The most demanding work—batiked skirts and tiny appliquéd pockets—were often purchased by Hmong in America from camp refugees, and therefore demonstrated not skill at needlework but the presence of money to buy it.

At the New Year, although older women began wearing Lao skirts or American dresses, exuberant versions of the traditional costume began to appear on unmarried women and girls. They often mixed Blue Hmong skirts bought from Thailand with White Hmong appliqué work or Lao needleweaving (which they took up) on the aprons, which now had bright nylon sashes. Over American blouses they wore the traditional jacket, now made from flocked velveteen or satin. A favorite embroidery thread was Day-Glo orange safety cloth, unraveled. New aluminum necklaces from Thailand duplicated the old style in a lighter and less expensive material. Instead of the quieter turbans, women might wear an enlarged version of the spectacularly pieced baby's helmet embellished with sequins and baubles. This costume was completed by stiletto heels, rings and bracelets, and much makeup. The men's costume might be worn by courting males and by performers, but Hmong men now nearly always wore American suits on special occasions. The economics of costume for New Year, emphasizing the marriageability of girls, represented a continuing area of Hmong values.

NEEDLEWORK MARKETING AND GENDER ROLES

Hmong textile production in Laos was attached to gender roles in several ways. Women produced textiles: they spun thread, wove cloth, made dye, sewed and decorated clothing and other textiles intended for practical uses, and provided finished textile pieces for ritual exchanges. They worked with tools that men provided—loom, spindle, batik pen, cauldrons for dyeing. Needles (and increasingly cotton fabric and embroidery floss) were purchased using money received from men. Thus both genders were important to textile work. Men not only provided the tools and used finished textiles, but also could be seen as generously allowing women the time to do needlework by taking on farm work, household chores and babysitting, and by helping wives strip strings from hemp plants. Female-produced thread, clothing, and fabrics used in ritual or given in ritual exchanges symbolized the cohesion of the male-dominated Hmong household, descent line,

and (ultimately) society, with textile exchanges occurring within and between patrilines. In textile work, then, there was a gendered discourse
in which men gave women raw materials (tools, time, fibers, and floss),
women gave men finished products (thread, clothing, ritual pieces), and
men and women both made statements about kinship relationships with
these woman-produced things. The topic of exchanges was textiles, but the
message was kinship. When, during warfare, some women began to trade
and finished textiles were sometimes available to buy, the paths of goods
still followed kin networks.

Resettlement altered the meanings attached to textiles. In the United
States, ethnicity was not obviously indicated by daily wear. The ritual role
of textiles was reduced among Hmong Christians, and even among those
who held to the old religion, since women were no longer making the
thread that passed from the spirit altar to the front door, or the thread that
was used in wrist-tying ceremonies.

The development of commercialized textiles produced a confusion over
how gender connected with needlework. The commercial textiles were
associated with Hmong women's identity. Hmong women made them,[15]
and purchasers, most of whom were women, wanted to buy at fairs from
Hmong women sellers, in the same way that American volunteers expected
to work with Hmong women. But the social aspects of production (compromise of designs and colors, quick sewing for efficient production, and
the intent to sell) moved these pieces definitely into the arena of trade,
which in Laos had been clearly male. However, Hmong men did not produce textiles and in America were nearly excluded from retail trading in
textiles, owing to the demands of the market. Women were thrust into an
area previously familiar only to a few. Whether the profits from needlework sales were a major contribution to household economy or a small
supplement, it was the first time most Hmong women had any profit to
provide.

I had expected that these new relations in production and marketing
would impel changes in household economic decision-making and produce
new attitudes about appropriate behavior for men and women. However,
in spite of the changes that took place, needlework among the Hmong in
Seattle remained within the same frame of gender discourse as in Laos. Men
stood behind the scenes to direct their wives. In HAA, though women
continued to sell in the market and at fairs, men took over the management
of the organization. Money had always accrued to the household, where
domestic power relations continued to favor male decision-making. Cooperation was still defined as taking place within a framework of patrilateral
connections. Finished textile pieces moved along kinship networks from

Thai camps to sellers in Seattle. The topic of exchanges was still needle-work, the message was still kinship. Needlework passed from hand to hand in one direction, and needlework profit passed back the other way, carry-ing the message that kinship still existed between the parties. My Seattle informants complained about how hard it was for them to find markets for the dozens of pieces coming from camp, how time consuming it was, and how irritating to try to answer continual demands for money—but they continued doing it, because these dependents were relatives.

The kinship dimension is a vital part of Hmong needlecraft production and marketing. In HAA, the right to membership (or in some cases, its political necessity) was determined by, or expressed through, the medium of kin ties, sometimes fictive, to Kue Koua or Vang My. The predomi-nant determining factor in membership was still a patrilateral connection. The true conversation was about Hmong cohesion through kinship and its alliances; its vehicle was needlework. Men and women, not women alone, carried on this conversation. The goals of doing needlework had altered to include making money, and the social paths through which this was achieved had shifted to include women in trade, but the internalized cultural model for social organization remained in place.

6

COURTSHIP AND ELOPEMENT

After initial connections with particular Hmong families, I found tremendous changes in the conduct of daily life. Change was proceeding at lightning pace, too fast to record. I supposed it must be impelled by interaction with the environment, particularly the economic environment. The Hmong had come from an agrarian setting to an urban postindustrial setting with essentially no preparation for their new lives. They had a background of self-sufficiency and ethnic distinctiveness in their homeland with very limited participation in state-based politicoeconomic structures, followed by war, which brought a short period of national participation for a narrow stratum of military elites and their families, coupled with the experience for many ordinary Hmong of long-term dependency on wartime air-drops of food followed by refugee camp experience.

I had expected that in the United States, further economic adaptation by both elite and rural agricultural Hmong would produce new cultural conceptualizations of how men and women should treat each other, of what maleness and femaleness implied. I looked at economic change in two ways, studying household economic behavior by helping family members get jobs, and studying the social organization of two needlework sales cooperatives. In the five-year period 1981–85, there were many adjustments in the way families survived economically. Men took what jobs they could, whether laboring, professional, or (rarely and tentatively) entrepreneurial. Women took similar jobs or began acting as producers and intermediaries in needlework-selling operations. Welfare was a financial resource like any other. The Hmong studied English language and American society from the very beginning, from simple survival English classes at church or the YMCA to more advanced courses at community colleges, and also through interaction with American society via television, store, street, and workplace.

I did not find economic change driving social change. For first generation Hmong women, new economic activities did not seem to engender more control of economic resources or a greater sense of gender equality, although the women made explicit economic contributions to the household. Men and women retained the cultural conviction that men's words were more important than women's, that men's decisions carried more weight than women's, and that a woman took on the social standing of her husband, never the other way around. Women's economic activities were perceived as being permitted by their husbands, and their wages or profits entered a household economy where decisions were dominated by men.

Yet in spite of all this, I could not believe that gender relations were remaining static. Through all these changes, a great debate was going on about the content of Hmong culture, the need to retain "Hmongness," and what that might mean in this new place. By all accounts, domestic violence and divorce had both risen among Hmong since resettlement. This must imply strain in relationships between men and women, shifts and disjunctions in attitudes, social flux, demands met with impatience.

If economic relations within households did not demonstrate changes in Hmong gender beliefs, other aspects of domestic life might be more revealing. Looking at economic behavior had been a way of looking at people's internal convictions. Other products of cultural systems, however, such as arts and music, rituals, literature and storytelling, equally express cultural convictions. Perhaps tracking alterations in such cultural performances would give a clearer view of alterations in cultural beliefs. A set of cultural performances central to Hmong social structure, and one expressing in idealized form the proper relations between men and women, is the events and ceremonies that take place when the Hmong marry or when marriages are dissolved. I had been recording marriage performances since 1981. Perhaps implications about shifts in Hmong gender concepts could be found in the events, processes, rituals, and ceremonies of marriages, and in the handling of marital disputes.

Hmong culture provides a strong ideology of pairing, promoting the idea that marriage is the natural state of adults, and that people who do not marry and produce children never attain true maturity. From a habitual emphasis on even numbers (trips taken on even-numbered days, even numbers of people participating in ritual events, a preference for even numbers of children in a family), from the myth of the primal couple who appear in the world even before the sun and moon, from the many orphan tales in which the solution to the poor orphan's problems lies in marrying (for instance, *Txiv Nraug Ntsuag Thiab Ntxawm Quam Ntuj*: The Orphan and the King of Heaven's Daughter [Johnson 1985: 1–39]), and from many other obvious clues, Hmong culture implies that marriage is desirable.

In Laos, getting married for the first time generally involved courting, choosing a mate, and an elopement (called catch-hand marriage) with the girl staying at the boy's house for three days; or alternatively the boy making a formal request to the girl's family, raising the bride wealth, contract nego-

tiations between families and payment of bride wealth, and formal conveyance of the bride to her husband's home. Formal courtship often occurred
at the time of New Year celebrations, although boys and girls might have
noticed each other before, especially at events that sparked boy versus girl
song contests. Parties and events drawing together clan members included
meetings on the groom's side to raise the bride wealth, the negotiations between sides in which the bride's family hosted the groom's representatives,
and a series of parties for both sides at the time the bride formally joined
her husband's family (although she may have been living there informally
already). The costs of marrying were borne by the groom's family.

These basic steps to a first marriage may be divided on the basis of who
acts. Courtship, mate choice, and elopement are in the hands of the young
people who marry (except in the case of arranged marriage); contract negotiations, bride wealth, and conveyance of the bride are in the hands of their
elders. The following analysis uses the same division, looking in this chapter for changes in how courting, mate choice, and elopement are handled,
and for changes in the elder-controlled process of formal marriage in the
next. I will try to cover these topics fairly thoroughly, since they have
not been described from women's perspectives elsewhere in the scholarly
literature. Hmong practices in regard to marrying have engendered many
negative stereotypes among Americans, so I will try to show their cultural background in Southeast Asia, as far as I have been able to learn
it. This will provide the basis for questioning whether the underlying cultural attitudes toward gender seen in marriage practice have changed since
resettlement.

COURTSHIP IN LAOS

Hmong courtship in the Southeast Asian context has been described by
Savina, Bernatzik, Lemoine, and Lee; there are brief accounts by Chindarsi, Cooper, Geddes and others. De Beauclair, Mickey, Graham, and
other writers have given accounts of Hmong courtship in southern China.
Refugee Hmong in the United States have also described the events of
their own and other people's courtships. Broadly speaking, refugee sources
and researchers in Southeast Asia are in agreement on the purpose, main
events, and permissible varieties of courtship. All assume that it leads
toward marriage, and that marriage is a decisive event in women's lives.
Where they disagree is on who chooses whom. Do families choose their
children's spouses? Does the young man take all the initiative and the
young woman follow passively? Does the couple choose each other mutu-

ally? Does each pick the other on the basis of personal liking, or with an eye to advantage? To what extent are young people influenced by known family preferences? May a girl reject a suitor she does not like? Thus the major question that arose when I inquired into courtship was to what extent a Hmong girl chooses her own husband.

In Laos many Hmong courtships were initiated at the time of New Year's celebrations, the traditional time of relaxation and parties. Each hamlet celebrated its New Year for a minimum of three days, and possibly as long as a week, whenever the harvest was complete, at different times in different places. Boys traveled from village to village in order to meet girls, participating in festivals wherever they had relatives. The main vehicle for meeting during the New Year was the ball game (*pov pob*) that went on during the entire New Year in each place. Boys in one line facing girls in another, they tossed homemade fabric balls (*khaub hnab*) the size of oranges back and forth, back and forth. Dressed in their beautiful batiked and embroidered clothing, tinkling with silver coins arrayed in rows on beaded strings, and bright with silver jewelry, they joked and sang. Songs (*kwv tshiaj plees*) could be exacted as penalties for dropping the ball, and as singing was improvised within a poetic and musical frame, young people who were otherwise shy with each other could show off their wits to their best advantage (see Savina 1930: 224; Geddes 1976: 92; Mottin 1980a: 2).

As days wore on, a boy might concentrate on a certain girl. Redeeming the forfeits from the ball game gave the two a chance away from crowd and family to talk and get to know each other. The New Year's game therefore provided a springboard for more intense romances. Mottin says:

> At night boys go see the girls [with whom they had played ball] in turn. They come back to several, talk to the girls they are courting, and demand a song of them. Their visit is thus not compromising and the approach is more natural. To encourage the girls, the boys sing in their turn, and the meetings are prolonged. If all goes well, they hope that little by little their melodies will mingle with those of the crickets in the bushes. (Mottin 1980a: 2; my translation)

The convention of casual public meeting at the New Year's ball games and the increasingly narrowed focus until a partner is singled out allow for marriage partners to be selected by personal taste. If a boy sang or played the flute or the mouth harp for a girl outside her house late at night and she slipped out to join him in the moonlit jungle, no one was supposed to take any notice of it. If marriage followed, it was often within a few days.[1]

The pleasures of courtship provided a counterpoint to a daily life composed of hard work and obedience to the elders' wishes. For girls especially, the years of adolescence, when most could throw themselves into
romances, appeared as a time of flowering and delight. Girls devoted themselves to being charming and beautiful. The magnificent elaborations of
costume so often represented in movies and textile books belong generally
to this period of life. Girls became extremely coquettish. Some of them
invented a sort of pig-Latin so they could say outrageous things without
seeming forward, to the delight of other girls.[2] Here is an example of this
code language that I recorded, by a Hmong woman from Xieng Khouang
Province, Laos. The statement "I tell you, go on home but do come back to
see me," which in the daily speech of Blue Hmong (*Moob Ntsuab*) is said:

Kuv has tas koj moog ob peb nub es rov qab rau saib kuv,[3]

becomes this rhyme (words of original sentence underlined):

Kuv tub nxhuv, has tab nxhab, tas tab nxhab, kos tob nxhob, moos ntuab
nxhuab, es teb nxheb, os tob nxhob, peb teb nxheb, nuus tub nxhub, es teb
nxheb, qas ntab nxhab, raus tuab nxhuab, sais taib nxhaib, kuv tub nxhub,
os tob nxhob.

The mechanism is clear: extra words are added that rhyme with each word
of the sentence, and the tones are changed to a sing-song rhythm, which
is said very fast. Here is another way she encoded the same sentence:

Kuv kev hab heeb tab teev koj kev moog meeb tsev tseev, lawm leeg os es
kuv keev nyuuj nyuub nyeeb kaw keeb, kooj kees moog me os, ob es peb pes
nub nes quos qees rov qab qais tus teev saib ses nkub kev os es.

In this example I have put commas where she paused to breathe. The
mechanism is a little different, but the original words of the sentence can
still be found embedded in the nonsense words. Not all Hmong girls learned
this joking language; a woman from Sam Neua had never heard of it, and
my younger informants appear to be unfamiliar with it.

In addition to nonsense talk, another sort of secret language was used
by boys and girls to communicate with each other, preserve shy politeness,
and confound their elders. By playing on flutes and mouth harps [*ncas*],
concentrating on melody and tone, they could approximate tonal speech,
and if the sentence was very simple the sense could be apprehended by the

listener. The mouth harp in particular lends itself to this use, as it sounds very soft if the singer's lips are held away from the blade. Catlin describes it as follows:

> The most typical instrument for courting, and also the simplest in con-struction, is the jaw harp (or Jew's harp) called nja (ncas). Made of a flat sheaf of copper [actually brass] in which a fine incision outlines the tongue which has been cut from its center, the nja is held by one hand between the lips. The other hand strums the end, horizontally, causing the reed to vibrate, while the player lightly inhales and exhales through his or her lips. By altering the shape of the mouth cavity, different partials of the vibrat-ing . . . reed are amplified, creating notes which again convey the tones of the words to be transmitted. The nja is often played in the night by a young suitor outside the house of his beloved. She may reply with her own nja or another instrument, and the dialogue can continue for hours. It is difficult for us to imagine the quiet which would allow a dialogue of these barely audible instruments across such a distance. (Catlin n.d.: 12)

Casual flirtatiousness could be public. Bernatzik, describing his sojourn in a Meau (Hmong) village in Siam, writes:

> We frequently had an opportunity to observe an open flirtation. My wife wrote . . . "May, the chief's daughter, is probably about sixteen years old and a typical 'teen-ager' in behavior. She giggles at the least thing or bursts into loud peals of laughter over a remark shouted at her by one of the boys. . . . It is gayest when Bun Ma, our Lao interpreter, is visited in his camp by three or four girls together. . . . They tease him about one of the girls, urge him to visit her because, they say, she is waiting for him, ask how the Lao make love, and so forth. . . . He is readily captivated by the pretty faces and the in-gratiating nature of the girls. In the evening Bun Ma sits in the house of the chief, and the girls teach him the love songs of the Meau in their language, and even the old chief joins in and, turning toward Bun Ma with a smirk, sings in the same register as the girls and amid general laughter: 'Where do you stay so long, I am waiting for you!'" (Bernatzik 1970: 128–9)

But in Lee's experience, serious courting

> must be done in the least conspicuous way, particularly for the girl's parents or relatives. . . . As in the old days, courting is still done with both the young man and the girl whispering to each other in the dark of the night through a slit in the timber wall of her house, the girl lying on her bed and

the young man crouching or bending himself to her level outside. . . . He often covers himself against the cold or prying eyes with a thick woollen blanket, which . . . must be of sufficient size to accommodate two persons in case the girl agrees to spend the night in the bush with the man. (Lee 1981: 42–43)

The old chief made jokes about the forwardness of his daughter and her friends, but Bun Ma was not actually an available suitor. Young people went to great lengths to keep their elders from knowing their actual affairs. Courtship is one area of life where the strong Hmong value on truthfulness is not enforced.

Many Hmong women have an extreme reluctance to talk about their courtship at all, even many years later, and some of my subjects would not talk about courtship at all. The women who spoke to me most easily about it were my closest Hmong friend, who was quite committed to making me understand her culture, and a risqué old lady who adored telling funny stories. The general reluctance to talk about courtship did not seem to be due to my status as an outsider among the Hmong. In the case of older women, it was a residue of their youthful reluctance to talk about courtship to their own families. My subjects, in talking about their courtships, all thought their families were entirely unaware of their activities.

He followed me one time as I was going with my father to carry rice from the field to our house. He followed talking to me for a few hundred yards, but I said, "Please don't follow me, because my father is right there. I don't want my father to see me with anyone." Xao said, "Are you sure?" I said, "Yes, I tell you, I'm very sure! I don't want somebody to just follow me when my father is around. That's not OK with me." I was shy, you see. All the girls were like that, no one wanted her parents to know if she had talked to a boy. (Xiong and Donnelly 1986: 215)

This girl was retailing household goods for her soldier boyfriend among her relatives (a very obvious occupation), but when she told her parents she was "helping the army" they evidently asked nothing further. In talking to me years later she still did not give any sign of thinking they might have been aware she had a boyfriend.

Cooper says it is "considered bad form" for parents to notice their daughters' adventures. He implies that parents are often aware but silent, which seems intuitively correct. At the time of courtship, a girl was preparing to shift her efforts so that they would benefit a different family, in the service of her own future. My informants tended to phrase their girlhood relationship to their birth family in terms of economic value, not affection, and thought their family would be angry to lose their labor contribution. Some of their stories convey a feeling of alienation from family that may have helped them want to leave. As my subjects had been taught to conceal nothing from their parents, their new secrecy, aimed at avoiding confrontation, imbued courtship with an anxiety that has persisted into their adult years, making them still shy about speaking of it, and helping to recreate this gulf between themselves and their own daughters. The secrecy game, with its pleasing air of conspiracy, wittiness, and excitement, thus has a sober side that links it with the requirements of Hmong social structure. The structural requirement that girls shift families upon marriage leads them into stealth and unreliability.

EMOTION AND COURTSHIP

There is another reason for shyness and the desire for privacy. Writers on the Hmong from Savina to Geddes, covering the area from China to Thailand, mention easy premarital sex as a fact of Hmong village life. My respondents (except the converted Christian Hmong) seem to agree with other sources that Hmong girls and boys play sexual games together, and that fidelity to one friend is not expected:

> Hmong people have many friends. Not only one boyfriend. It's many friends. Yeah, many friends. Some people who want to ask me, it's OK. No problem.

I have found Hmong subjects reluctant to make any statements about sexuality; they seem much more private on this topic than Europeans or Americans. But Bernatzik, who goes so far as to list techniques of Hmong lovemaking (making one wonder just how he got such explicit information) has much to say on this topic (Bernatzik 1970: 134–35). Cooper comments:

> It is perhaps surprising that in a society where women have so few rights, there is an attitude of tolerance towards pre-marital sex. . . . Young people mix freely in the evenings and from puberty (about twelve-fifteen years old), a girl is free to have sex with any man she wishes, married or unmarried, unless he falls within the clan taboo. These sexual encounters follow an institutionalized form in which the girl has every right to reject a suitor's advances. (Cooper 1984: 144)

Is this "perhaps surprising," as Cooper says? The financial and ethical consequences of early sexuality among Hmong in Southeast Asia seem to have

Mother and child, 1981, wearing traditional costume altered by new materials such as flocked velvet and jewelry findings. The coins on the child's hat, for instance, are stamped foil imitations of Roman coins.

Chay Xeng Xiong plays the traditional two-string fiddle in the New Year's program, Seattle, 1983. The drum set behind him is for a teen dance later that evening.

Courtship ball game, New Year 1982. Mixed costumes reveal changing tastes. Video tape being made by man in center will likely be sent to Hmong in other cities to show them what happened in Seattle at this most important yearly festival.

Courtship at New Year 1988. The ball game has not passed away, but casual connections are much more relaxed among teenagers than they seemed during the early 1980s. The young man has taken his style from the *Miami Vice* television show; the young woman remains traditional.

Wedding, Seattle 1981. The bride (*background*) is escorted by male representatives of the groom's family, who carry her possessions to her new home, and a female chaperone (concealed behind her) who is a friend of hers from the groom's family. There must be an even number of people on this journey so that the new couple will endure.

The bride and her chaperone waiting for the ritual portion of the wedding. Since the groom's family is Christian, the ritual consisted of prayer.

Wedding negotiations: bride's representative on the left, groom's on the right. The table is filled with ritual pairs of objects, including liquor, cups, plates, chickens, and forks. Negotiators perform paired acts (here, eating pieces of chicken).

Kialor *(left)* prepares greens in a bowl on the kitchen floor as Tou and his father, Yong Koua, talk. (Source: Neil Menschel, *Christian Science Monitor,* August 12, 1987; reproduced with permission)

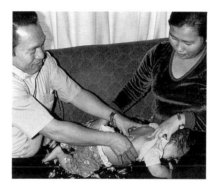

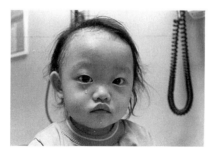

When Lisa Vang had pneumonia, her parents tried both allopathic and traditional medicine. The physician provided antibiotics while the traditional healer performed acupressure-based massage.

Taking the restaurant-worker's test, Seattle 1981, and later slicing zucchini in a French restaurant.

Income taxes.

Mee Vang *(right)* shows off the baby carrier her mother *(left)* made for her. The pattern includes a Hmong cross to ward off evil. It is batiked and has an overlay of red applique; the edging is pink satin. The coins are real Indochinese piastres.

The baby carrier in use.

A batiked and appliqued panel made for sale. This cross pattern appears most often on baby carriers. (Source: Mallinson and Donnelly 1988:50)

Haam Nhia Nruag (Doua Hang), Tsaab Ab (Ah Chang), and Haam Npis (Bee Hang) at a recording session of love songs improvised in the traditional way. The session was arranged by Marshall Hurlich and Doua Hang. The girl could travel unchaperoned with these two men, and the couple could sing love songs to each other, because she was already betrothed to the young man. University of Washington, December 1982.

Left: Crossroads batik pattern, with a fern pattern border. This skirt pattern was photographed from a piece produced for sale as a tablecloth or wall hanging.

Family of Xao Vang and May Xiong, Seattle 1984. This family moved to Wisconsin, where both parents could attend school. Now both are working, they own their home and a rental property, and they have one more son. Their eldest son is in college.

Family of Wa Her and Hua Lor, Seattle 1984. This family was newly arrived when the picture was taken, having joined the eldest son (*second from right*), who had come to the United States several years earlier. They followed Xao Vang, their close relative, to Wisconsin. The parents have not learned English or held jobs, and one daughter (*center*) died. But the eldest son has now graduated from college and the other boys are doing well in school.

Shaman and healer Cha Fong Hang and son, Stockton 1984.

Herbalist and batik artist La Xiong, wife of Cha Fong, Stockton 1984.

Leader and entrepreneur Ly Hang with her granddaughter.

Family of Mai Vang in Ban Vinai, Thailand, within two weeks of exiting Laos, 1978. Their many sufferings included the death of their husband/father.

Mai Vang's family in the United States, 1984. Eldest daughter had married and moved, and one son was off playing soccer.

been light. The sexual acts of unmarried Hmong girls had no practical impact on property relations. A woman did not bring real property, notable personal goods, or potential inheritance into marriage. Except for wedding gifts from her parents, such as clothes, silver, pigs and chickens—which in theory remained the woman's property even if her husband used them, to be returned in case of divorce—each patriline disinherited its daughters.

The financial burden if a pregnancy occurred was on the putative father, who paid a fine and lost the child, unless he married the pregnant girl. Even if he was unenthusiastic about this marriage, later if he could afford it he could marry again to his liking. Often marriage was the solution favored by his male relatives, who otherwise would be contributing to the fine (ibid.: 145). On the other hand, illegitimate pregnancies did not seem to inflict on girls the burden of a terrible moral flaw, since sex among traditional Hmong was not conceptualized in terms of sin as it is in the revised beliefs of Hmong Christians. One of my subjects used the term "fresh" for a girl before she bore a child, and "not fresh" for a woman after she had had children, but I have not heard that bride wealth was lower for unwed mothers. Cooper speculates that having had a child (proving fecundity) would even add to a girl's attractiveness as an investment. This view recognizes that the most valuable property a girl brought into marriage was herself, her labor and her fertility.

Hmong girls' and boys' sexual adventures, then, were not important to the maintenance of Hmong social forms, and were unimportant to the transmission of property or access to economic goods. Unintended pregnancies were not seen as terrible moral flaws, and child and mother were not without a place in Hmong society. However, girls' premarital adventures in Laos were not unhedged by cultural conventions. While boys (and girls) were looking for a good time, girls still assumed that if a youth made any gesture of interest toward her, he was considering her as a marriage partner.

> Xao was interested in me because I could read and write. He was learning to write Lao in the army. He sent me a letter; he said he wanted to make new friends. . . . If a girl is not polite, the young men make jokes about her. Even if you don't really want to meet him, it's more polite to say, "Sure!" It's better not to say no. But you always know if a young man writes you a letter, he's interested in marriage. Otherwise he wouldn't write. (Xiong and Donnelly 1986: 214)

Lemoine comments that the "pursuit of pretty girls" is young men's main diversion, and Bernatzik notes one father's delight at his son's "clever[ness]" with girls. We can consider sexual play, from the girls' point of view, as a series of trials leading toward the choice of a mate, but they too could see that boys might not be serious, but merely seeking conquests. Many misunderstandings no doubt arose because of this gap in how courtship by-play was perceived. Such feelings can be seen in the following song excerpt:

> At night thousands of crickets make their songs heard;
> At the fall of day Pe Koua retires,
> Then silently he goes to the peak across there.
> At the time we met each other
> You spoke to me of love, but your heart wasn't in it.
> And, during this whole time you have courted me
> In the way of an old Chinese couple
> Who, when the rice is ripe, leave half of it.
>
> Before leaving each other, let me sing to you:
> "Poppy dries in the sun, but flowers under the rain."
> We have loved each other without being married,
> Because you spoke of love, but your heart was not in it
> So you will have courted me only in passing.
>   I am sad enough to die!

(Mottin, 1980a: 23, sung by Zuag Thoj, Khek Noy, 23 May 1975, translation by Valerie Lewis; Pe Koua is the name of a bird)

Unmarried Hmong girls' feelings have not been investigated directly, but perhaps we can see them in reflection by looking at love songs. Among Hmong females, only single girls are supposed to sing love songs, and as most songs fit this description, women generally stop singing once they marry. Love songs were produced in an atmosphere of contest. Wittiness was very much emphasized in the verbal gaming that surrounded singing:

> In our country if they have a party, the young women and the young men make teams, and a woman sings a song, a man sings another song, another woman sings, another man sings, until one side wins and the other loses. They keep on going back and forth. Whatever topic one sings, the next person has to take that idea and follow with a new song. If someone cannot follow, he or she doesn't know very much! There is no judge, but whoever says, "Oh, I want to go home!" that one doesn't win. On that night five girls and five boys sang against each other, and everyone else listened. When the

older people got thirsty they just drank a little more wine, and the young people kept on singing. They sang all night, and in the morning the girls were the winners.

Mottin has an extended discussion of poetic form in Hmong love songs (1980a: 7–11), showing how complicated the rhyme patterns are, how phrases are built in parallel segments and ideas are stated in parts that add up to a whole. These songs are very intricate, especially in view of their improvisatory nature. Most are lost. However, working in refugee camps, Mottin was able to record some songs of Hmong girls and boys from Laos, which he then translated to French (see the previous and following songs). Girls' songs do not recount actual experiences. Their imagery abounds with mythical birds, dragons, and Chinese grandfathers. Some songs speak in the voice of a girl *ua nyaab* (already a daughter-in-law), and others take the girl's own adultery (impossible because she is not yet married) as their topic. Courting songs, invented and stylistically elaborated by singers, move within an oral tradition, subject to improvisation, like jazz songs. We can suppose that just as American love songs model and prescribe emotions that are really felt in certain situations, Hmong love songs do the same.

There is an overwhelming tone of sadness and a wrenching sense of loss in many of these songs; there is almost no example of a purely joyful lyric. The girl presents herself as vulnerable and helpless during courtship, and after marriage as a victim forced to do as other people dictate. She can only dream of happier times or wish that life had taken another turn. The reason for her woe is that she does not belong anywhere, because she has to marry and shift families. Her happiness is thus at the whim of her lover or husband.

Love songs represent a cultural fund known to most Hmong. They speak about the girl's perception of her situation, bringing her concerns, fears, and wishes to a quasi-public level where they can be negotiated without her having to confront her suitor directly. But whereas Mottin sees the songs as set pieces out of the past, I suggest they are part of a living social (as well as artistic) tradition, because they are improvised.

Little sister Ya Ndze has her dress of silk;
If Ka De doesn't marry her, she'll die of sorrow.

The trunk of the tree increases its size slowly.
If Ka De wants to keep little sister Ya Ndze,

He must be gentle to her, and then she can live;
Otherwise she will say to the dragon of the pools
To liberate their waters, after which she will drown.

You nibble the worm, I nibble the stem.
You say that all is well, how charming you are,
And I, I think also that I am the most beautiful.

(Mottin 1980a: 37; Sung by Maiv Nyiaj Xyooj, Ouinay Camp (Ban Vinai),
22 February 1976; my translation)

About this song, Mottin comments:

> The girl dreams of marrying her lover, although marriage drives her crazy.
> She believes that the boy will not prove gentle to her, so she threatens, if
> this should be true, to put an end to her days. She will liberate an aquatic
> monster who will loose a deluge in which she will drown. This mysterious
> animal (*ntaaj dua vuam*) is doubtless the dragon who rules over the waters
> and provokes the rains.
>
> This avowal is not to be taken lightly, since young Hmong girls do kill
> themselves following deception in love.
>
> In the last couplet, the loving girl sees herself as already romping in the
> fields with her love, searching for insects to nibble on. The Hmong are par-
> ticularly partial to bamboo worms, which they catch in the stems of certain
> plants. Graciously, she gives him the worm, while she contents herself with
> the stem. (Mottin 1980a: 37; my translation)

Most writers about Hmong courtship mention that girls are willing to
kill themselves if they feel enough despair. Suicide is also a possibility for
a young couple whose parents refuse permission to marry, and for married
women. It is an acceptable cultural option. The often repeated threat of
self-destruction (besides being an expression of despair) is a social tool for
the helpless, as they try to control the actions of others toward themselves.
It demonstrates Hmong girls' perception of their socially helpless condition, and their concept of themselves as romantically helpless within the
structure of Hmong society. The threat of suicide was a pivotal part of
courtship for one of my life-history subjects, discussed below. For her, the
threat of suicide came from an intense upwelling emotion, but also func-
tioned as a sanction with which she strove to gain control of a particular
series of events.

MATE CHOICE IN FIRST MARRIAGES

Qooh tsis zoo tsuas plam nyog ub cim;
Poj-niam tsis zoo ces plam tas ib sim
    (If the crops aren't good, you lose only one year;
    If your wife isn't good, you lose a whole lifetime.)

Vang and Lewis 1984: 82

Marrying a family already related by marriage was strongly preferred among Hmong in Laos, so that the best predictor of a potential spouse was a pre-existing marriage tie between families. This was not only because of the smallness of Hmong villages and the limited range of acquaintance in the Lao mountains. Marrying was called "becoming a daughter-in-law" because the new wife was almost certain to live with her in-laws and work under orders from her mother-in-law. Successful previous marriages between families might augur well for a couple's future, and in case of marital dispute might provide sympathetic counselors for both husband and wife.

The principal social constraint on marriage was the absolute requirement to marry outside the clan, which applied to everyone under all circumstances.[4] Lesser constraints were observed less carefully or ignored for pragmatic reasons. For instance, it was ritually out of order to marry above or below one's own generation. As one informant relates:

> My aunt who married my husband's brother said, "Why did you follow me? I'm already here. This is too bad, they won't value us. You're my niece and I'm your aunt, and they will treat us like crummy old bamboo buckets with the bottoms broken out, everything goes through and nothing stays in, and they will throw us both away!"

When this girl married her aunt's brother-in-law, it was inauspicious for both women; however, the second marriage was not invalidated. Violation of this constraint could be handled by a money fine paid by the husband's family.

Until the war virtually all Hmong families practiced farming, in which success was attributed to personal skill or character, luck, or avoiding bad spirits. Family position was not dependent upon marriage to someone equal in a status hierarchy, nor did the Hmong determine access to economic goods by ordering families within a class system.[5] I heard many times that the social position of a girl's family was irrelevant, although her family's pleasure at her marriage would be increased by vigor and success in the young man's family. Violence, opium addiction, communism (at least among refugee Hmong), suicide of a previous spouse, insanity or gross stupidity, physical deformity or terrible ugliness, barrenness, and being old all rendered males and females less marriageable. A man who was already married was also less marriageable. My informants commented that from the point of view of the girl's parents a bad marriage was one that would harm her through poverty or overwork, or would take her so far away they would not see her. From the boy's family's point of view, it was laziness and bad temper that made a bad daughter-in-law (such girls were "pitilessly bullied," says Lemoine). In general, individual reputation could be partially equated with the potential for economic contribution. Additionally, the sending family would be interested in their daughter's welfare, while the receiving family would be interested in her compatibility with their household.

HMONG YOUTHS' BASIS FOR CHOOSING A WIFE

Basic qualities sought in a wife were willingness to work and potential fertility. Over and over in the literature and informants' statements the ability to work hard is mentioned as primary. One of my life-history subjects told how her aunt listed her virtues in terms of work:

> Gia told my [future] husband. She said, "Mang, she really likes to work. She likes to cook and sew, she likes to pull weeds and take care of the pigs and the chickens. Can you marry her?" My [future] husband said, "OK, I'm looking for somebody who really likes to do things. I don't want to marry some girl who's lazy."

In addition, a young man might seek to please himself with someone young, beautiful, smart, or good tempered. In one instance, the youth was first attracted to the girl because she could read, and she tried to show him she could help him by selling things and giving him the money (Xiong and Donnelly 1986). One of my informants recalls herself as having been very beautiful and, for that reason, highly sought after even at the age of ten (she married at fourteen).

Social maturity depended on producing offspring, not simply on marrying, and it was difficult for a girl who might be infertile to find a spouse. Cooper tells the following story:

> One man in Pha Nok Kok had paid only 2,800 baht for a wife that he admitted was old and unattractive, and, although a good worker, was thought

unlikely to have children. Her father gave her two neckrings, a bracelet and clothes, the total value of which almost equalled the bride price. (After killing a pig to feast the groom's family, it is possible that the father gained nothing from the marriage.) The bride bore her husband four children in rapid succession and he is now very pleased with his investment and is planning to marry again—this time a younger wife. (1984: 140)

The socially approved qualities that a sensible young Hmong man in Laos would be likely to seek in a wife would include industry, obedience, fertility, congeniality, and attractiveness. He would seek initial approval for the search from his male relatives. He might also consider whether the girl's temperament would suit his mother and the other women in the household. He would favor a girl with family ties to his own family. In short, he would take a managerial approach to his marriage, considering his future family and his natal family as much as his personal pleasure, which however he would not neglect. That young men actually took this kind of approach is affirmed in the literature and in my research.

HMONG GIRLS' BASIS FOR CHOOSING A HUSBAND

In some respects girls' criteria for choice of a suitor came from the same body of cultural values. Girls valued a youth who would work hard, and whose family they knew. They liked cleverness and good looks and preferred someone near them in age. They disliked men who were already married. Some girls also tried to take into account the structural position they would occupy in their husband's family, and the personalities of his relatives, but since the young man often came from another village or area, they were at a disadvantage in trying to consider this aspect of their future.

Many of my informants were married by age fourteen, and the oldest bride I have come across was twenty-two. Bernatzik declares that "the first wife of a Meau is generally older, more mature, and stronger than her husband" (1970: 139). Geddes makes a similar statement, saying that boys marry between fifteen and sixteen and girls at about twenty. But this observation is not particularly borne out by life histories from Laos; only one of my subjects was clearly older than her husband. Cooper in the quote above considers the wife's greater age to be a disadvantage. Lee (1981) goes into this topic in some detail, listing the difference in age of husband and wife for forty-two couples in Khun Wang village and finding the husband older in twenty-seven cases, the wife older in eleven cases, and the couple of the same age in four cases. Even this is a small sample, but the preponderance of information seems to indicate that younger brides are favored.

Lee's point is not that boys prefer younger girls, but that girls prefer to marry a boy older than themselves, since if he is younger he may marry a second wife later. Lee perceives a shift toward marrying younger girls, resulting from increased romantic courtship and decreased rational parental arrangements.

A girl's goal was not merely marriage, but a marriage bringing her respect, despite her future as a relatively powerless worker and producer of children. But Hmong girls were not able to take a managerial approach to their marriages, even though, my subjects agreed, their most important decision in life was whom to marry. They had little practice in making decisions, having been raised to be shy and obedient. Making decisions was seen as forward and bold, a function of males, not of females. For instance, if a youth proposed and a girl didn't want to marry him, she was not supposed to insult him by rejecting him outright, for "she doesn't know her future." Instead of saying "No" she was supposed to say "Maybe next year." If her parents asked her whether she liked a particular youth, instead of saying "Yes" she should "just cry." If she said yes, it meant "she knows nothing"; the sign of being committed to a youth was possessing a token from him, some gift he had given her that her parents might demand to see. This token was the sign she liked him. Being tongue-tied and indecisive was appropriate to girls. A reputation for forwardness could even prevent a girl from finding a husband; calling a girl bold was a warning for her to mend her behavior.

There were several ways girls avoided an appearance of boldness in courtship while still striving to attract attention: feigning ignorance of a youth's interest, while showing compliance if he made any moves; playfully using the secret language; embedding their own concerns and wishes within songs; or dropping the ball accidentally-on-purpose during the ball game to entail a forfeit that had to be returned. One of my subjects was quite clear in her mind whom she wanted to marry, but when he came to marry her she "had not decided what to do" and "was not really ready." Another avoided deciding anything; she did not admit her potential husband was courting her. Kidding and joking were excellent ways for witty girls to attract boys without seeming demanding, as with the girl in the story told below, who went to grind corn accompanied by two youths, and "just laughed and talked until the middle of the night." Such strategies, often charming in their own right, arose because girls had to find roundabout ways to get what they wanted, being unable to go straight toward their goal. In fact, ignoring the goal was one way to achieve it.

The necessity for these strategies must have reduced the objective information girls could gain about their suitor. Choices had to be based on advice, usually from older relatives, but many girls, as part of the concept of shyness, kept their courtships secret. Many girls had to base their choice on the boy's manner and treatment of them during a very brief courtship, which might last only a few days.

So girls were at a disadvantage in exercising choice. The boy was expected to initiate courtship, the girl to follow (or not follow); a girl was under great constraint to be polite to every boy; she was taught less about social forms and so had less ability to predict the social outcomes of her own actions; she was not practiced in decision-making. Her family had less ability than a boy's to help her if she was hoping for a particular match, or to fend for her if they thought she was in trouble. The habit of refusing to marry anyone fits into this scenario because, by refusing to marry and putting the onus for action on the boy, a girl gained leverage in case he mistreated her.

Under these circumstances, rural girls tried to achieve a desirable marriage by making themselves attractive to desirable young men. They concentrated on beauty (especially through costume), on flirtation, and on personal skills. Also, they were aware of their labor value and tried to show that they would be rational investments as human capital. Even Hmong girls from educated families in urbanized areas do not appear to have had more casual relations with young men than their rural relatives, or more control over whom they married.

WANTED AND UNWANTED FIRST MARRIAGES

The accounts of elopements in Laos given to me by my Hmong friends make it appear that girls make no direct effort to choose their husbands, and are usually astonished by the event. Here is a story of an ordinary marriage, condensed from a life history:

> My husband, Koua, was from another village about half a day from my village. His older brother's daughter was married to my older brother. He came by himself, and stayed in our house to visit just only one day. He came four times in four months, and at night he went to stay with his relatives. But late in the night he came back outside my house, right near my bed, but outside the wall. Then he could play his mouth harp [ncas] and I could listen to him, and after that I played my mouth harp for him to listen to me. He didn't play the flute because it was too noisy, my mother and father could hear it. I visited his village one time with my brother and his wife about

three months before Koua married me. We stayed two days, and I met his mother and father.

The fourth time Koua came to visit was around the New Year, and his two cousins came with him. They made their visit. And when night time came, my mother and father went to sleep, and everybody else was going to sleep, so Koua and his cousins said they had to go back home. And they went to the door to go out, and they left the door open. They said, "Mee, come to close the door." So I went to close the door, and they just caught hold of me and pulled me outside and shut the door! That is the way Hmong culture is supposed to do, too.

I was very surprised! I didn't expect that at all! I never thought they wanted to get married to me! I just thought I was going to close the door, and then come back and go to sleep. But they caught me, and pushed me outside the door, and shut the door behind me, so I was outside with them. I was so surprised I had to yell. "Oh!" I cried. Then my mother and father woke up again and my brother and his wife and my younger brother and everybody heard me call out. They all came outside the house to see why I had made that noise. They said, "What happened?" My mother and father didn't know I was going to get married, either.

So then Koua's cousins said to my mother and father, "You don't worry, nothing bad is happening. Koua just got married with your daughter." This was so they would know the reason I was outside. My husband could not speak to my mother and father, because he had to be careful to watch me, and he was holding on to my hand. He wanted to be sure I did not try to run away or go back inside the house! And they were afraid that my mother and father would say, "Don't get married, we don't want our daughter to marry you."

But they said, "OK, you can get married to Koua." Then they went back to bed, and I just had to stay outside with my husband and his friends. That is an important part of Hmong culture. After the girl gets married, she cannot go back inside her parents' house for three days. Then she can visit her mother and father again.

But in Tang Koeui all the families were from the same clan, all had the same last name as me. We could not go inside any of those houses. It was night time, so we could not walk to his house. We didn't have any place to go. Hmong people always get married in the night time. The time of the month was early in the first quarter of the moon. That's the best time to get married, when the moon is growing. If the moon is already full, or if it is waning, people don't get married at that time of month.

I wanted to get married with Koua, but I was not very happy that night. I just sat on the porch outside my parents' house by myself, and I could not say anything to Koua or his cousins. I leaned up against the wall, and thought that I could not go inside again, and I would not ever live with my family again, and it made me very sad. I was not afraid of Koua, but I didn't know his family very well, and I didn't really know how I was going to be living after the next day. Also I felt very shy. For anybody on the first day you have to be very, very, very shy, you know? I didn't say a word to anybody all that night. And also he didn't speak to me either, except at the beginning he just said, "I marry you and you marry me." That's all. I think maybe he was shy that night, too.

Very early in the morning when the roosters crowed and people began to get up, we started to leave. I said good-bye to my mother and father. My brother's wife was very glad that we got married, because we would see each other often. Other people who lived near the trail came out of their houses and saw us going, and they said to me, "Well, if you are going to his village, you must come back to see us again!" I was crying and crying. Koua was happy and his friends were happy, and excited that Koua got a wife! He said, "Now you are married to me, why are you crying?" Then we got outside my village and were walking toward his village, and after that I didn't cry anymore.

These are the feelings Hmong girls are supposed to feel at the point of elopement—total surprise and confusion, shyness, sadness to leave home, and secret gladness to be married to this particular youth. This woman presents herself as passive, not acting on her own behalf. She should not have been utterly astonished to be taken in marriage by Koua, however. Their families were already intermarried; he had come visiting four times, and she had visited his family once. In fact, she did not discourage him, but gave him positive signals of her liking—this is the woman who recited for me the nonsense poems quoted earlier. But as a proper girl she would not admit recognizing such factors.

If we add certain ritual acts required of the young men (bowing to her parents, giving each person in the household a cigarette), the story gives a paradigm for elopement. Arriving at her new home, Mee was greeted by her mother-in-law:

We went inside the door, and his mother did the little ceremony to bring me into the house. She took a female chicken, and when I came in, she used the chicken to call my spirit [qab hu plig] to come out of my parents' house and to come into the house of Koua's parents. She said, "You have to come and live with us. . . . Spirit, come in with Mee. Don't stay at that house, don't stay at your mother and father's house. Come to our house. Mee has gotten married with Koua. She is my daughter-in-law now." She said something like that. All Hmong mothers do that, when their son gets married. Only women can do that, his father cannot do it. And when the mother is finished, they don't kill that chicken.

The ritual aspects of shifting a girl from her parents' home to her parents-in-law's home are very simple, as described by my Hmong informants, and small discrepancies do not invalidate the marriage. This is because the marriage rituals link clans and extended families; they are not supposed to divide them.[6]

Different women reported a range of self-knowledge and intentional behavior for their marriages. Bla was determined to marry at New Year's of her sixteenth year. She carefully assessed the range of boys who played ball with her, spending time with several before settling on one preferred suitor, a boy whose uncle had married her aunt. This aunt had drawn Chou's attention to Bla when he stayed at his uncle's during the village New Year. Chou and Bla played ball, talked evening after evening, and mutually decided to elope, even though her brother and mother, she said, wanted to prevent her marrying because the family needed her labor. But when he came tapping at the house wall in the night and she slipped out to meet him, once on the path she hung back. She wasn't ready to marry, she told him, she couldn't leave her family. "Do you want to marry me, or not?" he demanded. In her thirties she laughed to recount this moment of truth. Of course she wanted to marry him. After a fractional hesitation, she said, "Sure!" and they kept going. Propriety was not her first priority.

Another woman, Mai Xiong, had been urged by her grandmother to find a husband who was not a farmer, to make her own life easier. She was noticed by a soldier, who was intrigued because she could read, and she fostered the relationship by helping him sell small things and by sending him a medicine when he was sick. When he came with his friends to "kidnap" her, she resisted strongly, saying she wasn't ready, that she didn't want to leave her family. But they pulled her away, and when they had gone some distance she decided it was too late to argue, and went along. She wanted to go, in fact. Her furious father sent the grandmother to bring her back, but the old lady made only a token search and the elopement succeeded (see Xiong and Donnelly 1986). Her father had had a different marriage in mind, since nearly all the marriages in that extended family for generations had been with the neighboring Thao clan, whereas this soldier was a stranger. Ultimately his only satisfaction came from demanding a high bride wealth payment.

From these and other cases it is plain that in an elopement the bride's family has something to say in their daughter's choice of a mate, but their wishes are less significant than the girl's preference, when these conflict. However, in the case of arranged marriages, the opposite was true. There are no statistics on the frequency or success rate of arranged marriages. Lee says that formerly the custom of arranged marriage was practiced, but now it is dying out and being replaced by personal choice (1981: 43). Cooper, however, says that "most Hmong marriages are arranged between the fathers of the bride and groom and take account of the wishes of both marriage partners" (1984: 143). Of the dozen or so marriages I recorded, two were arranged and one was arranged but later broken off.

One woman's parents had been asked for her three times beginning when she was ten, but her grandfather's was the crucial opinion. Her parents would have taken the highest bidder, she said, but he made them wait until she was fourteen and liked the youth who asked. She described her marriage as a love match.

Another woman, now in her thirties, was living in Vientiane and going to school when she learned, at the age of fourteen, that her father had promised her in infancy to the son of a friend. This had evidently been a political matter. The weekend when the youth came to get her was the first she had heard of the arrangement. Vigorously she refused to go, so the young man took her outside to talk. "We have to marry," he said, "or our fathers will lose face, but if you don't like me, we'll just get divorced afterwards." This argument persuaded her, "but you know," she added with the wisdom of greater age, "it's not so easy to get divorced." Nor would she divorce now, being happily married after all these years.

All these arranged marriages involved a positive choice by the girl, even the first marriage where the choice was covert. It is a choice within a narrow range of possibilities, in one case between an unwanted marriage and embarrassing the father, but even so, the act of choosing means that the girl has not lost control of her future. This aspect of choice is crucial, for ultimately the wife must be willing to work, bear children, and contribute to her husband's family.

Power relations in Hmong society meant that girls had little ability to speak about or defend wishes that contradicted the desires of their elders. Girls were raised to be obedient workers. But in the matter of marriage choice, several safeguards were built into the cultural patterns that governed getting married. Serious courtships took place under a blanket of secrecy. The family had no recourse if a girl ran off with someone they disliked. Generally speaking, of course, they had her best interest at heart. But if they did not, she could subvert their plans. The following events took place when Mai was about fourteen years old, in northeastern Laos close to the border of Vietnam. The puzzle in this story was to avoid an unwanted marriage and achieve an acceptable future. At the time of recording she was in her sixties.

Well, a man was being promoted, and the district leader came. So the man's family called me to help them get ready. The leader had a new secretary that year, a very young man about twelve years old. The household was killing pigs for the party and we were carrying water to clean the pigs. My aunt Joua and I were carrying water together. When we went the third time to get more water, some of the visitors followed us, and they brought that young man.

The older men said to me, "Do you like this young man?" I thought they were joking with me, so I said, "Sure." They said, "Can you marry him?" I answered them, and I thought they were kidding, so I said, "Sure!" But when I got home to eat my dinner in the afternoon, they followed me to my house. I thought that if I went to sleep in my house, they would find me there, so I went to sleep at Joua's house that night.[7]

Then they went on to another village to promote somebody else, and sent back a letter to me asking for "One sweet word, only one sweet, sweet word," they said. I gave the letter to my uncle Chue [Tswb] to read, and he said, "They want you just to say one word for them." I said, "I don't know what to say." He explained, "They want you to say yes or no, because they want to marry you, but the one who is going to marry you is not the young one, it's the older one." I didn't know who they meant—I never even looked at him. He was about 30 years old, and when I learned he had a wife I thought, all his children are already grown up! I had my uncle Chue write a letter back to them. I said if they wanted me to marry the younger one, I would, but if they wanted me to marry the older one, they could talk until their heads broke, and I wouldn't marry him. And I burned their letter.

That old man who wanted to marry me sent another letter, but this time to the leader of my village, not to me. He said, "You must take care of that young girl until I come back and talk to all of you. If you will not give her to me, after that you can give her to someone else to marry, but take care of her until I get there."[8] I heard someone talking, they said, "If we give that girl to them, they will promote us to be a higher leader, so perhaps we will give her to the old man." The man who said that was my uncle Dju, who was the leader of the village.[9]

I thought, "I have no mother and no father, and he will use me to pay for his promotion. To die is better than to be alive." I was making a batik for my skirt, and I was making the creases and folds in the material, and I cried and cried until the material was all wet. My aunt who was the wife of my uncle

Pao, said, "Why are you crying? Don't die, just find another boyfriend and marry him. If you die, you're just dead and you have no life any more. Just marry somebody else."

But I said, "Now nobody wants to talk to me any more. How can I find a boyfriend?" She said, "If now no one talks to you, and you still won't marry that old man, if he comes to your house, boil some water to burn him. If someone comes to your house, just kick them! My daughter Joua is going to Na Moh tomorrow. If you don't want to marry him, just go with her and find some boy. Take a token from him and when you come back, send for him to marry you." [10] I said, "No! I'm not going to do that!"

My aunt May Kue said, "Mai, you have to be smart. You don't want to die. Look at me. My mother's brother made all the arrangements for me to be his son's wife, they even had the party, but I didn't like that man. The party was almost over,[11] and I went off with Chue. We just jumped. Nothing happened, that was the end of it. Now if you like someone, just do that, because they haven't even come to your house yet." But I didn't have any boyfriend, so I was very sad because there was no one to marry me.

That night I had to go grind the corn, and Chee and Tru [two brothers] came to keep me company. We talked about going to marry the old man, we talked about a lot of different things, and just laughed and talked until the middle of the night. They didn't talk about coming to marry me, and I didn't know anybody wanted to marry me. That night I stayed with my aunt Joua and my aunt Phoua, who came to my house to sleep. They were joking and said, "Tonight we will stay with you one night, and we think that old man is going to come and take you, so this will be the last time we can sleep together." But they didn't know about it, either.

We went to sleep. In the night I heard a noise and ran outside, but it was only a cow eating the thatch out of the roof. The cow ran away and I went back to bed. I don't know how long I was asleep until my husband [to-be] pulled my hand and said, "Get up!" I said, "What's the matter? What do you want?" He said, "Come outside to talk to my brother." Joua and Phoua didn't hear a thing, they didn't wake up. So I came out and Tru's brother and his uncle were standing by the door.[12] Chee said, "I heard somebody say someone wants to marry you, and you really cried, you want to die." I said, "That's true, they scared me and I'm afraid, that's why I cry." He said, "We don't want you to die, we want you to marry Tru, and I'll take care of everything, don't you worry."

I said, "That's not true. You can take care of his side, but I have no father and no mother to take care of me, and I don't want to run off like that. If you want to marry me, you have to wait until the old man comes to talk it over, and if I tell all the old men I don't want to marry him, and if I win, then you can marry me." But they said they couldn't wait! I said the old man could sue them and they would have many different problems. (He did sue them later in a different town, and their family lost one silver bar [twelve ounces of silver].) "Anyway," I said, "I don't want to marry anybody, I want to stay free."

My older brother had a bird (the kind called *yij*)[13] that he was raising in a cage, and that bird was outside the house just behind the door. We were talking by the door next to the bird, and it flew in its cage. My brother heard it, and said, "What's happening with that bird?" Tru and his brother and uncle pulled me around the other side of the house, and my brother came out and picked up his bird, saying, "What's the matter with this bird?" He took it inside and went back to bed.

We talked a little more, until Tru's uncle said, "Tru, what's the matter? Do your hands hurt?" We say that when we mean: "Why don't you do something you want to do." And then they pulled me down the hill to the bottom of the valley and up the other side to his house. All the way down and all the way up I said I didn't want to marry. I said, "If you really want to marry me, call my grandmother. If I marry you without telling her, my family might lose a lot of money and my grandmother will fight with me. You have to ask." But they wouldn't stop. Tru's uncle said, "If we tell her we certainly will lose money. We're not telling anybody. If anybody asks you, say you like Tru and you just followed him."

A Hmong girl always has to say she doesn't want to marry. Even if she wants to marry, she has to say she doesn't want to marry. But I really didn't want to get married to anybody.

When we came to his house his uncle said, "I'll go tell them to get the chicken ready." Hmong people use a chicken to call the spirits when a new wife comes into the door. His uncle let my hand go to go inside, and my husband pulled me up to the door. But I was very angry and very strong. I pulled him back down the hill into the valley. He said, "Stop! Don't do that!" His brother helped him and two ladies came out of the house to help them and his uncle came, and they didn't have time to get the chicken ready. All those people just pulled me straight into the house, and we just stood there, nothing to do.[14] All I could do was cry and cry. I was too young to marry!

This story was received as extremely funny, with the interpreter at times unable to interpret for laughing, and both the storyteller and her friend wiping away tears of laughter. The story lends itself to literary analysis. It has a complication, development, and resolution; conflict and danger; and more than one narrow escape. Furthermore, it has narrative tension arising from an unstated level of irony that depends on gender concepts for its force.

Mai would prefer to marry no one, but this option is not open. Once she comes to the attention of a man, having no father to defend her interests, she becomes a pawn, as she clearly understands. She can only try to arrange favorable action by another man, since any action she might take on her own would be ignored. The contrasting advice of her two aunts marks a plateau in the story and summarizes her problem in gender terms.

The story presents her as refusing to take any action at all. Tension in the story rises because her words and actions run contrary to her own interests, although she is not a stupid girl. There are underlying hints that she knows what she is about, in her reports of laughing and joking with Chee and Tru, the banter of her aunts who sleep with her, her disappointment that the first disturbance is "only a cow," and her silence when she could cry out as her brother takes his bird inside. But she must avoid all hints of acquiescence; she doesn't want her family to be liable for the money fine to come. Her firm refusals place all responsibility for action on the men—but she is not insincere. Two levels are present, her real wish not to be married, and her strategic failure to prevent marriage.

She succeeds despite the fact that she engages only in feminine actions: hauling the water, cooking for the feast, sleeping with her aunts, listening to their advice, crying into her batik, pounding the corn, cloaking herself in the refusal to marry. Without going outside her female role, she successfully manipulates the males who would control her. The model for female action set up by this story is clever and strong, but it is entirely contained within a male-ordered social universe, and for this reason the story is subversive.[15] Most of the women's stories of mate choice that I collected contain elements of dismissing formalities or ignoring requests. Thus the women in a sense made their own choices, which is the moral of the story above.

Girls were supposed to be shy and deny interest in any boy. This system carries the obvious problem that true dislike might not be believed. My subjects assured me this was the real beginning of many marriages, including a few of their own. One set of circumstances where this problem arose and the girls had no option related to certain wartime marriages. Actually this particular problem was reported to me in terms of an affront to girls' fathers. If a girl possessed a token the boy had given her, it meant she loved him, regardless of what she might actually say. Soldiers far from home with an eye for pretty girls were known to shove a token into their pocket and claim a marriage, regardless of the girls' response. These marriages, many resulting in abandoned young wives, prompted meetings in 1966 between military leaders and irate fathers, with the result that such marriages were officially deemed valid.

Marriage alliances are an important part of Hmong social structure, and cultural practices involving courtship, mate choice, and style of marrying have had a great impact on how Hmong society has been perceived in the United States.

COURTSHIP AFTER RESETTLEMENT

The new American environment clearly produces many stylistic changes in Hmong courtship. A boy can no longer softly play the mouth harp outside the house wall where a girl lies sleeping, because apartment walls are made of solid materials, not woven bamboo or unchinked boards. He cannot get her attention inconspicuously at night, nor can he slip into the house to wake her as before, because now the door is locked—so elopements no longer start from home as they traditionally did. Girls' Hmong-style costumes (worn mainly now at New Year celebrations) may be bought or partly bought, so the quality of workmanship no longer necessarily expresses the diligence and skill of the girl. The youth's automobile has become a vital tool of courtship.

But if these aspects of material culture change quickly, many practices appear to be more durable. First among these is the assumption that communication between eligible young people of the opposite sex is directed toward choosing a mate. Outside the household, unmarried Hmong go about in groups of one gender, spending little time with people of the opposite sex, except for clan relatives. In America, the Hmong adolescents I knew did not go out on dates. A girl may go with her friends to watch a soccer game if a particular boy is playing (as I saw in Seattle), or a boy may spend a lot of time visiting relatives on his mother's side if a particular girl lives there (as I saw in the Midwest). Usually, in the presence of family members, neither speaks to the other out of the ordinary way. Signals of mutual attraction between these eligible Hmong adolescents are still hidden from the older generation, or if parents observe such signs, it is still considered very bad form to take notice, as it was in Laos. This reserve between generations helps put a face of free choice on courtship, but also made it hard to observe.

I was told eleven contemporary courtship stories during my research period, and read several more, and I have also watched courting couples as the occasion arose. But I had almost no Hmong acquaintances of courting age, nor would they have let me do field work among them.[16] All but one of the eleven courtship stories that I was told led to marriage. The ones I read, on the other hand, never led to marriage, and in fact their problematic nature was what caused their publication. Besides a lack of direct observation, another problem is that the practices of Hmong court-ship are changing very rapidly, especially as young Hmong stay unmarried long enough to enter college, and educated girls make plans for careers. Even so, I can suggest one immediate structural change, following upon the observation that while Hmong girls attended American schools, educated girls quickly fell into disfavor as wives, since traditional parents wanted obedient daughters-in-law and urged their sons to choose compliant girls (often fitting their own preferences). This immediately widened the age gap between males who often waited to finish community college before marrying and girls who wed before finishing high school. Most Hmong girls in America are married by age sixteen—in one study of Hmong in San Diego, all were married by this age (Rumbaut and Weeks 1986:438). Many Hmong still define social maturity for girls in terms of passing puberty, but education is entering the definition of maturity for boys. Often the girls considered the most eligible had just arrived from Thailand for resettle-ment and had no American school experience; these girls were assumed to be more traditional. Between 1985 and 1988, I recorded several quick marriages, often within weeks of arrival, in families who had come to the United States under sponsorship from their relatives who had become citi-zens. Educated girls seem to have been marrying down the educational lad-der, or sometimes marrying non-Hmong.[17] The goal of such traditionalist families can be assumed to be maintaining traditional social relationships in the household.

I also recorded several marriages delayed from their inception in South-east Asia. Courtship had gone forward there, but the couples had not married. One of these delayed events involved a young man in Seattle and a young woman outside Paris. He had caught her hand in Ban Vinai camp in Thailand, but as was probably common they delayed the formal events of marrying so each could take advantage of their family's place in the re-settlement queue. Unfortunately they went to different countries. When he finally collected enough money to visit her and renew the courtship, she was no longer interested. He overstayed his airline ticket in an attempt to persuade her, but finally returned without her, to the devastating ironical comments of his older male relatives who had to buy the second return flight. This happened in 1987. A delayed marriage that actually took place, in 1981, is described in the next chapter.

In 1981–88 among the Hmong families I knew, marriageable young people were frequently introduced by siblings of the opposite sex. They might go to the same school, church, or New Year's parties as their poten-tial partner, or they might be related as cross cousins. A very common meeting ground was still the family visit, in which a boy went with his married brother or sister to visit their in-laws. This contributed to repeated marriages between the same families of Hmong in America as it had in Laos. In Laos, visiting was tuned to the agricultural year, increasing in the leisure period after harvest, when New Year was celebrated. American Hmong went visiting year round, but New Year was still the time of serious courting and the most likely time for marriages. Even if they had been interested in each other for some time, young people often delayed active courtship, which would lead to a decision to marry or break off contact, until New Year.

The week after Thanksgiving, 1984, my friend Bla was upset because her sixteen-year-old daughter Mai had eloped with a boy she met at the New Year celebration in the town of Carnation, Washington, about twenty miles east of Seattle, with a population of nine Hmong families. This boy had driven up from California with two friends, stayed with a relative in Seattle, and played ball (*pov pob*) with Bla's daughter both days of the week-end celebration. As far as Bla knew, Mai had never seen the boy before, but on Sunday evening instead of coming home from Carnation she drove with him and his friends to Portland (150 miles south of Seattle). About an hour out of Seattle they stopped at a truck stop to telephone Bla, so she would not worry. Mai stayed with her new husband at his cousin's house in Portland for three days before coming back to Seattle. It was only then that my friend met the boy, Chue, who was very tongue-tied and embarrassed in front of his new mother-in-law.

Bla (who has four younger children) said she was very sorry to lose her daughter's help, but she felt somewhat consoled because Chue was her father's brother's grandson. She had known him in Laos before Mai was born, when he was a small boy and Bla was a young wife. He had the same clan name as she, and the family connections meant that she was "sending her daughter home to her clan." This surprising scenario is one I would expect to find in many Hmong marriages in the United States.

Direct courtship (that is, conversations and touching) still appeared to last typically only a few days, with the boy initiating the contact. Before talking seriously to the girl, he still might go to his older male relatives, who would feel obliged to help him pay the bride wealth (*nge mis*). This contribution let them influence his choice, but they would not feel they could definitively reject any girl. This was unlike the situation in Laos, where many fathers had more power, especially since boys married before they were capable of supporting a family. They still might marry without work skills, but in the United States they had more sources of support than in Laos. I have several times heard from male relatives asked to produce bride wealth the complaint that a particular boy waited until after having married the girl to ask for help with the bride cost.

After New Year celebrations in Seattle, held Thanksgiving Saturday in 1982, my friend Neng was furious because of the way his wife's sister had been married the night before. The boy, Yee, was part of his *kwv tij*,[18] and he called him younger brother (see the earlier discussion of kin terms), so the marriage itself was quite appropriate—it consolidated ties already made by Neng's own marriage and other previous marriages between the extended families of the two clans. But the boy had gone about things entirely the wrong way. Instead of taking the girl from her home at night, he had persuaded her to slip away from the New Year celebration itself. Instead of having two friends stay behind and tell her father, he had made no arrangements at all. When the family wanted to go home, they couldn't find their daughter and spent several hours looking for her, which worried them since the celebration took place in a rough neighborhood. Furthermore, the boy had made no prior arrangements for the bride price. Above all, the girl was underage from the American point of view (although at fourteen she was marriageable from the Hmong point of view). Her family was still being sponsored by a church group, and Neng told me he was afraid that these sponsors would drop the family or put Yee in jail. He felt he needed to apologize to the Americans for Yee's "foreign" behavior.

Americans who work with Hmong are frequently aware of striking cases in which young men are accused of rape, although they staunchly declare they were engaging in catch-hand marriage. Sometimes these cases come to court, and the youth's actions may be defended on the grounds that they are within Hmong cultural practice; such a cultural defense may reduce the penalty somewhat. To blame the youth for sexual assertiveness is shocking to first-generation Hmong, especially men. Among the Hmong, pitfalls of contact between the two sexes are considered the girl's responsibility. Regardless of how wide or how limited her experience, no matter what kind of hints she is given (or not given) by her elders about her suitor, and whether or not she follows advice, a girl is considered to be making her own choices.

Premarital sex is thus assumed among the Hmong to be a matter of mutual consent. Rape does not seem to have been a social category of offense among Hmong in Laos, because if the boy steals the girl away, he obviously wants to marry her (Hmong have not accepted the concept of spousal rape). Responsibility for any misunderstanding is considered to be the girl's, since she should not have let herself be lured away from her friends (Goldstein 1986; Hang, personal communication, 1985). It must sometimes have happened in Laos that boys forced themselves sexually upon girls without their consent and then abandoned them without marriage, because the Hmong have a folk saying about this. If a boy is too persistent and the girl cannot deal with him, she is still responsible for the outcome, for didn't she put herself in the position to be attacked? "If the female dog doesn't wag her tail, the male dog doesn't follow" (Hang, personal communication 1984, in reference to a case explicated by Goldstein 1986. This saying also appears in Vang and Lewis 1985). The girl has the right, Hmong say, to turn a youth away if she is not interested; she is not expected to be truthful, only polite.

But the catch-hand marriage, or *mpeg*, contradicts this model of a boy respecting a girl's polite refusal. *Mpeg* was generally arranged by boy and girl beforehand, with the girl conventionally hanging back at the last moment to avoid implied disrespect to her own family. The youth would seize her, she would refuse to cooperate, and he would pull her away with whatever force was necessary. The girl's culturally prescribed prevarication was complemented by the boy's prescribed boldness. The young man was supposed to take the initiative, because:

> Girls are very shy, they will not tell you the truth. . . . The men, they are not shy, they will say what they think, but the ladies, if they like [him] one hundred per cent, they say, 'I like, and I don't like'" (*Kuv nyiam tsis nyiam*, "I like a little bit").

In the United States, where boys and girls receive different, mixed and ambiguous messages from the mainstream society, the subtlety of these traditional messages can be lost, depending as they do upon agreed cultural reinterpretations of statements which, saying one thing, mean another. Thus if the Hmong girl's protest is real, the boy does not necessarily know it. Even if his intentions are entirely honorable, a girl's careful politeness as she rejects him (e.g., "maybe a little later") can sound to his eager ears like acquiescence. I do not mean to suggest that Hmong boys always approach girls with honorable intentions, only that they may have done so in some cases where their actions proved as open to contrasting interpretation as the girls'. Often these cases are true rapes in the American understanding of that term, but sometimes they have been tragic for both young people and for their families.

American laws on rape, bigamy, and divorce have negated the earlier assumption that ultimately male power over females is always valid, so the

Hmong boy's power implied by a girl's inability to reject him effectively is diminished in practice. The relative ease of divorce in America has also rendered first marriages less nearly irrevocable. These changes strike at the heart of the Hmong social structure and the ideas of gender seen in the courtship forms.

An early example of American law being used to change a course of events within Hmong society took place in Seattle in 1980. A nineteen-year-old girl in Seattle successfully resisted an unwanted catch-hand marriage by threatening her elders with the force of law. This particular girl was from an elite Hmong military family and had had a good education both in Laos and in France, where she had lived several years before joining her family in Seattle in 1979. Ploa (not her real name) was "kidnapped" by the son of one of her father's former associates in Laos. The two families had known each other for years, and from the point of view of both sets of parents the marriage was completely appropriate. She was held at the home of her new husband's parents against her will for the prescribed three days, and in the usual way was made a wife in bed. After three days she came home and the four parents set about contract negotiations. But Ploa was furious. She didn't want to spend her life with that man, she said; she had known him since childhood and disliked him all that time. He had a bad heart (*tsis zoo siab*), in her opinion, as was obvious from his treatment of her. Ploa was not polite. She told her parents flat out that if they persisted in the negotiations she would call the police and accuse him of rape. She would get them deported. This stunning threat stopped the negotiations, but not parental efforts to persuade Ploa to be reasonable. Years of family connections were at stake. However, Ploa immediately arranged another catch-hand marriage for herself, and decamped for the East Coast, leaving her parents to work out their own problems. In Laos, such an event would have been interpreted as her father's doing, since women were seen as mere agents of men. A traditionally raised girl in Ploa's position might have accepted the marriage as a sacrifice to the standing and political aspirations of her family. In Seattle, her parents were blamed for her actions, for they were too weak to prevent them; they could not control her. Ploa presently reconciled with her parents, but the other family remained their enemies.

It seems that Ploa had absorbed new ideas about gender equality and used legal options at hand in the American environment to subvert Hmong social practices. This incident might stand as a signal of imminent decay in the underpinnings of Hmong culture. However, as shown by Mai's story earlier in this chapter, in which May Kue backed out of an unwanted marriage at the very last moment by running off with Chue, there is clearly a traditional Hmong reference point for Ploa's behavior. Mai's story itself is an account of rejecting an unwanted marriage for a more favored one. Ploa, like May Kue and Mai, did not avoid marriage, and the timing of her marriage depended on men's actions. She used the threat of American prosecution to get her way, but she nonetheless acted in terms of Hmong cultural categories.

7

WEDDING NEGOTIATIONS
AND CEREMONIES

The Hmong brought with them certain habits in marriage, such as marrying again with families married before, that are clearly surviving in the first generation of resettled Hmong. Indeed, the decay of other unifying activities throws a spotlight on patrilineal and patrilateral structure and marriage alliance as central to Hmong identity, and informants all identify marrying in the Hmong way as central to Hmong identity.

Weddings are basically the same across clan lines, since marriage links clans together. The emphasis is on continuity and on the participation of the extended family. Resettlement has produced numerous immediate changes in how courting and subsequent ceremonies such as marriage negotiations are conducted, but to my Hmong friends such surface changes, for instance in the location of courtship or the menu of the wedding dinner, do not strike at the heart of the meanings attached to courtship or marriage. Recreating a particular set of social relations identified by the Hmong as specifically Hmong is still a major condition of courtship and the goal of ritualized or formulaic marriage negotiations. Anomalous or altered performances are incorporated into "the Hmong way" (*txoj kev hmoob*).

WEDDING NEGOTIATIONS

Wedding negotiations for catch-hand marriages follow the elopement by several days, and for arranged marriage they follow the parental agreement, but sometimes by a considerable gap of time. Negotiations precede the final parties and the transfer of the bride to the groom's family and constitute making the contract of marriage. Negotiating marriage is a major event of interfamily relations. Lee (1981: 45) mentions negotiations that lasted one or two days in northern Thailand, while my male informants nostalgically recalled four or five day long events in Laos. Brides in Laos had only a small part in the negotiations for their own weddings, which, being concerned with contracts, were the province of men. Few of my subjects could give any specifics about their own wedding negotiation in Laos, and evidently they were not present. One said she fell asleep. From the bride's perspective the most important change, from unmarried girl to married woman (and from daughter to daughter-in-law), had already occurred. Older women from the bride's side often participated in strategy sessions, but they did not set strategy; women relatives of the groom could not participate because negotiations took place at the home of the bride, with only men (and a young, nonnegotiating girl chaperone for the bride) traveling.

While drinking and good fellowship accompanied most negotiations, their basic nature was legalistic and contractual. The bride's negotiators and the groom's negotiators represented two sides conceptualized in terms of opposition teams. A principal negotiator (*mej koob*), chosen for his reputation of previous successful negotiating as well as his close relation to the family, represented each side. White Hmong negotiators often have an assistant (*thiaj com*[1]). The negotiators strove first to reconcile any problems between the two families in regard to previous marriages or codicils to previous contracts between other couples from the two extended families, and second to achieve mutually satisfactory terms for the bride wealth and other matters pertinent to this marriage. If the families were friendly, joking and highjinks amused the participants; if they were not, fines for previous infractions, tense demands for high bride wealth, and specific contractual requirements for treatment of the bride or of the gifts she brought into marriage could result.

In the United States, the negotiations I attended lasted less than a day, because of the requirements of the American work week. This meant that ritual had to be abbreviated, especially the songs. A Blue (Green) Hmong negotiation that I attended with J. Mallinson in Seattle, June 1984, is typical. When we arrived at the bride's father's large split-level rented house at about 1 p.m. on a Saturday, we found a crowd, mostly men, sitting or standing in the living room, where three couches faced each other in a horseshoe arrangement. This wedding was between a Hang groom and a Chang bride. We already knew most people present, and were quickly introduced to the notables, especially two gentlemen from France and a very elderly man in a blue suit who had come up from Santa Ana; they were all members of the Chang family.

The groom was the only person in traditional Hmong garments. Doua Hang, who acted as our interpreter during the first half of the event, pointed out that everybody was holding a cigarette. As the first step in negotiations, the groom's party had just given one cigarette to each member of the bride's household and to the negotiating team. On the couch was a folded blanket tied up like a present in a woman's turban cloth. The

Hangs had brought it, along with a basket (actually a bright plastic imita-
tion beach basket) with two cooked chickens, now cut up on two plates
on the Formica dining table. In Laos, Doua said, they would have used a
pack basket and would also have brought a small bag of cooked rice, two
spoons, a knife, and some liquor to make a meal on the way, but these had
been omitted today. In Laos they would have cooked the chicken en route,
and if it were boiled slowly enough the toes would curl up parallel to one
another, indicating that the couple would walk together throughout life.
They would have eaten most of the chicken, arriving with only the legs
to show the position of the toes. Today, although they did stop the car on
the way and eat a "picnic," they had brought two store-bought chickens
without toes (these should have been male and female, but in the supermarket they couldn't tell). As Doua told us this, everybody listened with
the greatest interest.

The negotiators were Song Chang, a neat little man in his sixties, and
Cher Koua Hang, a much larger and heavier set man with graying hair.
More Hangs had come than were part of the negotiating team.[2] The visi-
tors from Santa Ana and from France were experts in marriage form, and
Doua was glad they were present, as everybody was nervous about making
mistakes.

The Hang team consisted of the negotiator, groom (*vau*), groom's friend
(*phij laaj*) who helps him bow to the bride's parents, groom's second friend
who carries the food (*txiv ntaas*), and a girl to chaperone the bride (*nam
ua luaj*). There had to be an odd number, so that the bride returning with
them would make an even number. They avoided odd numbers in the table
arrangements, where two plates of chicken each had four forks radiating
out from them; there were two bottles of vodka and an even number of
little plastic cups (see photo section).

The Changs all went into another room, leaving the living room to the
Hangs. Ten minutes later, Song Chang returned, and he and Cher Koua
sat at the table facing each other. Each drank a shot of vodka. They gave
each other a piece of chicken skewered on a fork. Cher Koua said, "You
and I are not the ones marrying; we only help these other people, so we
should not get mad at each other. We are like lawyers. So we should tell
each other if one does not do the right thing. If I do something wrong, and
you don't tell me, it's your fault, not mine."[3] They each gave the other two
shots of vodka, and Song agreed with Cher Koua's statement.

The groom was standing outside the patio door behind Song to run
errands or carry messages, but he remained silent throughout. The bride
was in the back bedroom. In Laos, Doua commented, the liquor would be

put into a shallow bowl and set before the negotiator, who was supposed to kneel (Hmong tables being quite low) and drink it off without touching the bowl with his hands. If he should spill, the bowl was filled again.

The two negotiators lifted cupped hands toward each other. (Hands held respectfully cupped together symbolize a basket.) Song said, "I'm going to talk to the girl's family. If I'm gone a long time, please don't get impatient, because I don't know how long it will take," and he left.

Only Blue Hmong use chicken in the ritual like this, according to Doua; White Hmong place only liquor and cups on the table and later have rice with chicken. In a few minutes Song returned, saying, "The parents are still talking, no decision yet." He and Cher Koua took a sip of vodka. Doua described previous intermarriages between these two extended families, including his own marriage.

Twenty minutes later Ying Chang (the bride's father's brother's son) appeared, and Song went off with him. Doua told me that in the morning the Hangs had held a thank you party for the negotiator and helpers. But they did not discuss conditions to bring up at the negotiations, as it is their position to follow the lead of the bride's family, "who have more authority."

Soon Song returned with Dang Chang, Ying's brother. Negotiators lifted cupped hands and sipped vodka. The Changs required that the Hangs should give a small party for the negotiators on both sides before the actual wedding party. The groom had not taken the catch-hand route to marriage, but had asked his father to propose the marriage to the bride's parents. They had had to call all their relatives to give advice to the bride, and now all these people deserved a party. Dang sat next to Song as witness, and Cher Koua poured him two little cups of vodka (each now had two little cups). He sipped; all three lifted hands. The first bottle was now half empty, and the room was very hot. Ying set up his video camera, pointing at the negotiators.

Cher Koua lifted cupped hands and went into the living room to confer with the Hangs about this party. He returned to the table; the negotiators lifted hands again. A pig is needed for such a party; by custom, it must be three hands high from breastbone to backbone. The Hangs wanted to give the party, but because the main party was set for the next day, there was not enough time to find a live pig and slaughter it. They asked to cancel this party and pay a fine instead, on condition that if a Chang boy should marry a Hang girl in the future, the same fine would be paid and the same party cancelled.

The Chang negotiator left and soon returned. The negotiators lifted hands and exchanged pieces of chicken. Song gave Jane and me some chicken and Dang gave us each a shot of vodka. The Changs were insisting on the party, saying that because the suitor came to their house instead of eloping with their daughter, they had had to get the entire family together to consider the proposal, and so they were entitled to this party. The Hangs went off with their negotiator, returning in ten minutes. There was a lot of coming and going, a lot of noise, women and children in and out as well as men. The Hangs agreed that the Changs were entitled to the party, but since the pig would be so hard to get on a Saturday afternoon, they very much preferred to pay a fine instead. The Changs suggested buying an equivalent amount of cut and wrapped pork from a supermarket. The Hangs pointed out that this would be much more expensive than a pig on the hoof. Everybody was talking at once. The Changs also wanted two bottles of vodka, not one; this was no problem. Song and Dang left and returned in about ten minutes, lifting hands, pouring vodka, saying the family was still arguing about it. Song gave two shots of vodka to Cher Koua, then changed this to two shots of Sprite. Dang drank off his vodka and made a face, saying he preferred Sprite.

The bride's father stamped in, shouting at the Hang negotiator, arguing. His wife, rather larger than he and a vigorous person, followed him, standing a little behind and talking loudly. Dang was also arguing, and Koua Hang, who had taken Doua's place as my interpreter when Doua had left to go to work, nervously crushed a soda can in his hands. The Hangs offered to buy an equivalent value rather than amount of pork. The groom and his father listened intently in silence, but everybody else talked loudly, even the boy operating the video camera.

Suddenly Song gave a thumbs-up sign, and everybody smiled. The Changs accepted one bottle of vodka, plus fifty dollars instead of the pig. The Hangs maintained that if they had bought a pig, the money would have gone not to the Changs but to the owner of the pig; therefore if in the future a Chang boy married a Hang girl, the Changs would have to provide fifty dollars, rather than a pig, and the Hangs could buy a pig or not with it, at their discretion. This was agreed, and the settlement toasted by the negotiators, who gave each other two little cups of Sprite.

Koua observed that at negotiations only matters pertaining to marriage can be discussed (not business matters for instance), and that all bad feeling had to be settled between families before the wedding could take place. Here there was no bad feeling between families, but this matter of the fifty dollars would have to be brought up at future weddings. I thought they were striving for balance between emotion and protocol. The Changs went out.

Song and Dang returned, lifted hands, toasted in Sprite. A song was sung: "Our girl is not beautiful, she is not worthwhile. But a Hang wants to marry her even so. Does the Hang family want to keep her and honor her as a member of their family, and not throw her away?" This was a conventional statement.

Cher Koua said, "There is no problem, they have known each other four years (later the bride told me two years), so if he didn't want to cherish her, he wouldn't have asked her," which was a conventional response. Koua whispered that this was a very important statement, as it will be the clan's responsibility to maintain marital harmony and "control the boy" so he acts honorably toward his wife. Song and Dang left, returning almost at once, lifting hands.

The Changs wanted to know how they could be sure the bride would be well treated and not "thrown away." The groom's father replied at length that if they threw her away and it were not her fault, he would return all the gifts her parents gave her plus 250 dollars (equivalent to a fine of one-and-a-quarter silver bars, the penalty in Laos, Koua said). Everybody was talking again; the bride's mother had come in once more and was talking too.

Song and Dang left and didn't return for over twenty minutes. Then they came with good news; the Changs had accepted this offer on condition that it be written down and signed before the main party, and the Hangs accepted this with a toast poured by Cher Koua of two shots of Sprite each. They went out again and returned to inquire (after lifting hands and drinking Sprite) whether the Hangs had any further conditions. The Hangs said they had no further conditions, but inquired whether the Changs were sure they did not. So Song and Dang went out to make sure. Returning, this time Song opened a new bottle of vodka (the first bottle was still half full, and there was a second bottle on the table, but this was a different bottle brought from the bedroom). Song filled four shots and gave them to Cher Koua, saying formally, "The Chang family has no more questions. Do the Hangs want to ask anything?" Cher Koua filled two shots from the half full bottle on the table and gave them to Dang. Then he reached across the table, first picking up Song's two shots of vodka and handing them to him, then picking up Dang's vodka and handing it to him, then picking up his own and toasting: "The Hangs assent to everything the Changs have asked." They drank it off, Dang making a face.

S. L. Chang, one of the visitors from France, came out of the back room with the bride's father, laughing. Song offered Cher Koua two more shots of vodka. Everybody talked at once, laughing. Koua commented that this negotiation was very easy.

The bride's father asked for a song from the Hangs, to request a "basket" for the bride wealth. Cher Koua, Song, and Dang stood with their hands nested in front of them. Cher Koua sang the request song (unfortunately untranslated). S. L. Chang at the end of the table stood with a white plate upon which two pieces of blank white paper had been laid crosswise. When the song was ended, this plate was put on the table, everybody standing. Cher Koua, Song, and Dang stood moving their nested hands horizontally in a circle.

Koua took the money out of an envelope, counted it, and, returning it to its envelope, handed it to Cher Koua along with seventy-five cents. Following S. L. Chang's suggestion, Cher Koua put the seventy-five cents (representing a tip of twenty-five cents to each negotiator and witness) on the plate. Then he recounted the money from the envelope and put it on the plate.[4] He poured two more shots of Sprite for Song and set them before him, took the two shots of Sprite already in front of Song and put them on the table before Dang, took the two shots already in front of Dang and put them in front of himself, and gave his own to S. L. Chang. These eight shots remained ready on the table. Song took the "basket" and gave it to S. L. Chang, and all the Changs retired to the bedroom.

Koua commented that the bride's father had asked for an amount equivalent to that given in Laos. This morning at the groom's party, members of the Hang family had contributed to reach the sum that they supposed would be asked, although they had not actually talked with the Changs about the amount beforehand. But in the last marriage between Chang and Hang (a sister of this bride, and a cousin of this groom), the identical amount had been asked. The Hang contributions were considered no-interest loans to the groom, to be repaid by contributions to future bride wealth sums.

S. L. Chang brought the "basket" with its bride wealth back and put it on the table, and all the Chang men came out of the back room. Song gave his two shots to Cher Koua with a speech: "The money is the full amount and the Changs accept it." Cher Koua gave the same two shots back to Song with a speech, and then, standing, sang a song lasting seven minutes: "The money is not enough, we know, to reward the parents for their daughter, but it is according to regulation, so I hand it over to you now." Another short speech by Song, who offered two shots to Cher Koua, was followed by another song by Cher Koua, who offered two shots to Song. Each of the three principals held his left wrist with his right hand, moving his hands, clasped in this way, in a horizontal circle in front of his body, in concert with the other two.

S. L. Chang was asked to sing, and he did so in a low breathy voice (the song unfortunately untranslated), nearly drowned out by laughing conversations in the living room.[5] The women came out of the back room and stood at the edge of the living room. Each of the principals drank off two little shots of vodka, and then two more. They exchanged pieces of chicken and ate them. Koua told me that White Hmong would have had two negotiators for each side. The women came into the kitchen and began cooking, and the negotiation was over.

This negotiation was friendly—both sides approved the marriage, and there was no bad feeling out of the past, and no acrimony in the event.

CONTRACTS

In Laos, contracts between clans were the concern of men. Women were not able to speak binding words, nor were they able to set the amount of the exchange. On the bride's side, where women were present at the negotiation, women's anger or dismay could be used by the men as leverage to get a better deal, or it could be ignored where convenient.

Among at least some nonliterate Hmong in Laos, the physical marriage contract consisted of a notched stick, each notch standing for a clause. The stick was split lengthwise, each side taking half. If anybody forgot the contents of the contract, he would have to "eat the stick." My informant told me this in a memorable fashion, shaking his fist at me, thrusting his face close to mine, and rasping out the words threateningly, as if I myself were trying to weasel out of a contract by pretending to forget a clause. The physical contracts that I have seen have been affected by their new environment. They are handwritten in Lao or typed in Hmong, and photocopied for both families.

I reproduce here a wedding contract from 1983. This particular contract was handwritten in Lao, with an attachment in RPA Hmong listing the money spent on the wedding. One of the bride's relatives translated the Lao for me, and I translated the Hmong. It is readily apparent that this contract attempts to seal a somewhat problematic union. The English translation follows (the names are changed):

Statement of Marriage Between Miss Mai Vang and Mr. Bee Keu

On July 23, 1983, relatives of the bride and the groom have made this mutual agreement and statement for future use between this couple as below:

1. Because Mr. Bee Keu had divorce 2 wives in the past, the relatives of the bride have some doubtful and concern that he will do the same way as he did in the past. Bee Keu promises that if he didn't love her or care for her and divorce in the future, he will pay some monies which equivalent $200.00 US and bring Mai back to her relatives with all assets that relatives have donated to her and the marriage fee will be cancelled.

2. Error and missing of proper notification:

The notification or declaration of Mai's marriage was not properly notified as the Hmong's culture. The groom's party notified her brothers and sister in law only and missed her mother. If in the future, the Vang's clan has someone didn't know the Hmong culture and has caused the same fault as this time, the Keu's clan has to forgive and not to penalty or ask for money. If the Keu's clan denie and want penalty, the action is to come back and reconsider this case and solve this case first.

3. Other fault or penalty:

This is a mutual statement and to be used in the future for both party, there is no penalty for fault of any reason to be applied to the Yang and Keu family if the family tree are the same from Bee Keu and Mai Yang.

Therefore this statement is written to be used for the guideline in the future, the statement was approved and agreed by both parties.

Signed by the bride's side   Signed by the groom's side
    [3 signatures]   [3 signatures]

Some Goods Used to Make Wife and Husband
All Given to the Bridegroom's Side for the Girl to
Take Along Into Marriage

1. American money: $3,120.00
2. Set of Chinese coins: 40
3. Gold chain (heavy)
4. Gold chain (light)
5. Pair of gold earrings
6. Pair of Lao earrings
7. Two silver finger rings
8. Two American finger rings
9. Two Blue Hmong skirts and one apron
10. One White Hmong skirt and a red sash to go with it
11. One flat Lao skirt
12. One length of Chinese fabric
13. One headband [for the turban]
14. Three short pieces of white cloth
15. Four short pieces of red cloth
16. One short piece of figured cloth
17. Two lengths of blue sash
18. Three lengths of red sash
19. One rice steamer

20. One large storage box
21. Chevy Nova worth $1000.00
22. American money: $100.00

Brother-in-law Neng Yang gives presents to bridegroom's side
for his sister to take into marriage:

1. White Hmong skirt with red sash
2. Gold chain (heavy)
3. American money: $100.00

Relatives give presents for the girl to take into marriage

1. Older brother [name]: 1 Lao skirt and $20
2. Older brother [name]: $50
3. Older brother [name]: $50 and sashes
4. Older brother [name]: $25
5. Older brother [name]: $30
6. Great uncle [name]: $20

Only Hmong clothes are identified in this contract; the skirts were made by Mai herself. The first list consists of items given by her immediate family, meaning her mother, who gave items 21 and 22 Mai told me later, her brother and his family, and her own savings. Missing from the contract is the amount of the bride wealth supposed to be forthcoming from the groom's side. According to Mai, this did not equal the value of these gifts. In fact, it was never paid. But not too much can be made of the imbalance and lack of payment—in Southeast Asia bride wealth was sometimes not paid for years, or never, and families pleased with a marriage might give large gifts. The gifts from Mai's relatives can be seen as validating cordial connections with Mai's brother Neng.

BRIDE WEALTH PAYMENTS

Bride wealth (nqe mis, cost of nurture, lit. milk money) is also often called bride price, but I prefer the less commercialized term. In defining nqe mis for me, women tended to emphasize the process of raising the child, while men tended to emphasize the cost in such things as clothes or food; all agreed the sum transferred would never cover the actual outlay in time, emotion, or expense of a daughter's upbringing. For all the Hmong I talked with, bride wealth stood not as a representative of market value but as a symbol of social involvement. It is at heart a symbolic return that balances the movement of the bride to her husband's home. It provides reciprocity so that the two families remain equal, for if only the bride moved, the groom's family would owe a social debt to the bride's family, a humiliating position and upsetting to the concept of independent extended families. The groom's family has tremendous reason for gratitude, for brides are essential to carry on the family line. In Laos, an extended patrilineal family could produce by labor or trade whatever it needed to survive, with the exception of children. Without outside women willing to marry in, the patrilineal family cannot reproduce itself. The bride wealth symbolically takes the place of a reverse transfer of another person to the family of the bride. Essentially a fund held separate from household expenditures, bride wealth circulates from family to family when marriages occur. Because of the expectation that all closely related men will contribute to the bride wealth of any family youth, bride wealth helps create interdependence, loyalty, and mutual support between related families.

Cooper speculates that the long Hmong history of warfare made women dependent on men for protection, and implies that this need for protection produced the "institutionalized 'selling' " of girls into marriage by their fathers (1984: 142). Furthermore, in husband-wife conflicts, the threat that if the wife leaves the husband for maltreatment he will lose the cost of the bride wealth can protect her from him. The conception that accepting bride wealth is equivalent to selling the bride bolsters Cooper's argument of the female submission to male control. He implies that with the bride wealth transaction, the girl's natal family and her family of marriage have entered into an economic relationship as well as a kinship relation, with the silver as hostage for the girl.

Lemoine's interpretation of this payment is much the same:

> Hmong practice what it is convenient to call marriage by purchase. Each union is the occasion of a gift to the family of the girl at the expense of the boy's family. The purchase does not have the complexity seen, for example, among the Kachin or among the Lao. It is composed essentially of a certain number of bars of silver and a pig offered by the son-in-law to his father-in-law for the nuptial meal. On the other hand, it represents a shifting of valuables that is considerable. The largest sum proposed at Pha-Hok while we were there amounted to fourteen bars of silver, that is, 12,000 kip (1200 francs). (1972: 182; my translation)

Hmong men I have talked to do use the language of the marketplace when speaking of marrying. The money that the groom's family raises to pay for the bride wealth and for parties comes from male relatives. Sometimes repayment may be expected—as with one bride wealth in Laos that was borrowed in cash by the soldier husband from fellow soldiers and repaid by the new couple over about a year through trade—but the closer the relative, the less likely this is. In America, sometimes the bride wealth is never paid, but this is not an innovation; Lee (1981) mentions nonpayment in northern Thailand.

In Laos the usual bride wealth in the families of my Hmong friends in rural communities where the two families were related was three silver bars (although Dunnigan mentions four [1980: 35]). It is hard to pin down the number of bars paid, the value of a bar (in kip or baht), or the exchange rates between Lao and American currency at the time my friends married in the 1960s and 1970s. The highest amount I have heard was fifteen silver bars, asked by an elite family that was very upset by their new son-in-law, and the lowest was none actually paid. Geddes recorded high bride wealths (equivalent to about two hundred U.S. dollars) in northern Thailand in the 1960s, which he says, "would be more than the savings of most households for at least one and possibly several years" (1976: 58). The amounts were calculated in Indian silver rupees and paid in silver rupees, ingots, or ornaments. My female informants sometimes did not know (or would not tell) the amount paid, and in most cases could not make the conversions from one currency to another. Lemoine states that the Indochinese piastre at 27 grams of silver was worth 600 kip, and the silver bars poured by the Hmong contained about 380 grams of silver, that is, just over 13 piastres worth about 8000 kip (1972: 153). With three silver bars as the standard bride wealth, this would yield 24,000 kip. But, as he emphasizes, currency was very unstable, with two relatively independent systems of valuation: silver, which was stable; and paper currency, which was not. Between mid-1960 and mid-1974 the Lao kip fell from 84 to the U.S. dollar (84:1) to 630 to the dollar (630:1); by mid-1975 its value was no longer tracked by the *Far Eastern Economic Review* (FEER 1960:40; 1974:39; 1975:52). From 1965 to 1970, when Lemoine was in the field, 24,000 kip would have brought $39 to $62 (its value varied between 387:1 and 608:1). But I present this exchange rate, current in Hong Kong, simply for its curiosity. Kip could not be freely traded for dollars in upland Laos, and silver was strongly preferred to kip in any case. Silver carried ritual significance beyond its monetary worth. Kip would not have been a satisfactory substitute in bride wealth exchanges.

The values above for bride wealths in silver would have been current among rural families engaged in farming. After 1960, however, more and more Hmong joined the army and were paid wages. D. Hang, who had been a soldier in Xieng Khouang, told me that bride wealths in his experience amounted to about one month's wages. This seems to accord with the bride wealth I recorded for the first wedding in this chapter.

Geddes believes the high bride wealth among Hmong in northern Thailand fulfills social aims:

> The transactions are not aimed at economic gain, nor do they yield it to any extent. In the first place the price is offset to some degree by the fact that, according to the best Miao [i.e. Hmong] traditions, the bride's father should give her a dowry of an ox, a pig, silver neck rings, and a new embroidered costume. Secondly, the need for women is reciprocal so that what a clan receives for its daughters is more or less counterbalanced by what it has to pay out for its wives. Thirdly, the amount gained for a girl by a family is not usually equal to the loss of her value as a worker.
>
> The high price serves a number of social ends in addition to marriage itself. It displays the status of a family which can amass the bride-price. . . . It gives a family temporary prominence and its head leadership in the small circle of clansmen who are called upon to help in arranging the marriage. It bestows prestige on the bride and her family. It cements friendships in a party atmosphere. In short, once subsistence needs are provided for, it offers one of the most satisfying uses of wealth.
>
> The main utility of bride-price, however, is the symbolization it gives to a new creative act in the Miao social universe. The symbolization is both general and particular. There is probably significance in the fact that the price should be paid in silver and not in ordinary money, thus setting it apart from a commercial transaction and relating it directly to the traditions of Miao culture. The most precious metal, the material of ornamentation as well as wealth, silver symbolizes the most important occasion and celebrates the worth of the woman. The way the price is contributed by a group of the husband's relatives and distributed to relatives of the wife gives particular significance to the new relationships brought into being. . . . Marriage is the creative act at the centre of almost all new kin relationships. . . .
>
> In attempting to set the Miao bride-price in its wider symbolic context, [however,] we do not wish to argue away its meaning as a price. Miao clans are exclusive groupings in several respects and women are important assets to them. Through marriage, a clan gains new spiritual adherents and its constituent households [gain] mothers, housekeepers, and workers in the fields. It is appropriate that these assets should be paid for to validate the transfers in the public eye. (Geddes 1976: 58–59)

The earliest marriages that I know about in this country took place in 1980, when I was told that the *nqe mis* was around $400. The latest amount that I have heard of changing hands, in 1988, was $3,850 (from the same informant), nearly ten times more, but only twice the $1,900 paid in Kia's marriage (see p. 163). Other contracts that I have range between these amounts, listing donors and detailing amounts given. Bride wealth has risen with the rising fortunes of the Hmong community. But since the money usually comes from more than one source, it does not reflect the economic position of particular families. The $3,850 example came from a family with only a tiny wage-based income, for the wedding of their non-working cousin (to whom they stood in place of parents). Bride money does not seem to be derived from a wage-based scale. Instead families appear to strive for the highest amount that can be generated. Geddes calculated that in Thailand the bride wealth probably exceeded a year's savings. If it returns to this standard in the United States, its aspect as a symbol of the groom's family's pride balancing the bride's family's pride will become more apparent.

Geddes' assessment of bride wealth as having both a pragmatic economic motive and an abstract symbolic motive seems to be accepted by both male and female refugee Hmong. Mrs. C. Ly, for instance, when she gives the standard women's reason for bride wealth—that it makes the groom's family value the bride more, treat her better, and not "throw her away"—voices this dual motive. Although the language of exchange molds her ideas about bride wealth, she still sees it as essentially a protection for the wife as she ages:

> Our idea is, "When I marry your daughter, I'm the one that getting the person, so I have to lose my money." His parents are the ones that say they got me, and they lost their money. Because my children all belong to his family, so they have more chance to build up the family.
>
> And another problem is, the lady gets old quicker than the man. I mean, the chance you'll be married all your life is fifty fifty,[6] and maybe in five or ten years we are not living together, we got divorced. He didn't lose very much, because he's a man, he's not that old, his body is still healthy. But the lady lost, her body's not so healthy. Maybe another man will say, "Well, you were married already, your body is not strong, not really like a girl."
>
> My husband can marry another woman, younger than I, he can make a good life, but for me that's hard, my life has lost more than his life. That's what we compare, and so if the husband really want to marry you, he has to lose something to get you. He really has to know he made you into his wife, not that you made him marry.

Here are several ideas linked together: that *nqe mis* is exchanged directly for the person; that the high amount makes the man value the woman; that it commits his parents to accepting her; and that it contributes to the permanence of the union. The argument is that financial commitment ensures moral commitment to the marriage, providing security for the wife's future. Bride wealth does not pay for the girl herself, but it is a sign, a demonstration of seriousness and good faith. Later the wife cannot recuperate her losses; bride wealth makes the husband's family think carefully about what they are doing, and not toy with her life.

It is a complex and multivocal symbol, indeed. Although the wife felt the bride wealth stood for her giving the best part of her life, the bride wealth recompenses her father, not her. Although the payment is spoken of as if the groom paid it, in fact his senior male relations negotiated and paid it. Although the transfer of silver bars of money and goods went from male to male, the very name *nqe mis*, or milk price, recognizes the mother's role in raising the bride. By young men, bride wealth often seems to have been taken as a price, a transaction underwritten by father and uncles that purchased the bride's services; perhaps older men also retained this concept. Nonetheless, it was often balanced or even exceeded by the gifts the girl brought with her into marriage, which were seen as a thread of legal interest in her retained by her natal family, which could be used by her husband and his family. Thus the exchange, which might be seen as girl for wealth, could also be seen as wealth for gifts, with the girl not part of the monetary calculations but instead included in an emotional calculus. How the bride was interpreted depended much on where the speaker stood.

As a transaction between older male relatives of the bride and groom, the transfer of bride wealth signals the subordination of bride and groom both to their elders and actually has more to do with a hierarchy of age and power than of gender. When my life-history subjects talked about the superordinate status of Hmong men over Hmong women, they talked about daily decision making, social structural lines of obedience, the responsibilities of men, and assumed ties of reciprocity. They ascribed greater value to males because of their perceived central role in maintaining family structure. From the burial of the son's placenta next to the central housepost (while the daughter's was disposed of by burying it anywhere), to the education accorded to sons in ritual and farm management (as well as greater formal education when it was available), to the unreciprocated need for girls to obey their brothers and for wives to obey their husbands, to the more careful choosing of a burial site for a man than a woman, the reason given was always the greater support the male gives to his family—and thus to Hmong society as a whole, for "family" and "society" seemed hardly separable concepts to Hmong. But in this litany of women's subordination, bride wealth did not appear.

Hmong women in the United States have expressed to me inconsistent ideas about the meaning of bride wealth. I have heard that bride wealth should be given, along with the matching gift from the girl's parents, to the new couple to set them up in their future life; that there's something wrong with bride wealth as an institution; that it's good to give bride wealth for your sons' brides so they will be beholden to you, but not good to accept bride wealth for your daughters, because they will think you do not love them. Clearly the concepts behind bride wealth are not uniform. This may be because of the generally negative suspicions that Americans express about it, or it may come from new, competing ideas about what it means to form a couple. As time passes, what marrying means, who actually forms the new couple, and what "couple" means, seem to be changing. A real and visible difference in the performance of the final round of wedding parties leads to a new view of young marrieds.

THE PARTIES TO TRANSFER THE BRIDE TO THE GROOM'S FAMILY

The final events in a wedding are parties given by the groom's family in honor of the marriage: one for the bride's family when the groom and his supporters go to pick her up for her formal shift of residence to his family home, and the other for his family when the couple arrives. I attended such parties in a Hmong village in northern Thailand in 1988.[7] Chiengmingmai was a small village, dusty and hot in June, west of the Mekong within sight of the Lao border. Settled for twenty years, it was visibly integrated into the Thai state, with a primary school, health clinic, soccer field, Thai flag and Buddha statue, paved road, and a headman proud of his shortwave receiver for national news. While I was there, wholesale buyers for the cabbage crop came to town, as well as a regional political candidate and a seller of frozen tofu on a stick. The village was White Hmong and Christian. It retained such traditional aspects as customary housing construction, rice pounders, primitive kitchen arrangements and other material aspects of managing daily life such as the forge, a residence pattern based on extended-family compounds, and dependence on the stream for drinking water and bathing.

The girl who had gotten married was the headman's eldest daughter by his senior wife. The elopement and negotiations had taken place months before, and she was already living with her husband's family and about five months pregnant. Only the final round of parties, committing her formally to her new family, had been delayed. Early in the morning pigs were killed at both the young husband's family compound and the headman's compound. Cooking proceeded, with the men of the households butchering and the women killing chickens and steaming rice. Long tables with chairs and benches waited in the headman's reception hall and side porch, and in the groom's house and dooryard under the trees. All the village women dressed up. Their long black pants, black aprons with bright blue borders and long sashes, black blouses with embroidered collars and front panels, and necklaces reminded me strongly of New Year's celebrations in Seattle. But these women had much less embroidery and jewelry; they leaned toward metal clips for hair decoration; and their turbans were terry-cloth towels loosely wrapped. The men wore ordinary Western clothing and flipflops.

The day turned very hot as morning wore along. People stood around talking and waiting. Girls took each other's pictures with plastic box cameras. Women sat in the shade and complained. On the headman's front porch, a man at a card table received gift donations from male relatives, recording amounts in a ledger. I was introduced to the *mej koob* for the bride's side. Important people here were to sit at a special table inside, under the village map and list of households on the wall. At the groom's house, male relatives from out of town ate a preliminary luncheon. This was an upscale house with a wood floor and a glass-fronted case to display enamel dishes and a clock.[8] Outside, less important relatives feasted under a tree. People here seemed to find everything hilarious.

Finally the groom's party set off for the bride's former home, a quarter mile away uphill. The groom, carrying a blanket on his back, and his helpers, one with an umbrella and the other with a basket containing freshly cooked chicken, preceded the bride and her girl chaperone. Halfway there, they stopped and ate part of the chicken, squatting by the side of the road. The girls stood a little way off, eating too. Arriving at the headman's compound, where they were greeted and surrounded by the crowd, they avoided the front door, going instead to the back, where they were not permitted to enter. For about ten minutes the groom begged in barely audible song for permission to enter. Inside, the headman responded in poetry. Between them on the threshhold, a stool supported two shot glasses of corn liquor.

The groom drank off the liquor and entered, followed by the others. The bride, greeted by her weeping mother, disappeared into her grandfather's bedroom, walled in by a crowd of sobbing well-wishers. The groom and his father-in-law hosted the feast of roasted pig, blood pudding, spicy chicken in broth, rice, and corn liquor, which now began, men inside, women and children outside at long tables. Eventually the bride came out of the bedroom and sat with the groom under the village map, at the card table, which had been moved inside. On the table was a bowl of sand and flowers with burning incense sticks, white cotton good-luck strings for the guests now lining up—honored guests first, men second, women third—to tie the couple's wrists to each other, and a big bowl for money offerings. The pile of bills rose higher and higher as the couple smiled. The groom was very drunk indeed.

This was the last event of this wedding that I saw. Gradually guests drifted off; the party was over. The conventional ritual or traditionally repetitive segments visible to me included receiving contributions for a bride's dowry, a short prayer before the meal at the groom's house, strict separation of groom's and bride's parties, the trip from groom's to bride's house, the pause to eat chicken on the path, the groom's request to enter the bride's house and the poetic response, paired shots of liquor, the bride staying out of sight in the inner portion of the house, the menu omitting vegetables, the separation of men and women, the groom's drunkenness, string-tying, and good-luck cash. There were also moments I thought were idiosyncratic, such as the bride following the groom back to her father's home, where she would normally have been waiting.

In the United States these wedding parties have taken on a different style. At one such party, the 1981 marriage of Kia Her and Tsu Ly (both pseudonyms), the guests were church members and what took place were formal prayers of welcome and a supper of chicken and rice. Kia Her and Tsu Ly grew up in the same locality in Laos. When the aftermath of the war made them refugees along with their families, they promised each other that if they ended up in the same country they would marry. Tsu's family had been resettled to Stockton, California, while Kia's widowed mother resettled with her five children in Seattle. In October 1981, Tsu was twenty years old and studying English at the University of California at Fresno, while Kia, about eighteen years old, was a sophomore in high school. Because Tsu could not afford the trip to Seattle, he asked for the help of his clan relative, Chou Neng Ly, to set up a wedding by proxy.

Chou Neng's wife Ker asked me to help receive the bride at the Lys' house and act as photographer. Arriving in the late morning with my camera gear, I waited with the family until midafternoon. Hmong finery was unpacked from suitcases stored under the beds and a girl related to the Lys was carefully dressed. Cooking was being done by Ker, Chou Neng's brother's wife, Ker's mother, and Chou Neng's mother's sister's son's wife (that is, women related to Lys mainly through female links). It consisted of at least one whole pig and a great many chickens, lots of rice, and boiled tofu. There was a large party at the bride's house and another in a public park to which about one hundred people came. Ker was very excited to have cooked for these feasts following methods she had learned from her mother, but neither she nor the other Ly connected women nor I went to these parties. Chou Neng also did not go because he had to work, and my notes do not reveal whether any Ly connected men went.

The total sum that the groom's family in Stockton had provided for the two parties, plus plane fare for Kia to fly to Stockton, came to $1,100, and on top of this sum, $800 had been sent for the bride money, as I knew because I had cashed the money orders through my bank account. This bride wealth was approximately equivalent to a month's salary for a worker at five dollars an hour.

In midafternoon Ker's father (again, not patrilineally related to Ly) and the traditionally dressed girl (who beside being a Ly was also a friend of the bride) drove off, returning with the bride and five other men, one of whom was a stand-in for the absent groom. The bride wore Hmong costume but all the men wore Western suits. At the time I didn't know them very well. My notes call these men "relatives of the bride" because that was what Ker called them.

Their arrival brought the number of people in the small apartment to at least fifteen. Kia was treated civilly but without any special ceremony and without particular warmth. The pastor from the Hmong Missionary Alliance Church offered prayers as all the adults sat on the folding chairs that lined the four walls of the cramped living room. There was a supper in preparation.

Two days later I drove the family with the bride bound for Stockton to the airport. She had all her clothes and jewelry in two huge suitcases and carried a large black plastic purse, but I had persuaded her to take out of the purse and strap about her waist the $1,800 that the Her family had provided her to take into married life. This sum would be used by the husband's immediate family, but in theory it remained Kia's property in case the marriage failed through no fault of her own. The amount almost equaled the bride wealth plus plane fare, and the Lys expressed some satisfaction about the amount.

The latest version of this type of party that I have attended took place in September 1988. The bride's family and the groom's family had known each other back in Vientiane. Both families, already linked by marriage (bride's female cousin to groom's brother) and by many other ties (such as being Christian), had resettled in Seattle. So the youth and the girl had known each other all their lives. But though the groom's family remained in Seattle, the bride's family had moved to California two years before the party. The young man, a house painter by trade, in his middle twenties, was the second brother of three. He was known for being quiet and my women friends commented that he would not have had the nerve to propose had his elder brother's wife not acted as broker by contacting the girl's family for him. The bride was nineteen years old and had graduated from high school. Negotiations between the families had already involved a transfer of cash bride money. The bride had come up from California three weeks previously.

The elder brother's wife, Zer, invited me, along with Siu-Woo Cheung, a Chinese friend who was learning Hmong preparatory to field work in China. We arrived at the split-level suburban-style home in south Seattle just at dusk. The yard and the shoulder of the street were parked full with cars. We entered on the lower level into the recreation room, which had been decorated in the style of a church social, with twisted crêpe-paper ribbons radiating out from paper wedding bells hanging in the middle of the ceiling. Wedding presents wrapped in gift paper filled a table in the recreation room.

A line of men and women in no particular order snaked up the stairs from the recreation room, through the living room, and around the table in the small dining room. We had arrived late, so the formal greeting of the bride was over. People had begun to eat, filling their three-compartment paper plates with rice and spicy chopped pork, cole slaw, cabbage wedges, Lao style chicken soup with coconut milk, and canned lichee fruit. Most of the older women took their plates into the kitchen and ate standing up. All the older men took theirs into the living room and sat watching television. Teens, young adults, and a few older women ate sitting on the folding chairs that lined the recreation room. The bride and groom were both in this room, but not together. He sat in his work pants and striped billed cap with a crowd of young men; she sat in her beautiful Lao dress with gold thread and her gold jewelry talking to women. Every once in a while all conversation stopped as a jet went overhead.

Fifty or sixty people attended the party, mostly church-connected friends or relatives. Some of the guests wore regular daywear, others wore suits or very fancy polyester lace blouses and very high heels; no one wore Hmong clothing. Besides me and my friend, four other non-Hmong were present—the Vietnamese, Lao, and Anglo-American husbands of three Hmong women, all in their twenties, and a middle-aged American woman who had been the ESL teacher of the bride years before.

When the food had been eaten, more people, mostly young, drifted into the recreation room and sat down. Zer's teen-age brother put on a tape that played, through giant speakers, a mix of Lao rock music, slow moving and decidedly romantic. Picking up a microphone that also fed through the speakers, he declared that now was the time to start dancing, beginning with the bride and groom. He wanted them to demonstrate dancing, he said, and the groom led the giggling and pink-faced bride into the middle of the floor, placing his arms around her and patting her behind while she cuddled into his arms and gave him a little kiss. The announcer kept talking English cheerfully, making slightly risqué comments, calling the dance sexy and so forth, while the watchers on the sidelines smiled and the groom said softly but quite clearly to the bride, "I love you" in English.

The next dance drew out four couples, the American husband and his Hmong wife, Zer and her husband, the bride and Siu-Woo, and the Lao husband with a Hmong girl (not his wife). The music was similar, but the style of dancing shifted. Couples danced separated, without touching or eye contact, deliberately looking elsewhere, their hands describing improvisatory gestures that the announcer called Lao. People switched partners from dance to dance, as song followed song. Meanwhile, upstairs the older men still sat watching television; a few young men had joined them. Many of these men spoke no English, and my friend joined them to speak Hmong. The kitchen was empty at this point, and leftover food sat on the dining table. People began to leave. The teen-agers downstairs continued dancing. Family groups left. We left.

Almost all the surface events of this party were innovations, compared with such parties in Laos: the bride's Lao clothes, everyone else's American clothes, the layout of the house, the church-social style of decorations, the vegetable food which would have been thought unlucky in Laos. Women planned as well as executed this party, and the bride and her mother-in-law, not the males of the household, stood at the doorway greeting guests. Men did not precede women at supper (the order of serving was entirely mixed), although the older people separated themselves in traditional style to eat, with the men taking the formal part of the house and the women the kitchen. While some older women watched the dancing, the older men stayed upstairs. There was no string-tying. The ritual part of the evening had been Hmong Christian, while the celebratory part owed more to high school dances and music video than to any Hmong cultural practice.

The most intrinsic Hmong meaning—that the bride was now part of her husband's family—remained intact. The couple did not establish a new household but took up residence with the groom's brother and his wife and children, and the men's mother. But the kind of life the bride was likely to lead, how she was conceptualized as a gendered person within this family unit, seems to have changed. She was more outgoing and spoke her own opinions much more often than Kia Her did in 1981. In the events of this party she was less of an icon of fertility and more a person with something to say, part of a couple dancing together for all to see, within a mixed and shifting cultural frame that demanded English to express itself. This seemed to be the lesson of this party: that this extended family, consisting of younger couples and their children and their aged mother, was in fact comprised of cooperating nuclear families, not of brothers and their peripheral wives. I will come back to this point later.

8

DOMESTIC CONFLICT

A functional argument is generally made for unequal domestic decision-making among Hmong in Southeast Asia (Lemoine 1972; Cooper 1984; and Lee 1981). The cultural definition of family as built around a core of related men reinforced and was reinforced by agricultural process and religious ritual. Men, as heads of families, negotiated between themselves through discussion and consensus. Within the household, although discussion between husband and wife was usual, the husband operated as leader of the family enterprise. Since men's farming decisions determined the prosperity of the whole household, men had to be able to command the labor of wives and children to carry out their decisions. Thus a rationalized model of the Hmong household in Southeast Asia placed men in key ritual and economic positions, and at the heart of the very definition of family. Women's obedience was crucial for the survival of all.

What is happening among Hmong now that the functional explanations for these lines of command within the household are no longer reinforced by the local economy? In marriages what seems to be very important are propriety and loyalty to family. For women in particular in this new ambiguous environment, these factors may be seen as making or breaking marriages. Actual actions or events appear as variations on these themes.

This assertion is based on cases involving conflict and dispute. The 1981 proxy wedding of Kia Her and Tsu Ly, described in chapter 6, for instance, became an example of such a problematic situation. In March 1983 I visited Kia Her and Tsu Ly in Stockton, where they lived in public housing with his father, the father's second wife and infant daughter, and the father's sister. The father's second wife was younger than Kia and did not speak English; she tucked in her chin and gazed unsmiling at me. The middle-aged unmarried sister, red-haired and freckled, had a bleak and cold eye, and frowned intently without speaking once during my visit. Also visiting were a young distant cousin of the father from Kansas, and Kia's mother and young brother (who loudly practiced his English on me, telling me how he and his mother and siblings had moved to Stockton "to be near Kia" although he was intending to return to Seattle where his brother had stayed).

Of the people in this household, only Kia and Tsu spoke English; I had come to see them, so my visit was not based on an invitation from the household head and was thus not entirely politely framed, especially as I could not converse with him. Kia had a baby girl, Sharon, four months old, and we sat playing with her as I talked with Kia and her mother. Kia was in school three days a week, thought Stockton was "OK," and liked being a mother. She wanted "a small family, four or five children." Presently Tsu rather peremptorily indicated that she should get me something to drink, then took her vacated chair. Kia's mother and brother went home, and the three women of the family laid out a cold meal of chicken, rice and vegetables without salt or other spicing, and thin instant coffee. Men and women sitting together, we ate politely, after which Tsu's father, stepmother, and aunt left the table and Tsu, Kia, the cousin from Kansas, and I talked about Tsu's life.

Tsu was a very tiny man, less than five feet tall, pale and freckled like his aunt but with black hair. He was still in school. I tried to think of him doing farm labor (a typical source of employment in the Central Valley), and couldn't. He said he had been a soldier as a child, engaging in jungle fighting from about age eleven. I was very struck by his sudden stiffening, fiery eyes, and clamped jaw and fist, as we talked about it. "But what can a soldier do now?" he demanded as if despairing the futility of life. So I introduced Simon Fass's idea that former soldiers could do guard work, describing the job as driving around at night to make sure business property is safe. "Do you get a gun?" he asked. "Yes, but you are not supposed to kill people." He lost interest and said he didn't care about property—if you couldn't fire at robbers, you couldn't defend property anyway. I mentioned Chao Fa, the messianic guerrilla force supposed to be operating in Laos, and his eyes lit up. "Yes, I know it," he said. We talked late into the evening, and I went on my way.

In July 1986, I happened to be in a Hmong grocery in La Crosse, Wisconsin, with my friend Ker, when to my astonishment Kia Her appeared around the end of an aisle. We said hello warmly, but as I asked her about moving to La Crosse she stammered and seemed embarrassed and quickly left the store. Ker coolly told me that Kia had separated from her husband "for no reason, just quarrel with her mother-in-law." Kia, it seemed, had taken some of Tsu's money without permission, packed when Tsu was not home, and with her two children slipped away by bus from Stockton to La Crosse. Tsu suspected her destination (because Kia's mother and sister had lately moved with the sister's husband to La Crosse) so he called Ker's husband Chou Neng, who found Kia in her sister's household. Once Kia admitted she was not on a mere visit, her family refused to harbor her for fear of offending the Lys, and insisted she enter the police shelter. She lived there two months, Ker said loftily, and now had her own little apartment "by herself, nobody talk to her." Tsu was refusing to come to La Crosse, denying any fault in the matter, in case her family demanded the bride wealth back, and was telling everybody Kia could find her own way back, but she had no money and had gone on welfare in Wisconsin. Ker thought she was stupid and should get some American friends to help her, because she had no reputation left among the Hmong. She considered that Kia had been trying to make some point about how her mother-in-law should treat her, and it had backfired. She also thought Kia's mother had been telling her that Tsu was a bad husband and Kia had listened, so that at bottom this problem had been caused by Tsu's mother-in-law. Kia did not go back to her husband, and the marriage broke up. Although Kia's marriage had begun with ceremony and propriety, when it ended, she found herself excluded from Hmong society.

American gender practice affects Hmong lives. Marriage conflict and its outcome exemplify the problems involved in trying to retain Hmong gender hierarchies in the American setting. Since remaining Hmong includes keeping the traditional household relations between men and women, many Hmong fear that new ways of interacting mean the end of any meaningful Hmong culture in the United States.

During July 1988 a conference took place in Seattle, put on by the National Coalition Against Domestic Violence. After it was over my friend Zer called me, disturbed by one session. She had attended the conference to sell needlework, but was invited to sit in the audience for various sessions. In one workshop, delegates from a Midwestern coalition for battered women were to present a videotape of a Hmong woman who had come to them for help. Before the showing they asked if any Hmong were in the room, and when Zer raised her hand they asked her to leave. This demand caused an uproar as audience members rushed to her defense, and ultimately the video was not shown at all.

Zer said that her presence had hurt the workshop and she felt sorry and embarrassed to have caused such a problem; probably the Hmong woman in the video didn't want her face seen by other Hmong, which was only to be expected. Evidently the Midwestern group introduced the video in a rather lurid way, because she went on to say, "Why do people criticize Hmong men all the time? There are so many wonderful men, they are beautiful people. American people don't understand Hmong culture. Families do not sell their daughters, that's ridiculous. Parents cherish their daughters, the bride money shows that. Hmong people depend on each other. If a husband does the wrong thing to a woman, her family can come and get her. It is not true that Hmong do not care for their Hmong women!" She couldn't understand, she concluded, why people try to break apart Hmong and prevent them from helping each other.

Clearly she perceived the coalition's shelter as something that came between Hmong who would otherwise negotiate with one another. Hmong conflict management, in the hands of elders, includes counseling mechanisms for dealing with violent husbands and unhappy wives. The goal of Hmong counseling is always to keep the family together, which means persuading the wife to reconcile herself to her situation as well as persuading the husband not to be irresponsible. Accepting family responsibility is a keynote of Hmong counseling. If this involves swallowing bitter pills, Hmong elders recommend doing so, rather than divorcing, since there is no place in Hmong society for divorced people. Divorce is truly the path of last resort in Hmong society.[1] Taking the uncomfortable advice of Hmong elders implies a high degree of respect and trust in their wisdom. It means sharing a Hmong vision, being part of a Hmong community, being Hmong.

A DIFFICULT SITUATION

Family politics are not apparent when everything is going well. Lines of power become much clearer during disagreements. Already several examples of domestic conflict within resettled Hmong families have been described in chapters 6 and 8. The case from chapter 6, in which Ker lost the argument with her husband's young male relatives, illustrates what we already know, that among the Hmong, household authority is vested in men, while it is women's responsibility not to hold themselves in opposition to masculine dominance.

My friend Neng moved his family away from Seattle in 1985, and in 1986 and 1987 I visited them in their new home in the Midwest. Many families had moved to the new location, and during my second visit I wanted to visit his wife's cousin Kua (specifically, his wife's father's father's brother's son's son), who was also Neng's relative on the female side (specifically, his mother's father's brother's daughter's son), and whom I knew slightly from Seattle. But Neng would have nothing to do with the idea. The families were not speaking to each other, because a marriage had gone awry. Neng told me at length his feelings about the case.

In 1986, Kua had been in charge of the New Year festivities. He set up ball playing and Lao dancing by young people as a cultural display. Among the dancers was a young man of Neng's clan ("same last name only, we are not *really* related, and his family comes from Sayaboury but I am from Xieng Khouang"), who still lived in Seattle but had come visiting for New Year. The youth was staying at Kua's house. Every day Kua and his wife

Ly went off to work on a farm while their only daughter, Mee, and her friends stayed at home to babysit her little brother—"partying" as Neng acidly commented. Presently the boy, Song, went back to Seattle. A few months later Kua's daughter turned out to be pregnant. She called Song, who called Neng, who suggested that Song marry her. "If he really love her, they should get married. They get along fine."

Mee was fourteen, Song sixteen and in high school. This was where the problem came up. Song was the only child in a household headed by a widow. When they came to the United States, for some reason they gave his age as older by two years, so at this time his legal age was eighteen, no longer eligible for public assistance. So, as he was still in school, he and his mother were both living on her welfare check of about $380 a month. Their rent was $250 a month. Neng and his relatives who participated in the wedding negotiations naturally expected that Mee would get herself on welfare once she arrived in Seattle with Song. But Kua and his relatives objected that Mee was under legal age to marry, so although in Hmong culture she could marry Song, in American culture it was not possible. Thus this marriage should not be registered at the courthouse and Song's family should not let any official know Mee was living with him. The marriage contract therefore included this provision. So when Mee went to Seattle, she joined a household whose income was $380 a month. She was not allowed to see a doctor during pregnancy, nor was provision made for the expense of her confinement, although after much negotiation by telephone between Song, Kua, and Neng, Mee was permitted, as she neared term, to get in touch with a Hmong hospital translator. All this was according to Neng, who commented that Kua "hated" this marriage because Song was so poor.

These inadequate financial arrangements were not the only problem in the household, for Song's mother, being as Neng described her "old fashioned," saw no reason not to make all sorts of demands on her new daughter-in-law, ordering her about "like a slave" and never bothering to be polite to her. Kua's clan relatives and Neng's clan relatives had many meetings about these problems, which Neng called "too difficult." Kua would not agree to any official recognition of the union. He may have been trying to force Neng and his male relatives to help support Song and Mee, which they would not do. Nor would they agree to Song simply breaking the contract by signing up for welfare. Meanwhile, Mee had her baby as if she were single, and continued to live unhappily in Song's mother's household.

Finally, Mee ran away after a quarrel with Song's mother over laundry money. She called Kua's former American sponsors in Seattle and asked for help. They had known nothing of her return, but immediately picked her up with the baby and took her to a shelter and called Child Protective Services. Kua had to send air fare to bring her home. Now Kua was furious with Song and all his relatives, and although Song had come to get Mee back (admitting that the fault lay with his family, not with Mee or her family), Kua wouldn't let him in the house and Song had to stay with Neng, who didn't want him. Neng told me that to be quite correct Kua should have given Song a room in his house but not let him sleep with Mee. This is how he said it would have been done in Laos. (Lemoine [1972], however, recounts a case where a young husband who is at fault stayed with his clan relatives, so Neng seems to have been too punctilious.)

Finally in negotiations both sides softened. Neng's clan proposed that Kua's clan permit Song and Mee to take welfare, and if in the future any girl from Neng's clan should marry any boy from Kua's clan under similar circumstances, Neng's clan would permit that future couple to get welfare. This was acceptable to Kua, and the couple had returned together to Seattle only three weeks before my conversation with Neng.

This was why we could not visit Kua. Neng commented that the real problem lay with the two mothers of the young couple. Song's mother had said "probably not nice" things to Mee, and Mee's mother "probably said bad things" to Mee about Song. So Mee's reluctance to stay in Song's household was really the elder women's fault. I said American parents probably would have tried to prevent the marriage because we would consider a fourteen-year-old girl too young to get married, even if she were pregnant; we would think she should stay in school. Well, Neng said, the boy and girl like each other. "The marriage can work if people let them alone."

That marriage survived its early problems. Hmong counseling depends on being able to persuade the husband and wife to follow advice. If they will not, a new situation arises that in Laos had to be resolved by one spouse giving in to the other. As the wife lived under the control of her husband's clan, it was frequently she who yielded. I would link the power dynamics within Hmong households, in cases of insoluble conflict, with Hmong wives' frequently mentioned suicide rate in Southeast Asia, for it was not only courting girls who killed themselves (see chapter 6). There are no statistics, but many stories, about women's suicide (see Lemoine 1972 and Cooper 1984, for instance). Among my subjects, the old lady who told her obstreperously funny story about marrying to avoid a worse marriage (chapter 6) had lost in rapid succession both her mother and her father's second wife to suicide by poison, before she was eight. Her father could not find another woman to marry him, so he was forced to do all the farm work and much of the household work himself. The household then consisted of himself, his second wife's old widowed mother (Mai's stepgrandmother), and five children, of whom Mai was second. Hmong would generally say that the stepgrandmother should not have been living with her daughter's family, but with a male clan relative (preferably a son), but in this case she remained in her son-in-law's household. The eldest child, a son, married as soon as possible, when Mai was about twelve. But then her father died, orphaning a household that was almost unviable, consisting of one old woman, one teen-age couple, several girls, and one little boy. This was the family Mai didn't want to leave when she was forced to find a husband. At that point she, too, considered suicide.

Life is physically easier in the United States than in Laos for Hmong. I propose that it is also psychologically easier, in that women do not have to choose between suicide and unhappy marriage. This is a non-Hmong thing to say, and I do not suggest that divorce never occurred in Laos.[2] Divorce was rare, however, perhaps rarer than women's suicide (which does not seem to have been rare). In the United States, divorce among Hmong must be much more common than women's suicide, and one reason is that the grounds for divorce are more permissive than under Hmong custom in Laos.

THE SEPARATION OF MAI YANG AND BEE KEU

On a Sunday in May 1986 I happened to call Neng Yang who said, "Oh, I'm so glad you call, I need your help for my sister!"

Three years before, his sister Mai had married Bee, a man of the Keu clan. I hadn't seen her much since then. They had never had a peaceful marriage, Neng told me, and frequently argued and fought, usually over the husband's many girlfriends. Frequently Mai came to her brother to ask his help.

All his efforts did no good. The situation went from talks between Neng and the husband, to talks between clan leaders, to Neng telling his sister to call the police. The goal of the talks between Neng and the Kue clan leaders was always to reconcile the couple by advising the wife to be more patient and the husband to be kinder to her, and by reminding them both of their marital duties. None of these tactics helped reduce the arguing, Neng said; the husband kept on having girlfriends. He had hit her in the past, and just last night he had hit the little boy. Mai called the police, after which her husband ran out of the house.

The police took the boy to the hospital. Mai went with them, but then the police left her at the hospital by herself. She called Neng at 3 a.m. to come get her. He told her to call her husband's clan, but she didn't want to do that, so he had to get her and take her home. Then this afternoon she had come to stay at Neng's house with her two-year-old boy and five-month-old girl. Neng did not want her in the house, as this would make his relations with the Keus deteriorate even more. Also, he had given up his own apartment and was living with his wife's sister and her husband, prior to leaving Seattle. It was too crowded for three more people. So he needed my help, because Hmong culture had no more answers for this couple. They needed a divorce. He was very worried about his sister but he could not help her, and he did not want her around. Another friend, Jane, had found a shelter where his sister could go, but Jane was going on vacation. Neng could not tell Mai to divorce her husband because it would be wrong to say this to a woman married to another clan—but she had no choice. He really wanted me to help her.

All this came tumbling out with hardly a word from me. Of course I had to go over there. I called Jane, who was willing to help line up a lawyer, but said she had no experience with battered women, and would rather I handled the problem. But I had no more experience than she.

I went over to Neng's wife's sister's apartment (which was also Neng's cousin's apartment, for she was married to Leng, a cousin of Neng; but Neng was emphasizing the social awkwardness implied by all these female links). I had been there before for a baby-naming party, but now the living room was filled with mattresses, and all the furniture was shoved against the walls. The one-bedroom apartment now had nine people living in it, plus Mai and her two children. Leng's wife, a cheery young woman named Ah, said she liked having so many people; it was fun.

There was very little floor space. In the dinette Neng moved several chairs into a semicircle. Mai Yang sat with her baby girl; her boy was asleep on a mattress. Neng and I sat, and the family stood to listen. Mai whispered that she wanted my help. Her voice was very high and childlike and soft. She was small, maybe four foot ten, stocky, dressed in slacks and flip-flops, with her long hair wrapped in a knot at the back of her head.

What did she want? I asked. A divorce. Her husband always argued and did not come home from work on time. When she went to find him, she found him with his girlfriends. Once he went to California with a girl and didn't even tell her he was going; she found out from his brother several days after he left. He hit her last year, and now last night he had hit her little son. They went to the flea market yesterday and she bought a motorcycle toy for her son because he wanted it. It was a big police motorcycle with battery-operated flashing lights, about ten inches long. In the evening her husband got very angry about spending two dollars on this toy, took it, and broke it over the head of her little son. She called the police, as Neng had told her to do, and her husband ran out of the house. She was afraid of her husband and did not want to see him any more. He was always telling her he wanted her to leave, that she was a bad wife. She cooked for him and everything like a Hmong woman was supposed to do, but he kept telling her he could find much better wives than her. She thinks he is not a good husband. Sometimes he is very nice, and he can say nice words to make anybody believe him, but he is lying, and later he always goes back to the same way and gets very angry and says terrible things to her. She asked Neng to help her but he could not do some things, and anyway he was moving away. She was very firm that she wanted a divorce, and she would not change her mind. Her son, Hu, woke up then and laid his head in my lap. I had never seen a child so spiritless. The sadness of this little boy made me want to help his mother.

We spent Monday getting an order of protection. As we sat filling out the papers, she worried that her husband might try to get the children, either to spite her or because normally the husband's clan would want the children. In the Hmong way, they might let her keep them while they were small but could insist on taking them away when they were older. She said he did not like to hold the children. If she asked him to hold them he was very awkward and soon gave them back to her, especially if the baby cried or something.

At one point we stood in line near a woman who had just gotten her permanent order of protection, who said she had been well prepared in court with papers and evidence, a good thing as her recently divorced husband had told a lot of lies to make himself look good. Mai was very impressed with such competence. She wanted to follow her brother and live again with the Yang clan, go to school, improve her English, and learn how to make a living. Yes, I said, she would need to learn to support her children. At last we had only to file the statement. I left Mai to stand in the line while I fed money to my meter. She was excited to have filed it alone.

Jane talked with a woman named Zer about translating for Mai when she filled out divorce papers. But Zer said she could not help because she was related to Mai's husband: her husband's brother's wife's brother was married to the sister of Bee Keu, so she was unable to interpret for either side. She said that Neng and Bee Keu had gotten into a big argument at the party to give needlework to Mai's mother (a ritual after the birth of a daughter's children). Bee left the party without eating, a terrible breach of etiquette. His family had migrated as a group of brothers and sisters, without parents or elders, and never joined Hmong community activities. Zer thought they "weren't very Hmong."

I went to take Mai to the shelter. Neng talked about this and that. Someone called, and he got into a long conversation. Clearly he was ambivalent about this venture, not wanting Mai there at his home, but not wanting her to leave either. At last, while Mai and her children stood at the door in their winter coats patiently waiting for Neng to hang up, I stood right next to him as a hint, and finally we were able to load the gallon of milk and the big bag of Pampers in the car, with many farewells.

Eventually we arrived at the shelter pickup point, Mai driving behind me. The shelter people never permitted anyone except staff and residents even to know the true location of the shelter. I telephoned them. Mai and I waited, and I wrote my phone numbers for her. Mai was excited and happy, banking on her ability to make a new life for herself, jumping off into the totally unknown with tremendous bravery. The shelter woman arrived, with tattered clothes and stringy hair. I began to wonder what Mai would find at the shelter. The shelter woman and I shook hands and thanked each other for looking out for Mai. Mai was really ready to go.

Later I called Neng to report that Mai was safe, I hoped. It took a long time to get through, as the line was busy. Finally I reached him, and he said fine, and immediately went off into talking about the insurance woes of his male cousin. I reminded him after about five minutes that I was calling about his sister. Yes, he said, he was sorry that he could not help her, but he had really tried to help. The Hmong culture provides for negotiating, but this couple made him crazy because they never changed.

"Well, you can't say your sister is at fault here, it is the husband who is wrong."

"That's true, the whole family is hard and that man has a bad reputation."

"I heard you had a quarrel with Mai's husband."

Yes, he said, at the party for his mother when she moved, Mai's husband wanted to do the ritual the White Hmong way. Neng told him when he went to Keu's, he would follow them in the White Hmong way, but now Bee Keu was in a Blue Hmong house and should do it their way. Bee Keu hit his fist on the table and said he would not eat at Neng's house, and then he left. Nobody knew what to do and it spoiled the party. Neng said he could not stand the sight of Mai's husband. This is why he would not want to offend him or his clan by helping Mai, because it would make bad blood between the clans. "I couldn't have her here."

"Why do you care?"

"Because my son may want to marry a Keu girl and then that clan will bring up this marriage and will fine me if I help her."

"But your son may not marry a Keu, he may marry Xiong or some other clan, while your sister's problems are here in the present moment."

This comment made him very angry, and he could hardly be polite to me. A Hmong wife really was considered legally the possession of the husband's clan. Neng was concerned about his political relationship with the Keu men, and the women were pawns in this, not participants. Despite the formal Hmong ideology that claims that a woman in trouble can call on her clan, in fact Neng was too worried about offending Mai's husband's clan to give her overt help. Our conversation was a kind of argument.

As the case developed, Mai managed her male relatives, the legal system, and her American friends to free herself from her husband. Neng and his cousins were willing to cover legal fees, as long as they could act covertly. Mai stayed a month in the temporary shelter but then had to find another situation. Leng and his young wife invited her to stay with them, but Neng's wife, who was still living with Leng, thought Mai 'belonged' to the Keu clan and should not live with the Yang clan. Still, Mai moved in temporarily, until Leng and his brother Sw found an apartment for her. Leng and Neng paid the deposit, and she moved again June 15.

Meanwhile, I was hearing gossip from other Hmong women about Mai's character. She was said to be forward, bad tempered, and unwilling to take advice. "She will not listen to anybody. Nobody can do anything with her. She is nice to people not in her family, but always fights at home." These comments came from nonrelatives. Her husband fared no better in gossip. He was said not to care about his children, to be willfully stupid, not to try to understand his situation, and not to want to listen when people gave advice. I took it he was getting a lot of advice.

Zer, the translator who had refused to help either side, invited me to lunch to tell me that couples should try harder. Mai and Bee were not trying to understand each other, she said. Then she went on to say that a man needs to understand the problems of women. Life in Laos was very terrible for women. Her husband's mother was a case in point. His father had taken a second wife only a few years older than his son. The son was fifteen then, and he and Zer were not married yet. This greedy woman got the keys to the family strongbox and care of all the family's money. When the first wife complained, her husband beat her and told her to get out if she didn't like it. So her son built an entirely different house for her, but though she had her children with her, she had no means of support, nor would her husband divorce her, and as a woman she could not take a lover. Within a few years the young wife's extravagance had ruined the family finances, but meanwhile the son had learned how to support his mother and siblings by selling things.

Her mother-in-law suffered terrible grief at that time, and none of the children can forgive their father, even though he now realizes what a mistake he made in his pride. Now he lives in Canada with his second wife and five children. They have had a very hard time, as he had all these young children to support while he was aging, and now he sees that they are not hard working like his first wife's family, who had to struggle and get educations on their own. He came to visit last year, and all he could do was cry, he could hardly speak. The wife really belongs to the husband's family after marriage and is not part of her own family anymore.

I took this story as a condemnation of her father-in-law, a statement of her own position in her husband's family, a comment on Mai's behavior, and also a rejection of American divorce and our efforts to help Mai get divorced. She thought it was disreputable for Mai to go "back to her clan," and she wished that Jane and I would not help her.

Neng came back from the Midwest to visit. He was perfectly willing to pay for a lawyer, an apartment, or anything else. "In my heart I want to help her, but I'm not supposed to help her because she married Keu already. She can never live with me. So we don't tell anybody, but I do it." Neng's wife was greatly irritated by these expenditures.

As the summer wore on and divorce papers were filed, Mai spent weekends with an American friend from her shelter days, and I investigated the idea of school for her. Nothing lasting resulted. In July she told me about some Hmong neighbors in her new apartment. The husband was related to Leng's wife in some way. The couple had gone by car a week earlier to visit her parents in Spokane. While there, they took the car to a gas station close by. The husband smoked, and the wife was arguing with him, Mai said. The wife got out of the car and "ran away" to her mother's house, saying she couldn't stand the smoke. Her husband was so mad he came right back to Seattle (350 miles).

Then he said she was a lazy wife and he didn't want to be married any longer. He told the landlord they were separated. The wife called Mai from Spokane to tell her husband she wanted to come back, but he said she could find her own way. She was nineteen years old and about three months pregnant. Mai said that at the time of the marriage, the husband paid no bride wealth and there was no party. "Are they married then?" I asked. "Yes, I think so," said Mai. "Is she lazy?" "Well, she sleeps until noon."

Mai found this disagreement amusing, and was not surprised that the wife came back soon after. But when her own husband began making overtures to her late in July, she was terrified. I had called her about childcare. She picked up the phone but said nothing. "Mai?" "Oh, Nancy, my husband called me and I don't want to say anything." Her voice was trembling. He had called her twice the day before. My notes recall:

Last night she dreamed he was killing her. Four days ago when she went to Leng's, her husband came over and tried to get in. He has an aunt living in that building, and Mai thinks this aunt called him. He came to the apartment of Leng's wife's sister and asked her husband to help him get Mai back. The husband called Leng, who said the case was now in the court and nothing could be done, and Bee Keu should go home. Instead, Bee knocked on Leng's door and said he wants to see his children, but Leng told him to go home. About twenty minutes later he showed up at Sw's. Sw told him to get a court order if he wanted to see the children, and Sw will not tell Mai to go back to Bee. So Bee left. I said if he comes to her place and knocks on the door or window, Mai should call the police, and I made her repeat after me: "I have an order of protection. My husband is at the door and I am afraid. Can you help me?"

The marriage was dissolved in a court hearing in August. Mai was awarded custody of the children, while Bee Keu received carefully controlled visiting rights and was ordered to pay child support. It takes three months for a divorce to become final in Washington State. At the end of September Mai's cousin Sw, who had a job helping with refugee resettlement, received a note, which roughly translated by Sw reads:

Sw—Why is my entire penis unable to straighten out, it turns sideways and when I pee it goes crooked? Why didn't you do your job right, but only help your own relatives? You think no one can replace you, but someone from our clan can take over your job. You don't have many relatives here, just a few, so if you don't quit your job and leave Seattle, we will come beat you up. [Four signatures of local Hmong known to Sw] If you receive this letter and you disagree, you can go to any court or any lawyer and they will follow and support us.

Sw's work supervisor also got a copy of this letter. Sw's male relatives in Seattle called a well-known man related to both sides, who called the four signatories to say that if Sw had any accident his relatives would publicize the problem to all the Hmong in the country, and in any case they intended to call the police. The four denied any knowledge of the note, saying, as Sw recounts: "If you call the police you will cut off our life here, because we just came. Can't you understand us, because we have known each other seven years, you even set up the party for our brothers when they graduated from high school. We will never forget you, and we never did this!" Sw and his relatives decided that these four undoubtedly had no part in the affair, and in the end both groups gave fifty dollars to the Hmong Association of Washington, which sponsored a party "to tie up both sides together to trust each other again." At this party the threatening note was ceremonially burned by a shaman who cursed the writer to suffer the same fate Sw had been threatened with. The president of the Hmong Association announced in church that whoever wrote the letter should come forward and apologize, but no one did.

Toward the end of October, Sw commented that he felt certain he knew who the author was: Bee. He had spoken to Bee's younger brother, who had said that his family could not control Bee because he was the eldest brother. Being allied by marriage to this family was bad for his family's reputation, Sw said. He thought Mai should move somewhere safer. Sw thought Bee Keu was engaging in these odd tactics because he really loved her and imagined that if he could drive Sw out of Seattle, Mai would be deprived of support and would come back to him. Bee Keu attacked Sw rather than talking to Mai because he believed Mai only did what her male relatives told her to do. Sw said this was a tactic that someone would try in Laos, but "here it cannot work."

In the aftermath of these events, the cumbersome visiting arrangements meant in effect that Bee had little contact with the children. He failed to pay his child support, and with his younger brother's family moved to California. Just before they left, Bee's younger brother called me. Bee thought if he was expected to pay for the child, he should be given the child. He wanted the boy but didn't care about the girl—but in any case making this monthly payment ought to be in exchange for the child; having to pay and losing the child too made no sense to Bee. Mai moved to be near her brother in the Midwest, and married again in 1988.

ANOMALOUS GENDER PERFORMANCE AND MEANING

This case is one of several with similar logistics that I have in my notes. It clearly shows how American attitudes toward and laws about marriage change the potential outcomes for unhappy Hmong couples, and how Americans can be used by Hmong to accomplish tasks that are impossible within the framework of Hmong social structure. There are two ways to look at the case: that Hmong patrilineal social forms are subverted and destroyed by the American legal system, which, as Hmong are fond of pointing out, "favors women"; or alternatively, that a possibility and prescription already present in Hmong society (in this case, the notion that when a woman is in trouble her natal family should help her) can be more efficiently carried out by making careful use of the American system. Physical violence has become, in the United States, an acceptable reason for a wife to leave her husband.

Keeping alive a sense of being Hmong involves retaining the activities and ways of thinking that permit interactions that the Hmong think are necessary to Hmong society. Since social structure and family structure are nearly identical domains for them, remaining Hmong means retaining the traditional hierarchies of interaction within and among Hmong families. "Building the family" continues to be a source of praise, while the destruction of families through divorce compromises the alliances that constitute the Hmong social fabric. Yet Mai Vang was able to use American divorce laws to rid herself of an unwanted husband and still retain membership in the Hmong community, unlike the Hmong woman mentioned by Ker in chapter 4, and unlike Kia Ly.

Mai had several advantages. She and her husband had followed the cultural prescription of letting family and clan elders try to reconcile them, so Mai, her family thought, respected Hmong customs. Her brother also hated her husband, so he was willing to help her covertly. Bee Kue had a bad reputation, and his immediate family was already marginalized in the Seattle Hmong community, while Mai's brother was a vigorous and central figure in his clan and in community leadership, so ultimately the men of her family were willing to ignore Bee's importunities and the criticism of his clan members. Finally, Mai's natal family was in the process of moving to another region, where any repercussions would be minor.

Despite these advantages, Mai's actions were criticized by most of the women I spoke to, including her brother's traditional wife, because of the cost, and by two more sophisticated women on the basis that Mai was not fitting her wife's role but was too bold and impatient, which they saw as clearly the case because instead of accepting her husband's behavior as an ideal wife should, she was striving to end the marriage by turning to the American legal system. These criticisms were made within acceptable interpretations of Hmong womanhood—it is appropriate for a wife to want to save her family's money, and for Hmong women to recommend traditional values for women. Even so, Mai's use of the American legal system could be subsumed in the cultural subtext of "going back to her clan," so a Hmong framework was available to justify her actions in Hmong terms.

This was not true for Kia or the woman in chapter 4. In Kia's case, the stronger extended family was that of her husband. Kia ran away, not to her brothers, but to her sister and her mother, neither of whom could shield her from the criticism of the strong Ly clan. The divorced woman in chapter 4 had no helpful relations in Seattle and had to lean on her American sponsors, taking her right outside the Hmong community and making it impossible to interpret her divorce in Hmong terms.

Mee, the daughter of Kua, also invoked her tie to American sponsors, but did not damage her place in Hmong society because her father was eager to receive her. Mee's problem, too little money to survive, could be brought to a solution by precipitating a crisis in the form of outside intervention, forcing her stubborn and quarrelsome elders to find a workable solution. So Mee, like Mai, used the American legal system and sympathetic sponsors to improve her situation within Hmong society.

These cases have elements in common. Each crisis was launched by the woman leaving her husband. In each case, the woman's particular position in relation to the men of her natal family determined whether she could retain respect within Hmong society; the comments of women about her had less force. Mai and Mee used American methods after failed negotiation within Hmong social forms; Kia and the woman of chapter 4 had not tried Hmong negotiation, which also probably contributed to the perception that their behavior was improper. In the latter two cases, the husband's acceptance in Hmong society remained undamaged after his wife's flight.

In these cases of conflict, interpreting anomalous actions within the framework of Hmong social roles meant the event did not threaten Hmong social structure. It minimized dissonance between Hmong and American ways of dealing with domestic conflict by subordinating the American process to a Hmong goal, legitimated by subtexts of acceptable gender roles for Hmong women.

9

WHAT DOES CHANGE MEAN?

In this book several topics intertwine: the refugees' desire to retain a sense of being Hmong even in America, gender and age hierarchies as the main skeleton of Hmong social identity, the impingement of American convictions about gender on Hmong lives, and marriage forms and practices as exemplars of the problems involved in trying to retain Hmong ethnic hierarchies in the American setting. What were the Hmongs' lives like in Southeast Asia? What are some of the consequences within Hmong households of moving to the United States? Do men and women treat their relationship to each other differently after this experience in the alien environment that has become their permanent home?

The range of ways to make statements about being Hmong narrowed for refugee Hmong after arriving in the United States. In Laos, Hmong language as one's native tongue, a life high in the mountains as farmer-entrepreneurs, particular rituals especially at New Year's, particular treatment of the dead, dressing in a certain style, political loyalty given on the basis of family ties, and certain assumptions about social hierarchy within the household provided the backbone of Hmong identity. During the war, economic and military experiences broadened possibilities for some Hmong, who began to identify with Laos in dress and politics. Lao was the language of education for a small percentage; a small percentage became Christian.

In the United States, Hmong-Americans live mainly in urban areas, dress like Americans, and make their living in our class-based society however they can, from welfare to laboring to teaching and interpreting work. There has been an upheaval in political loyalty as they strive for effective leaders within a new political system. Now English is the language of education. Rituals are very much abbreviated, and probably more than half the Hmong have become Christians. What then remains as touchstones of Hmong identity? Wearing Hmong clothes on special occasions such as New Year or weddings—but this too is in decline; speaking Hmong at home— but some Hmong children do not speak Hmong at home; and maintaining particular forms of social structure within the household.

This study's most basic goal was to comprehend how changed circumstances create new social arrangements. Social change means more than surface accommodations to a new environment with new material things substituting for significant items no longer available. The internalized cultural framework with which members of Hmong society assign meaning to what they are doing is also undergoing strain in the new environment, accommodating itself and producing new interpretations for old actions, constructing new meanings out of daily interactions in a new environment.

However, although the environment is so different that time-tested explanations for reality must find new ground from which to integrate thousands of new experiences, in explanations of what in their culture is important to retain, first-generation Hmong over and over say it is important to retain the shape of household interactions, of family relationships. In the search for underlying change in how resettled Hmong explain their experiences to themselves, we seem to have come up against a stubborn resistance to change. It is reasonable, then, to ask whether these household arrangements and lines of respect and authority are indeed remaining the same; if so, why; and if not, in what ways change is occurring, and what explanations are available for change that provide a sense of continuity and imply that the people who have changed are still Hmong.

The key to understanding gender attitudes among first-generation Hmong refugees lies in their universal insistence that they will remain Hmong as long as they can maintain a certain set of social relationships within the household—an insistence on continuity, on nonchanging social structure. The particular social forms can be identified not by the actual content or goals of actions, but by the lines of respect and authority that they embody. These place each person in two hierarchies: gender and age. Old men are given more respect than young men, who receive more than boys. Old women are honored and their wishes catered to by their families, but while old men and women are more nearly equal than young men and women, the amount of respect accorded old women is still less than that accorded old men. Females in each age category are placed beneath male contemporaries, because they are female, and women always owe respect to men.

Hmong, like other refugees resettled to a new location, reconstruct as best they can their already understood social worlds, and overcome imperfections in the reconstruction by substitution and overlooking difference. In general, incoming Hmong refugees do not seek new lives, they seek the same lives in a new location, and where possible they use their new opportunities to bolster preexisting social conceptions. This is clearly illustrated by their needlework sales. The beautiful batik, appliqué work, and embroidery made by Hmong women were not marketplace items in Laos, but were intended for household use and ritual exchanges signifying social and emotional attachments. In the profoundly different environment of Seattle, however, traditional sources of family subsistence and of wealth (farming, opium trade) were in short supply. Hmong men could not easily turn to economic use in America the military and political skills they had developed during wartime. Meanwhile Hmong women, encouraged by American admiration for their needlework, and having available to them the cultural model of the effective and clever Hmong wife, turned their sewing skill to money by selling adapted pieces in a market economy mediated mainly by American volunteer advisors.

This activity illustrates a recombination and reconstruction of bits of strategic activity already available in Hmong culture, turning them to fit a new set of needs and opportunities. In the process, needlework intended for the market changed stylistically, alienated as it was from social and ritual use in Hmong households. Family and ritual exchanges continued, with new objects as well as old carrying the burden of social attachments; for instance, sisters-in-law made up coordinated outfits by exchanging store-bought clothes (a new set of objects), even as gifts of baby carriers to new mothers continued, unaffected by the marketing of baby carriers. Meanwhile, the profits of needlework sales entered the family economy, where their use was determined by traditional ideas of authority within households. Underlying cultural meanings were not damaged or reshaped by this shuffling of the objects used in symbolic behavior or subsistence support. The definition of Hmong women as creators of beauty, skilled in devotion to their families, and embedded in a social order dominated by men, remained intact.

The politicized nature of two needlework cooperatives can be included in this pattern of taking the materials at hand and restructuring them to conform to existing cultural models. Here the materials were the cooperatives and the model was hierarchical control. Using familiar strategies, accepted (even when disliked) by other Hmong, local Hmong leaders experienced in the former power structure in Laos strove persistently to coopt the cooperatives to a vision of Hmong social structure directly derived from their old-country experiences. Their complex statements of motivation and their persistence even in spite of unprofitability, lift their actions beyond simple self-interest. They acted as they knew how, *because* they knew how, and did not change methods although they recognized their inadequacy, because they did not know how to change. The problematic results of their endeavors demonstrate that control over people depends on the quality of the available rewards and threats. This is evidence, not of newly developing meanings to explain changed behavior in a new setting, but of old explanations transplanted.

Underlying gender constructs seemed not to have been threatened by Hmong women's textile marketing. But another arena of cultural action appeared promising in the search for possible shifts in the symbols that support behavior. Overt differences in the rituals and events comprising Hmong marriages were immediately apparent, but whether these indicated underlying change was not. Kia Her and Tsu Ly's marriage was arranged using conveniences like the telephone and money orders. The groom's family bridged distance with cars and airplane, and offered Christian prayers rather than spirit offerings. These innovations, however, were entirely subordinate to the older meaning attached to the process of marriage—that the bride was now under the protection and control of her husband's family, and her children would be legitimate members of his clan.

Again, in the wedding negotiation discussed in chapter 7, many small differences arose in procedure because of the new milieu, some appearing to hinder and some to facilitate the preservation of traditional form. Prognostications could not be made from the toes of the gift chickens because supermarket chickens have no toes. The negotiators preferred nonalcoholic Sprite over vodka, so a source of cleverness and fun in setting terms of the marriage (befuddling the other negotiator to benefit your own side) was not available. A dispute arose over the value of butchered pork compared with a pig on the hoof, the standard of value in Laos. Because time was short and one side lacked a seasoned negotiator, songs were abbreviated and a clause excusing errors had to be added to the contract. Bride wealth was paid in cash, not the silver of tradition. While these aspects of the negotiation do not seem to accord with tradition, other new elements appeared more congruous. Faraway but significant relatives had come by air, one from Santa Ana, one from France. The contract could be typed, meaning its terms were more securely set down than the verbal contracts usual in Laos. The negotiation could be videotaped for distant relatives. Many such differences could be cited, but ultimately the meaning of the negotiation itself remained constant. The bride was honorably shifted to the care of her new husband's family, with the offer of bride wealth demonstrating the approval of the husband's elder relatives, and its acceptance signaling the approval of the bride's. The contract reinforced continuing relationships between and within the two families. The elder men of both families indicated their status in regard to the young couple, since only they could make the contract. The young people accepted the propositions that without this contract they would not be married (no other could suffice), and that with this contract no other was necessary (this one was sufficient). Despite its flaws and abbreviation, this negotiation provided an acceptable framework for reproducing and validating Hmong kinship ties.

The same appears to have been true even of the troubled negotiations over the wedding of Mee and Song described in chapter 7. Nearly all the actual circumstances of life, the topics covered in the contract, the later subjects of dispute, Mee's method of escape from her unsatisfactory situation, and the financial difficulties differed from those of life in Laos. Yet even in this conflict, vital elements of Hmong social structure were reproduced. The young couple placed themselves under the vigorous control of the older generation. Song's elder, a traditionalist, took a romantic attitude—if the children loved each other, their marriage could not fail. But Mee's father, who was working diligently toward economic security, felt quite differently. To him, poverty was hateful. His emphasis on economic progress and his despair over his daughter's poor future looks Americanized until we remember how well his new son-in-law fit the Hmong cultural model of the poor orphan who marries up, and how well he himself fit the model of the infuriated father-in-law impotent to prevent it. There are Hmong cultural models for these behaviors. The girl's model in this case is the King of Heaven's daughter, solving all the orphan's problems with her magical powers. This was where romanticism ended, when the disillusioned girl, instead of striving by her labor and generosity to improve her husband's lot, decamped. Hers was a dissonant act, which had to be reinterpreted in Hmong terms to become the result of female meddling, before the elder men could take the initiative again and a formulaic face-saving compromise could eventually be reached. Since the acts of girls "do not matter," Mee's disturbing flight could be smoothed over. As with Kia Ly's defection, the individual act of rebellion posed more hazard to Mee's place in Hmong society than to Hmong society. Such incidents were part of life in Laos, with no structural change required to accommodate them.

What happens when motivations seem to run contrary to the ideals of Hmong social life? In chapter 8, we saw Mai use the American legal system to free herself from her husband and go back to her natal family. In Laos this would have been an impossible goal, given the feebleness of her complaints compared with traditional grounds for divorce (Cooper 1984; Lemoine 1972), the primacy of the social rule that women upon marriage join their husband's clan, and men's preference not to offend other clans. Hmong strategies to resolve domestic conflict failed, as neither husband nor wife would take advice, and an anomalous strategy succeeded, as Mai's male relatives covertly helped her utilize American legal processes and

Americans who could guide her through the courts. Mai expressed the unusual wish to be more like her brother, literate and self-reliant, and she
wanted her children but not her husband. Although strongly criticized
by proper Hmong women, she retained the support of her male relatives.
Her use of outside resources was incorporated within an acceptable Hmong
strategy for unhappy wives, seeking the protection of her own clan. This
would not have sufficed if her male supporters had wanted social ties with
her husband, but he was both weak and disliked. They overlooked the conventional strategy that required urging her to return, since Mai emphasized
her propriety in other ways, giving up her desire for education, spending
her time in childcare, sewing and cooking, and placing herself under her
brother's control. If Mai had not had relatives willing to help her, if she
had pursued her nonwomanly desire for personal strength, or if she had
relied more heavily on her American friends, she might have been forced
out of Hmong society. In this configuration of mixed strategies, however,
the overriding image was of a troubled Hmong woman seeking the help of
her natal family.

In looking for the manner in which lives change, it is important to look
not only at changing goals, but also at how such goals are achieved (see
Swidler 1986 for a full exposition of the theory on which my argument is
based). Particular goals are themselves in part determined by what possible
strategies can be used to achieve them. This is apparent in Mai's efforts to
escape the threat of domestic violence and her husband's expressed contempt for her. She focused her efforts on divorce, while in Laos she might
well have had to be satisfied with oral assurances of physical safety. Her
ultimate goal—freedom from fear—remained the same, and she achieved
it in the United States by using the same strategic style she would have
used in Laos, putting herself under the protection of her male relatives.
The actual lines of action she and they constructed, however, included new
elements in the form of non-Hmong assistance and the American court system. Only because these elements could be subordinated to an overriding
Hmong strategy could they be acceptable action for a Hmong woman. For
the same reason, the range of acceptable actions for Hmong women has expanded to include divorce. Although divorce is still confined, in the eyes of
"proper" women, to "improper" women, divorced women can nonetheless
be improper *Hmong* women.

The reason divorce is improper behavior seems to be related to women
crossing over the age and gender line that assigns contracts to the sphere of
elder males. If a woman meddles with divorce to benefit her own life, this
is improper behavior because she was not one of the people making the
marriage contract. In the traditional view, the contract linked two families

of men. Family ties are strongest between related men, and women think of themselves as the glue that holds these families together. The long-range implication of divorce initiated by the wife is that the marriage contract is between husband and wife. This is the American view, assumed by American courts, but it opens a Pandora's box for Hmong social structure. Where the society itself consists of links between families, the definition of family is crucial.

Other hints of change in the definition of family are visible in the very proper wedding party described at the end of chapter 6. There were echoes of the format seen in the Chiengmingmai, Thailand, wedding party, with the older men and women eating separately, but, especially among the younger people, changes in the symbolism of marriage seemed evident. Women had a more central role, having arranged the party, and the bride stood at the door with her mother-in-law greeting guests. In Chiengmingmai, the party and its exchanges were arranged by men, who greeted the guests, while the bride stayed reticently well behind her husband and deep within the house. In Seattle, English was the language used to celebrate the formation of the couple, who danced publicly together to romantic Laoized rock tunes, whispering romantic phrases. The effect of such modernized behavior is to emphasize the presence of a couple, the basis of a nuclear family, rather than (as in Chiengmingmai) the creation of a daughter-in-law with her potential for continuing her husband's descent line.

Over time, the Hmong families I knew in America were coming to seem more like nuclear families based on married couples and less like extended families based on ties between brothers. I attribute some subtle changes to the effect of the larger American society, which had clear assumptions regarding individuals and did not assume family solidarity at any cost. Wives, even children, are expected to have opinions and individual goals in American society. Teachers, doctors, social workers, co-workers, and employers all expect individual family members to speak up, decide for themselves, and look out for their own benefit. Christianity, especially the fundamentalist Protestantism espoused by many Hmong in America, assumes individual salvation and responsibility, and the equal value of all souls. American legal process assumes that women are equal to men before the law, and in problematic cases deals with catch-hand marriage in terms of kidnap or rape.

The aspects of life in which traditional Hmong can most easily resist change are those where a tally can be kept. This is clearly visible in terms of money exchanges and control of money within the household; it is easy to see who brought home how much, who made spending decisions, and where the money went. In these areas—income, household expense, bride wealth, financial contributions to relatives' projects, expenses for future planning, travel, education—power over decisions, which was in male hands in Laos, could be guarded by men, because there was a convenient and precise measure through which the amount of control could be determined.

But other areas of life were less amenable to close accounting. What did it portend if Hmong women promoted Christianity, especially when they said it was because Christianity rejected polygyny and taught the equality of all souls? How visible was that to the men who might be jealous of their privileges? Would the men object if they recognized these reasons among other, more spiritual ones? What if women no longer sewed clothes for men, but strictly their own festival wear and commercial exchange items? If a mother signed the child's school permission slips instead of a father? If the mother, not the father, conversed with a child's doctor? If children of both sexes were outside parental control most days? If a woman successfully ignored an oral contract? If women as well as men learned the requirements of citizenship and the language of the dominant society? If a girl cried foul when a youth forced her into an unwanted marriage, and successfully avoided marriage? If wedding gifts were given directly to the young couple instead of being channeled through the bride's father? If bride wealth was sometimes not paid? If the durability of a marriage could not be foretold from the toe curl of toeless supermarket chickens? If a few Hmong girls began to marry non-Hmong, while the few divorced women forced from Hmong society did not perish? If the King County Superior Court assigned child custody on the basis of parent's closeness to the child rather than parent's social power?

All these instances are alterations in the expression of social power and the capacity to express it. Most of them are hard to calculate in terms of actual advantage—which is the point. Because they cannot be measured, they became ambiguous, ungraspable. Often they seem trivial or are even invisible to the people involved. Still, whether large or small, unavoidable or discretionary, they taught their participants something about the possibilities for action in a new environment. As these and a thousand other incidents multiply in the lives of resettled Hmong, their weight tends to lead toward more egalitarian interactions between men and women. The more nearly equal conceptualization of men and women current in the United States has entered Hmong households via such changes. Some Hmong ideas of gender are being reexpressed, and the idea of family itself has changed in ways that echo the new environment. American cultural concepts about romance, the expectation that both men and women will work and make decisions, the individuality stressed in public schools, and new ideas about how to conduct a wedding can be pointed out as influences from the new society, especially on younger Hmong.

If this viewpoint is true, Hmong might be expected to adopt new tenets of egalitarianism as part of Hmong identity and reexplain Hmong social relations in terms of gender equality. The seeds of gender equality are present in Hmong folk tales and in the concept that both men and women need each other to achieve maturity, even if they are not always expressed in Hmong social practice. From these seeds, novel lines of action might arise to fit new experiences, without Hmong having to invent wholly new and idiosyncratic personal interpretations of events, without the need to justify new behavior by stepping outside their native culture, without resorting to alien ideas. Since submissiveness was usually called for in the lives of Hmong women in Laos, this capacity was woven into the social behavior of Hmong women generally; but when assertiveness was demanded, a different, yet still appropriate, cultural model—the vigorous Hmong wife promoting her family's benefit—was available and could be taken up. The two styles of action contradict each other, but both are available within the range of models available to Hmong women.

Cultures abound in such an overrichness of possibilities, of inconsistencies and contradictions in cultural models. This provides the resiliency that may let the culture itself survive even traumatic shifts of circumstance. The way action is organized survives even as its goals or ends change to accommodate different surroundings, different needs. But perhaps it is not appropriate to be too optimistic about Hmong culture. The contested ground of control over women's lives engenders terrific bitterness and pain for first generation resettled refugees, as assumptions shift about propriety and possibility for women and men. Perhaps this can be called cultural lag.

> People do not readily take advantage of new structural opportunities which would require them to abandon established ways of life. This is not because they cling to cultural values, but because they are reluctant to abandon familiar strategies of action for which they have the cultural equipment. Because cultural expertise underlies the ability of both individuals and groups to construct effective strategies of action, such matters as the style or ethos of action and related ways of organizing authority and cooperation are enduring aspects of individual, and especially of collective, life. (Swidler 1986: 281)

Even when the values or goals of a community shift or surface behaviors change through interactions with a new environment, the basic organization of a society need not necessarily be changing. Change in this deeper sense must include alterations in cultural capacities or the symbols that give them meaning. These are what produce all the different strategies of action that are manifested in behavior. Overt actions illustrate the contact points between cultural capacities and the exterior world.

This study, based on work with mostly middle-aged refugees resettled less than eight years, found less culture change than expected. It would be very helpful to study the lives of adolescents, especially Hmong who came to the United States as quite young children, to record how they are faring in their mixed milieu. Future research on the attitudes of the next generation, particularly if undertaken by the very Hmong now growing to maturity in the American educational system, will provide a fascinating comparison for this and other studies now appearing on the Hmong.

Gender attitudes are only one area of the research into social change that could be undertaken among resettled Hmong. This study is incomplete because systemwide explanations are most likely to satisfy questions such as the ones that begin this chapter. In particular, inquiry into Hmong Christian religious ideas would be very useful in trying to understand changing Hmong ideas regarding gender, but Christianity is an area I have hardly touched. Every aspect of life partakes of the experiences and demands of every other aspect. Hmong can change their economic and educational goals, their clothing styles and household paraphernalia, parts of their vocabulary (in some households, the language itself) and still be certain they are Hmong. In the chameleon world of surface change, goals shift and strategies of action gradually accommodate to tasks rephrased in a new environment. Dissonant symbolic messages picked up from outside Hmong culture jostle against ideas taught at home, and must be reconciled. Religion may provide a major mechanism of resolution (in Keyes' phrase) in helping people struggling with change to reorder their ideas in new symbolic shapes, integrating their new lives with the old. Christian influence is a complex issue in these resolutions that needs future exploration.

NOTES

1: Discovering the Hmong

1. Directed by Renee Taylor, funded first by the Northwest Area Foundation, and then by a Seattle City Block Grant, the Indochinese Women's Project began in 1980 and ended in 1985.

2. Hmong girls, like boys, are given one or two personal names (*Mai* and *Chia* are both given names, treated as a single name like Mary Ann in English). Young married men, when their wives have produced a child or two, receive another personal name, which is granted by their wife's father. This honorific, which signifies maturity, is generally the name of an honorable antecedent in the wife's natal family. Thus in the name Nhia Doua Hang, *Hang* is the clan name, *Doua* is the child name, and *Nhia* is the honorific. The man will then be known as *Nhia Doua*. But Hmong speaking to each other or about each other especially within the family commonly use teknonymy. That is, if Nhia Doua and his wife Mee have a child Kong Meng, usually Nhia Doua will call his wife Kong Meng's mother and she will call him Kong Meng's father. This is an affectionate way of speaking. Teknonymy replaces names most of the time in ordinary conversation. Nhia Doua's mother, for instance, might well call her daughter-in-law Kong Meng's mother, Nhia Doua's wife, or daughter-in-law, depending on what aspect of the relationship she wanted to invoke, but she would not generally use Mee. Since relational terms replace names in domestic settings, as time passes mothers' personal names are rarely spoken; my subjects often did not know their grandmothers' names. Men's names are more often used and remembered because they are important for figuring descent, and in formal or political settings.

3. A section of the Seattle City Department of Human Resources, the P-Patch program began in 1973, and provides garden sites in twenty-two locations within Seattle. Each garden site is divided into plots which are rented to individuals for the cost of services. The program, which provides no-cost plots to needy families, did not charge any of the refugee families I signed up in 1981.

4. The following analysis owes a great deal to the ideas of Collier and Yanagisako (1987) and Swidler (1986).

5. However, no society is fully consistent in its ideas. Actions sometimes contradict explicit statements about gender; various statements may contradict one another; actions can be inconsistent. A society's resilience, hence its ability to sur-

193

vive, depends on having a variety of different models that can be brought into play when necessary. This is equally true of individuals and families. Finding inconsistencies in behavior does not necessarily mean finding social or cultural change, as I was to discover.

6. This research was assisted by a grant from the Indochina Studies Program of the Joint Committee for Southeast Asia of the Social Science Research Council (SSRC) and the American Council of Learned Societies, with funds provided by the National Endowment for the Humanities, the Ford Foundation and the Henry Luce Foundation. The project, entitled "Research on Hmong Women" (1984–85), was my collaborative effort with Jane Mallinson, Ly Hang, and Corinne Collins-Yager.

7. The Indochinese Farm Project (IFP), a bootstraps operation that strives to train Hmong and Mien farmers in growing and selling market produce in the climatic and economic environment of the Pacific Northwest, is the most underfunded and the most durable of all the various projects that have tried to set up Southeast Asian tribal people as commercial farmers in America. Not without many problems and miscommunications, the farmers and the IFP have persisted together. Its spin-off, the Indochinese Farmers' Association, is a successful Hmong/Mien farmers' marketing cooperative.

8. The King County Refugee Forum, formed before 1980, consists of representatives of agencies and volunteer organizations striving to assist refugees. This large and effective body struggles to coordinate helping efforts, resolve interorganizational conflicts, announce the availability of public or private funding, and encourage accountability among all its members. As refugees themselves began to form organizations, they were invited to join the forum, but soon split off to form the Refugee Square Table, composed of representatives of refugee mutual assistance associations.

9. The collection included some one hundred fifty waxed batik samples, a number of batiked skirts, and taped interviews on technique, the transmission of knowledge, the stories contained in the patterns, and the uses of the batik-decorated textiles in Laos, especially as skirts, and their importance in costume. Interviews were done with herbal healers and forty-six samples of medicinal plants were collected in the United States and in Ban Vinai refugee camp, which are now deposited in the University of Washington Botany Department's herbarium. The Linnaean classification of most of these has been identified by botanists either at the University of Washington or at Harvard (where the samples were sent in 1988 for this purpose). We shipped SSRC copies of 130 one-and-a-half-hour cassette tapes, copies of the batik patterns, some photographs and slides, and verbatim transcriptions of the English portions of the tapes. These will be available to other researchers through the Smithsonian Institution, where they are permanently housed. Other products

of the research to date are: Donnelly 1989a; Mallinson 1985; Mallinson, Donnelly, and Hang 1988; and Xiong and Donnelly 1986.

2: Hmong Society in Laos

1. Also called the Vietnam War, which in Laos ended in 1973 with the formation of a coalition government. That government fell in a bloodless coup in May 1975, and then the Hmong began to leave.

2. In this description of Hmong life in Laos, I concentrate on practical day-to-day matters and on gender conceptions because my subjects concentrated on these in telling me about their lives. Two of my subjects had been shamans in Laos, but I did not feel I had learned enough about cosmology or shamanism to make any definitive statements about how it had redefined their lives. Two books are essential for an account of the Hmong religion and how it affected their conduct of their lives: Chindarsi 1976 and Tapp 1988.

3. Cousin, the term Mrs. Ly uses, appears frequently in statements about kinship. It is the English word that best translates the kin terms npawq and muam npawq (grandfather's brother/sister's daughter's son/daughter, father's sister's son/daughter, or mother's brother/sister's son/daughter). It is not used for father's brother's son or daughter, who would be called kwv or tij laug (older or younger brother), and muam (sister), which are the terms for one's own brother or sister. The important thing is that the children of one's own father and one's father's brothers are all called brother and sister, and same-generation relatives through other links are called by a term signifying greater distance, translated cousin. These are terms men use.

Grandmother's brother's or sister's daughter's sons or daughters are not considered related to oneself, and therefore no special kinship term for this relationship exists. People who would fit this category, if it were a category, may be related in some other way that has a term, however.

Women's kin terminology is different and slightly less differentiated. Women call their sisters viv ncaus and their brothers txiv hluas and nus (older or younger brother). These would be the children of one's own father or one's father's brothers. Women use the term yaum dab for the relationship men call npawg; the relationship men call muam npaws they call viv ncaus. Thus the term viv ncaus has a wide application, since any woman related by descent (terms for in-marrying women are different) is called viv ncaus, sister. (See Heimbach 1979, Ruey 1958.)

The word cousin, besides having this application to relatives at middle distance from the speaker, has other uses, as a catch-all term for any distant, supposed, or fictive patrilateral tie, and can be used up and down the generations. Cousin can also be used when you cannot, or would rather not, specify the exact tie, but want a kin-based relationship. Without a kin tie there is no strong basis for any relationship.

In 1987, I watched an older White Hmong woman married to a Thai and living on the East Coast and a Blue Hmong man from a different political faction who had left Laos quite young, who had never met before, struggle to find a kinship tie, comparing their family trees and places of residence in Laos until they found a tenuous thread of kinship through female cousins who had married the cousins of other cousins (I never really got it straight), whereupon, delighted and relieved, they sat down to socialize at a picnic. That incident epitomized to me the usefulness of cousins.

4. To maintain the purity of this Christian Hmong girl.

5. Quotes that are not attributed come from tape-recorded interviews with an informant, edited by me into narrative form, and later corrected and approved by the speaker for her life history. I have omitted the names in some cases to maintain the speaker's privacy.

6. I think she means "twelve or thirteen."

7. Her grandfather's first wife and second wife, whom she also calls her father's mother and second mother. In the same way, Va's grandmother, Nyia Yi and Tse Ling's mother, and Nyia Yi's wife's mother-in-law are the same person. Her second grandmother, who had to cook, was a young woman who had married an older man and produced several children, all of whom, except the last daughter, had died before the death of her husband, the narrator's grandfather. This left the young widow without enough children to support her in her old age, yet unable to produce more. She soon married a new husband, therefore, and moved away; she had to leave her small daughter behind because of the social rule that the girl belonged to her father's family.

8. For instance, one of my informants was the child of a second wife. The first wife, being sterile, had suggested a second marriage to her husband, and then was "given" the first offspring (my informant) to raise as her own.

9. I had gotten, from reading ethnographies of Hmong, particularly in China, but also in Southeast Asia, the idea that polygynous wives usually accepted one another and cooperated extensively in domestic work, but I quickly learned from my women friends that polygynous family dynamics were emphatically not like this. First wives commonly hated it when their husbands took second wives, but there was nothing they could do. Women (according to the women) had to do what they were told, but men did what they wanted. The only exception to this rule was when the second wife improved the life of the first wife, as in the case of Chao's foster mother, a sterile wife who encouraged her husband to take a second wife for the sake of producing children. Because Christianity frowns on polygyny, conversion was attractive to a number of my women friends.

10. There was nothing foul about sucking this blood, Ntxai Vue said, because

she was in trance at the time. It wasn't she who did it, but rather her spirit helper who occupied her body during the trance. My Christian translator later confessed to being quite shocked by this account. I asked Ntxai Vue if she still entered trances, but she had also joined the Christian Missionary Alliance church by then and given up shamanship.

11. Regarding "The Woodcutter, His Rooster and His Wife," this message was not explicit enough for the translators of Johnson's volume. They add: "In real life, Hmong men in general believe that men are smarter than women, apart from a few rare cases. Traditionally, a Hmong woman defers to her husband's opinion, initiative and authority, at home and especially in public. While a Hmong woman has the right to discuss with her husband such grave issues as whether the family will move, and where, or which marriage partner they will choose for a son or daughter, she usually does not enter into discussions when a group of men are present. This is not her role. Her job is housework and child care, and she will generally not come into the room and speak up in family and clan discussions 'unless her work is all finished.' . . . Hmong women are not accustomed to going to meetings to discuss and resolve problems. They tend to feel timid and ashamed to assert themselves in public" (Johnson 1985: 264–65).

12. The daughter of an elite military family who spent her time in school. I talk about her in chapter 5.

13. As refugees, White Hmong women have taken to the elaborate and expensive Blue Hmong skirts. Skirts have become less useful political indicators, and instead have picked up other meanings that will be discussed later in the chapter.

14. I am not going to discuss needlework technique per se. The technology of spinning has been partially described by Lemoine (1972: 118–24), and clear scenes of textile processes such as spinning and weaving can be seen in the film *Miao Year* (Geddes [1967] 1971). Techniques of batik dyeing and detailed information about the Hmong process of creating and waxing batik patterns can be found in Mallinson, Donnelly, and Hang (1988). Pang Xiong Sirirathasuk and Sally Peterson have documented traditional techniques and needlework skills needed to create White Hmong appliqué and embroidery designs (Peterson 1989).

Pattern elements carry names, like "mountain," "pumpkin seed," "elephant foot," and "stone flower," that derive from the shape of the pattern. In Xieng Khouang province, stone flowers stood for good luck ("may you have good luck until the stones sprout flowers"), but I have not heard of any system of symbols linking design fragments together or creating oppositions between them. Individual women may attach particular stories to particular patterns. One of Mallinson's informants said that in Laos, as she waxed her skirt panels and baby carriers, she told herself stories. The shell elements represented babies and the circle elements represented parents. But these personal fantasies did not refer to shared cultural symbols; Mallinson thinks there are no shared symbolic meanings for pattern elements; Vang and Lewis, in a project to record cultural meaning, come to the same conclusion (1984:128). Peterson has decided that intellectual pleasure in the process of pattern construction motivates Hmong needleworkers (Peterson 1989). It could be that an extensive set of symbolic meanings for the building blocks would interfere with the free construction of patterns, and so such meanings have not developed.

Pattern names show a slightly more developed set of notions. Mallinson found "old lady pattern," "short cut," "baby-carrier pattern," and "grandmother's pattern," as well as many descriptive titles, such as "coins and shells," "open connecting links," "small horn pattern," and "bells ring in a circle." The first pattern taught to girls learning batik was usually the "divorce" pattern, an ironic title for a pattern intended for a courting skirt. The story was that a woman wanted to get divorced, but she was in the middle of waxing her skirt panel. She knew she could not leave her husband until she had finished, so she invented this particular pattern, the easiest and fastest of all. This tale may be supposed to reduce girls' anxieties regarding courtship, by making marriage seem less permanent. Seen in this light, it links with girls' conventional inability to make up their minds whom to marry, and recalls one suitor's promise of divorce if the bride didn't like him. As we will see, however, divorce was all but impossible for Hmong women in Southeast Asia. So we find that the story of the "divorce" pattern is consistent with a group of ironic messages surrounding marriage.

15. This habit of abbreviation contributed to confusion in the spectacular controversy over so-called yellow rain. In 1981, the U.S. government accused the Soviet government of having used chemical weapons in Laos and Cambodia. Hmong refugees were interviewed about effects of yellow rain and told lurid tales of poisoning and death. But researchers questioned the adequacy of these interviews. Doubt arose on several grounds, including linguistic: "Another major problem is separating events actually witnessed from hearsay information. It has been noticed that Hmong tend to use the first-person when reporting both types of accounts" (Crossland et al. 1984: 9). Yellow rain was later demonstrated to consist of pollen overloads shed by flying bees, not chemical weapons at all. The Reagan government's accusations came to be seen as part of its view of the USSR as an "evil empire." Hmong interviewees, though some undoubtedly believed they had suffered from chemical warfare, may also have been motivated by hope for early resettlement or an improvement in their political or legal position in refugee camps. Thorough reviews of the yellow rain controversy appear in Ember 1984 and Seeley et al. 1985.

3: Changing Times

1. William Smalley, however, noting that the missionaries had had only very short contact with the converts, and did not know the language, suggests a miracle (Smalley 1956: 47).

2. The political history of that war as it affected the Hmong has been expounded by authors of varying quality and attitude (a good, brief summary can be found in Dunnigan [1986]). For an extended account of Hmong political and military events from the Hmong point of view, see in particular Larteguy (1979), whose principal informant was Dr. Yang Dao. A very different account of Hmong motives can be found in McCoy (1970; see also Schanche 1970).

3. Jitney bus. Long Tieng and Sam Thong are separated by a mountainous area.

4. She was taught to pray with her eyes shut, but in this case she was searching relentlessly for food.

5. I found this account deeply distressing, partly because I could not believe soldiers would bother with the infants as described. Children in wartime perish from all sorts of deprivations and illnesses, particularly cholera and other waterborne diseases, but she was attributing all childrens' deaths to the soldiers' malevolence. It seemed to me that the fears and hatreds experienced during the war had persisted in the memory of this family living safely at last in California. Hunger, terror, a fierce desire to protect her children, and a conflict (described below) with her nephew over how to quiet her dangerously noisy infant seemed to have produced in this unfortunate mother and daughter a hysterical paranoia that had shaped their perceptions and continued to color all their memories.

6. Almost two hundred dollars.

7. Smalley, in a very interesting article based on the lives of the former residents of Moos Nplais now living in Minnesota, proposes six stages of Southeast Asia experience for the Hmong who eventually resettled in the United States. They are: 1. Laos penetration stage; 2. Laos traditional stage; 3. Laos adaptive stage; 4. Laos resettlement stage; 5. Thailand camp stage; 6. U.S. resettlement stage. See Smalley 1986. For another account of a Hmong family's wartime and resettlement experience, see X. Xiong n.d. [1985].

4: The Hmong in Seattle

1. Recorded 29 June 1984, in the Ethnomusicology Department of the School of Music at the University of Washington. She sang four songs. The tapes were translated orally on tape two separate times by different Hmong translators. Laura Keisker transcribed the translations into typed form. I then correlated the two transcripts and produced written poems.

2. The Seattle-Tacoma Statistical Area, which includes three counties, had a population of just over two million people.

3. Only 11 percent of Chinese families fell below the poverty line, and 3.3 percent of Filipino families. This data is from 1980 U.S. Census, unpublished data tapes run at the University of Washington Academic Computer Center.

4. Other than Vietnamese.

5. Bureau of the Census, *Census of Population Subject Reports: Asian and Pacific Islander Population in the United States: 1980* (Washington, D.C.: U.S. Department of Commerce publication PC80–2–1E) vol. 2, sec. 1, says: "The data are estimates of the actual figures that would have resulted from a complete count. The basic sampling unit for the 1980 census was the housing unit, including all occupants. . . . Approximately 19 percent of the Nation's housing units were included in the census sample" (1988: iii). The census was conducted prior to 1 April 1980.

6. Some married girls under fifteen, for instance, might not have been in school.

7. *Qeej*, pronounced "geng" with a falling tone, is a musical instrument. The player blows into a tube that carries his (never her) breath into a chamber held at arm's length. Through the chamber at right angles to the airflow pass bamboo pipes with resonating reeds similar to harmonica reeds. These pipes vary in length, producing different notes, and the chamber has finger holes that let the player influence how much air each pipe receives. The pipes are often three or four feet long, and the player may dance with the *qeej*, scooping the pipes back and forth in circular patterns, even leaping into the air or rolling on his back to demonstrate his acrobatic musical prowess. The *qeej* is also used very solemnly, in funeral and ritual.

8. Rumbaut and Weeks found that in 1983, Hmong women living in San Diego who were past childbearing had an average of 8.63 children; women twenty to twenty-four already had an average of 2.5 children. No Hmong girl over fourteen remained unmarried. They projected an uncorrected total fertility rate of 11.9 children, commenting that the Hmong seemed to be about as fertile as the Hutterites, the world's most fertile group (1986: 445–46).

9. The bitterness with which Hmong at the second Hmong Research Conference (Minneapolis, November 1983) attacked Cooper's observation that some men make a good thing of the *yao jua* (father-in-law/son-in-law) relationship (Cooper 1979) demonstrates how disfavored and thus covert it must be.

10. Only twenty-two Hmong lived outside families. Family size and household size were nearly identical (5.82 and 5.86), so in the text I use these terms interchangeably.

11. That is, 529 men worked at all, and 131 men worked all year.

12. Later it turned out Xee had lost husband and children during flight and, terrified of growing old without children to take care of her, had begun reconstituting her family regardless of marital status.

13. My interpretations of her behavior.

14. There were also absurd events, as for instance when a newly arrived family looked on in silent confusion while a man walked right into their unlocked apartment as they were watching television, unplugged the set and walked out with it. They thought there must be some reason he was supposed to do that.

15. It was also difficult for nonliterate people to open bank accounts.

16. A recent article on Hmong responses to social stress reports that Hmong almost never turn to their sponsors for help (Hirayama and Hirayama 1988: 101). This was not at all the case in Seattle before 1986, which raises questions about the methodology of that study, in which twenty-five male household heads in Tennessee were asked to speak for their entire families about events as long as two years previous to the research; observational techniques were not used for data collection.

17. This quote is approximate, not verbatim.

18. In Hmong levirate marriage, a widow marries her husband's younger brother. If he is already married she becomes a second wife. The term comes from Latin *levir* (husband's brother); numerous societies have practiced levirate marriages, for instance the ancient Hebrews. The levirate is rooted in the need to define a social place for widows. In strongly patrilineal tribal societies, children belong to their father's family. If a widow remarried outside his family, she would lose her children. Different resettlement countries take different stands regarding the levirate. France admits preexisting levirate families but prohibits new levirate marriages; the United States requires a husband to discard a levirate wife before immigrating, causing much anguish, or perhaps preventing families from coming. However, social beliefs are not discarded easily, and informal levirate marriages persist. Since the levirate is not legally recognized in the United States, second wives must represent themselves as independent heads of household, sisters, or some other acceptable category.

19. The same scenario was enacted in September 1988, when the eighteen-month benefits were cut to twelve months, this time with only two weeks' notice and no effective public protest.

20. For an interesting parallel, see Tapp 1988: 207. A Hmong mother in Thailand describes her offspring as five sons, five sons-in-law, and five dead; Tapp comments that her daughters count only as providers of sons-in-law.

21. The problem of describing refugee populations has vexed other researchers, partly because refugees are not fixed in place after arrival; they move around. Yu and Liu, for instance, had trouble finding Vietnamese for survey research: "Faced with the challenge of obtaining a current roster of Vietnamese surnames, we finally resorted to a public source available in California: a special street directory published every six months by the Pacific Telephone Company. . . . To our dismay, approximately 60 percent of the Vietnamese we tried to contact in this way had already moved elsewhere. We soon discovered that it was not unusual for many Vietnamese refugees to move six times in seven months, especially unattached individuals. . . . Some refugees would move across the street if only to save ten dollars a month in rent. Others would move to another district and pay more for rent, just to live close to a countryman they liked. Still others would move without leaving any forwarding address. . . . In the end, we had no choice but to use as survey respondents the remaining 40 percent of the population listed in the telephone company's street address" (Yu and Liu 1986: 491).

22. The Seattle School District, Office of Student Information Systems, provided me with cross-tabulations of home language with census tract of residence for 30 Asian languages and 121 census tracts for a nine-year period, 1980–88. The languages are: Chinese, Cantonese, Mandarin, Tibetan, Taiwanese, Fukienese, Pilipino, Tagalog, Ilokano, Sebuano, Korean, Japanese, Samoan, Fijian, East Indian, Bengali, Hindi, Malayalam, Panjabi, Urdu, Malay, Indonesian, Thai, Burmese, Vietnamese, Cambodian, Laotian, Mien, and Hmong. The language names follow the choices of the children or parents filling in the form.

23. For the Hmong students I have students' addresses, and therefore can identify number of students per household. Sometimes children gave the same address, even the same apartment number, but different telephone numbers. In this case I considered that they probably lived in different households but wanted to get mail at the address given.

24. For a contrary Hmong experience with allopathic practitioners, see *Peace Has Not Been Made*, a video about a disastrous medical misunderstanding in Providence, Rhode Island (Finck and Yang 1984).

25. Like other kinds of migrants, Hmong elders seem to be losing this struggle, at least in Seattle. Perhaps a Saturday school, such as Chinese and Latvians among others maintain, is essential for language survival.

5: Selling Hmong Textiles

1. At the time this split occurred, I thought that events would fit one of two models, Bar-Yosef's model of rematuration (1968), or the straight patron-client model following Paine (1971) and others. Bar-Yosef describes a process that she calls *dem
aturation* undergone by immigrants (some of them refugees) to Israel; immigrants floundered for a time in their new setting because they had lost the underpinnings of their former identity—their jobs, material possessions, and familiar round of daily activities. In Bar-Yosef's view, the Israeli bureaucracy assumed a parental role, while the immigrants perforce occupied the status of children until they could remature by one means or another. In becoming capable, immigrants threw off, in what Bar-Yosef terms a "coping mechanism" (27), the parent-child relation that they had accepted in order to survive. As I tried to fit this explanation to the events of the split, though, I found that I could explain events more straightforwardly by referring to concepts from the literature on patron-client relations.

2. An earlier version of this section, published as Donnelly 1986, was based on a presentation I gave at the Second Hmong Research Conference, held at the University of Minnesota in November 1983.

3. The Indochinese Farmers' Association (IFA), the marketing arm of the Indochinese Farm project (of which I was a board member), had a similar problem. Most farmers understated their retail sales to avoid the IFA markup of 20 percent.

Since wholesale sales to supermarkets and restaurants generated enough markup to support IFA, the board avoided this issue by simply turning all retail sales over to individual farmers. But without wholesale sales, such a course was not open to HAA.

4. At the end of 1983, the highest seller had earned over $4,300, the lowest earner around $68.

5. *Muam npaws* (classificatory sister) signifies a woman who is not a sister in the sense that she has the same father and mother as a man (in this case the daughter's husband), but whom he calls "sister" in kin terminology. See also note 3, chapter 2.

6. I had seen something like this at work in other situations, for instance with my friend Ker (not a seller of needlework). Often in my long friendship with her I would suggest she do something to benefit herself, but she would find multiple (and inadequate) reasons why she could not do it. Even if I answered every objection, and even if she apparently sincerely wanted to do whatever it was, she would not until I *told* her to do it. Then with every appearance of gratitude she would go right ahead. It was as if she could not initiate an action to benefit herself, but only to benefit others; action to benefit herself had to be initiated by someone else. This habit perhaps operated as a tactic of social cohesion. It is also strongly related to the patronage structures of AN, and fits with my conclusion that HAA was also a patron-client organization.

7. *Ginkoes* are stylized flowers strung together with plastic beads and baubles to make bright little pieces that can dangle from rearview mirrors or Christmas trees. The term comes from *nkiib nkos* (sp?), which were used as good-luck gifts in Laos.

8. Impact Aid, of which the Lao Highland Initiative was a part, was initiated by the Office of Refugee Resettlement as a stopgap measure of support after the thirty-six months of resettlement aid were cut to eighteen months.

9. About the resulting project, Yang et al (1985: 76) says: "The Seattle project sought to create a cooperative sewing project to subcontract with clothing manufacturers. The work to be done consisted of mainstream garment manufacture, not *pa ndau*. The Seattle project provided training in power sewing to women from each of four Highland Lao ethnic groups. The women found the training process a difficult one. Most of the women had little background for the work; insufficient time was allocated to the training; there were not enough machines; and the training had to be conducted in four languages. The notion of a manufacturing cooperative was new to all concerned, and the project did not materialize."

10. This men's organization included Lao Theung and Mien members, but was principally Hmong. Although it had begun as a Hmong group, Kue Koua argued that the membership should be expanded when it became clear that federal Impact Aid projects such as the Lao Highland Initiative would favor the more inclusive groups.

11. These points are mutually contradictory on their face, but his stance is con-

sistent if we recognize that his goal is to retain status by retaining both money and membership.

12. That is, they forgive her a little bit, make a face-saving gesture. This, it seems, would have been done in Laos. It fits within Turner's paradigm of conflict, as an offer of reincorporation.

13. "That's important, isn't it?" I said to Ker, Chou Neng's wife, "Yes, Hmong never steal," she answered. This indeed is an identity marker for first-generation refugees, a strong point of ethnic pride, for Hmong in America nearly always find themselves living in high-crime neighborhoods and have been subjected to repeated robberies. Thus this charge against Chee Her is extremely serious.

14. One extra indication of how clearly everyone in the Hmong community saw HAA as Vang My's private operation was that she herself had no reluctance to take money from the till for food. Throughout the entire quarrel about Chee Her taking money, no one ever said that Vang My should not do so.

15. In refugee camps, where time hangs heavy and few men work, an occasional Hmong man engages in needlework production. Their specialty is generally king-sized bedspreads with political stories of the Hmong experience of war and flight. Sometimes they draw the images which then are stitched by women; sometimes they sew, too. I have also seen men working on smaller pieces in camp.

6: Courtship and Elopement

1. No similar scenario is described by those who have written about the Hmong (that is, Miao) in China. Clarke (1911), Mickey (1947), de Beauclair (1974), and Lin (1941; translating materials from the twelfth to midnineteenth centuries) describe spring (not harvest) festivals at which young people meet and keep company, but no ball game is mentioned; instead, the boys play the "kreng" (qeej) and the girls ring bells. Graham (1978), in his collection of stories and songs for every ritual event or life change, has no songs for New Year's games played by eligible young people. Norma Diamond, who has done field work among Miao in Yunnan, has not seen ball games played by contemporary Miao (conversation, April 1987). Perhaps the game used to be played in China and then passed out of use after Hmong migrated to Southeast Asia, but it is just as likely that it was invented by Hmong once they were living there.

2. I am indebted to Dr. Timothy Dunnigan for pointing out this "secret language" to me.

3. See the note on Hmong orthography.

4. Lemoine (1972) mentions a pariah group of Hmong who married each other for ritual reasons, but who were so ostracized they gave it up.

5. Owing to intrusions of French, Lao, and American values linked with cash

income and military control, the well-known political egalitarianism of the Hmong was gradually changing. Still, I think growing differences of wealth, power, and education among Hmong families had not yet hardened into a class structure by the time the war ended.

6. The great elaboration of funeral ritual, on the other hand, is used to differentiate clans and extended families one from another.

7. To avoid a catch-hand marriage.

8. This statement, being the first request for the girl, reserves her for him and prevents anybody else entering into negotiations for her.

9. Her uncle, as village head, would be the local leader of her clan and therefore responsible for her wedding negotiations, since she was an orphan.

10. An irrefutable sign of having made an arrangement to marry was possessing a token, such as a piece of clothing, belonging to the other party. These suggestions from the wife of Pao are ridiculous and comically risqué—a young girl could never do any of these things.

11. After the negotiations between families have been settled, a party seals the contract.

12. An odd number of men is required so that when she joins them there will be an even number.

13. "A species of small wild bird similar to the quail" (Heimbach 1979: 426).

14. Crossing the threshold marks the moment that the marriage becomes irrevocable. Until then, in theory she can go back to her parents' home.

15. I thought there was probably some embellishment of detail in her tale, but I confirmed it (as above) twice at intervals separated by over two years, the second time in the context of checking her draft life history for errors, about which she appeared quite serious (April 1987). Thus even if she were embellishing, her ambiguous and bidirectional behavior survives as the heart of the story. Within her social space, moving in two directions at once was as close as possible to a straight line.

16. Since I am old enough to be their parent.

17. I am sure there are many individual exceptions to this generalization.

18. *Kwv tij*: group of brothers, including siblings and patrilineal first cousins. The term is a combination of *kwv* (older) and *tij* (younger) and is similar to a woman's term for her female relatives of the same generation (*viv ncanj*). See also chapter 5, note 5.

7: Wedding Negotiation and Ceremonies

1. Dunnigan and Vang's (1980) spelling, not in Heimbach (1979).

2. In Dunnigan's excellent and detailed account of a White Hmong marriage

negotiation in Minnesota (Dunnigan and Vang 1980), the negotiating teams also included a negotiator's assistant (*thiaj com*); this role was not pointed out to me in the event I am describing. Dunnigan's concern with rituals of language includes reproducing the negotiators' poetic paraphrases in rhyming verse, used to avoid an appearance of bluntness in these delicate negotiations. Each side politely declines to control the terms of the contract, humbly pointing out their own unworthiness and offering control to the other side, carefully permitting the other side to retreat if for some reason the contract should seem unappealing. In these verses, poetic language overlays exchange with a deep layer of romance. My account provides only paraphrases of this poetic language, so Dunnigan's article is an important enrichment.

3. All statements are translations from the Hmong by Doua Hang or Koua Hang.

4. In this negotiation the symbolic seventy-five cents was all the negotiators received. According to Dunnigan's account negotiators in the Twin Cities were receiving about twenty dollars (Dunnigan 1980: 43). In both cases, the amount is basically symbolic of the gratitude owed to the negotiators by the families. For this negotiation, I was asked not to reveal the amount of the bride wealth.

5. Later Cher Koua sang this song again for Jane and me. Yee Hang renders it thus in written Hmong:

1. Ib siv yig tuaj lag mej kev txwj los kev laug,
    zoo le kws yog lawg yog peb lawg laag lig yaug wb lub moog lawg rooj tshoob,
      kua txhaj taab kaum mej kev txwj yuag kev laug kev zej yuag kev zog naj ib
        nub qoob,
    ib yuj vi yuag tub los tsheej yuag mej puas los zeej yuag,
    ua tsaug yuag mej puab quas laug.
      Vi lawg laag lig yaug ib lub rooj kug,
        txha taab kaum mej kev txwj yuag kev laug kev zej nrug kev zog lawg naj ib
          nub moog
      yuav mej kev txwj yuag mej kev zej yuag kev zog.

2. Zoo le kws yog lawg vim laug laag lig yaug wb lub moog lawg rooj tshoob,
      txha taab kaum mej kev txwj yuag kev laug naj ib nub qoob,
    tshai ha rua mej rug tau paub,
    muaj nub dleg dlwg lis dlo tsis sis ntsib ces,
      zoov hlaav zoov quas xab tsis sis cuag ces mej paaj tsoob yuag kev kug tsis ncig lis
        yeev tuaj
    txug peb tej ntug zej,
    cev peb tsis muaj leej tub nrug lawg mej to ntsej,
    yuag mej kev txwj yuag kev laug kev zej nrug kev zog.

Ntsai muaj nub zoov hlaav lis xab tsis sis ntsib dlej dlwg lis dlo,

tsis si cuag ces,

mej lawm paaj tshoob yuag kev kug tsis cig yeev tuaj txug peb tej nutg zog,

ces peb tsis muaj lawg leej tub dug lawg mej to dog yuag,

mej kev txwu yuag kev laug kev zej dug kev zog.

3.   Zoo le kws tshai muaj nub dlej txawj dlwg ces clej clwg lis dlo yuav sib ntsib,

zoov txawj hlaav ces zoov hlaav li xab yuav sib cuag,

ces mej paaj tshoob yuag kev kug ncig lis yeev tuaj txug peb tej ntug zej,

kus ntsai peb tsis muaj leej tub nrug mej to dog los,

peb yuav muaj lawm leej tub nrug lawg mej to ntsej,

yuag maj kev txwj yuag kev laug,

kev zej dug kev zog.

>   Ntsai juaj nub ces zoov txawj hlaav zoov hlaav lis xab tuaj sib ntsiv dley
>   txawj dlwg
>
>   dlej dlwg lis dlo tuaj sis cuag ces.
>
>   Peb mej paaj tshoob yuag kev kug ncig lis yeev tuaj txug peb tej ntug
>   zog ces.
>
>   Peb tsis muaj leej tub nrug mej to ntsej los ntsai peb yuav muaj lawm leej
>   tub dug
>
>   lawm mej to dog nua lag,
>
>   yuj vis los tub los tsheej yuag mej puas los zeej yuag.
>
>   Ua tsaug yuag mej puab nquas laug. . . .

According to Doua Hang, the meaning of the song is: "We are having a negotiation today, and many of you have lost job time today during the time of negotiations, because you came to the negotiations, so you could not go to work. So thank you for your time to come. Someday, if any of you who are helping us this time, if you have a son who marries some other girl in our village, I would like to come to the negotiations and help you the same as you have helped me this time, unless you marry into another village so far from my home I would not be able to do it."

6. She is speaking about life in America.

7. During a visit arranged by Professor Marjorie Muecke as part of the Thailand-Indonesia Study Tour in Primary Health Care.

8. Most houses were built directly on the ground, with uneven dirt floors.

8: Domestic Conflict

1. The fact of increased divorce in the American context, however, is likely to produce accommodations over time that may help to integrate divorced women

into Hmong communities. Compare the situation of the divorced woman in chapter 4 with the case in this chapter. Note also the assumption by the Americanizing Hmong woman quoted in chapter 5 of increasingly frequent divorce.

2. See Cooper (1984: 141, 141n) for a discussion of Hmong divorce in Thailand. He maintains that divorces are initiated by women much more frequently than they are obtained, noting Bernatzik's earlier statement (1970: 147) that divorce must be initiated by the husband, and only for a wife's adultery. He presents initiation of divorce as one of women's tactics to reform a husband's bad behavior. Actual divorce, he says, is rare.

REFERENCES CITED

Bar-Yosef, Rivka. 1968. Desocialization and Resocialization: The Adjustment Process of Immigrants. *International Migration Review* 2(3):27–43.

Barney, George L. 1957. *Christianity: Innovation in Meo Culture. A Case Study in Missionization.* Master's thesis presented to the Department of Anthropology, University of Minnesota.

————. 1970. The Meo of Xieng Khouang Province, Laos. In *Laos: War and Revolution,* edited by Nina Adams and Alfred McCoy, 271–94. New York: Harper Colophon Books.

de Beauclair, Inez. 1974 [1972]. *Tribal Cultures of Southwest China.* Asian Folklore and Social Life Monographs, vol. 2, edited by Lou Tsu-K'uang. Taipei: Orient Cultural Service.

Bernatzik, Hugo. 1970. *Akha and Miao: Problems of Applied Ethnography in Farther India,* translated by Alois Nagler. New Haven: Human Relations Area Files. (Reprint of *Akha und Meau,* Innesbruk, 1947.)

Bourdieu, Pierre. 1977. *Outline of a Theory of Practice.* Cambridge: Cambridge University Press.

Bureau of the Census. 1981. *1980 Census of Population: Volume 1, Chapter C, General Social and Economic Characteristics (Part 49, Washington).* PC80–1–C49. Washington, D.C.: U.S. Department of Commerce.

————. 1988. *Census of Population Subject Reports: Asian and Pacific Islander Population in the United States: 1980.* PC80–2–1E, vol. 2, sect. 1. Washington, D.C.: U.S. Department of Commerce.

————. 1991. *1980 Census of Population: Profile 7, Race.* Washington, D.C.: U.S. Department of Commerce.

Cain, Mead. 1984. *Women's Status and Fertility in Developing Countries: Son Preference and Economic Security.* World Bank Staff Working Paper 682, Population and Development Series 7. Washington, D.C.: The World Bank.

Caplan, Nathan, John K. Whitmore, and Quang L. Bui. 1985. *Southeast Asian Refugee Self-Sufficiency Study: Final Report.* Washington, D.C.: Office of Refugee Resettlement, U.S. Department of Health and Human Services.

Catlin, Amy. n.d. [1981]. *Music of the Hmong: Singing Voices and Talking Reeds.* Providence, R.I.: Museum of Natural History.

Cerquone, Joseph. 1986. *Refugees from Laos: In Harm's Way.* Washington, D.C.:

U.S. Committee for Refugees Issue Paper, American Council for Nationalities Service.

Chindarsi, Nusit. 1976. *The Religion of the Hmong Njua.* Bangkok: The Siam Society.

Clarke, Samuel R. 1911. *Among the Tribes of South-West China.* Shanghai: China Inland Mission. Reprint, London: Morgan and Scott.

Collier, Jane Fishburne. 1988. *Marriage and Inequality in Classless Societies.* Stanford: Stanford University Press.

Collier, Jane F., and Sylvia Yanagisako, eds. 1987. *Gender and Kinship: Essays Toward a Unified Analysis.* Stanford: Stanford University Press.

Conquergood, Dwight. 1985. *I Am a Shaman: A Life History of Paja Thao, a Hmong Healer.* Pamphlet, collection of author.

Cooper, Robert. 1979. The Yao Jua Relationship: Patterns of Affinal Alliance and Residence Among the Hmong of Northern Thailand. *Ethnology* 18(2):173–82.

———. 1984. *Resource Scarcity and the Hmong Response.* Singapore: Singapore University Press.

Crossland, Andrea, Douglas Hulcher, and Richard Harruff. 1984. Preliminary Report of Questionnaire Evaluation of Hmong Accounts of Possible Chemical Warfare Activity in Laos. Unpublished manuscript, 20 pages.

Dab Neeb. 1974. Vientiane: n.p. Collection of University of Michigan Library.

Defense Mapping Agency Aerospace Center. 1979. Tactical Pilotage Chart TPC J-11D: Laos, Thailand, Vietnam. St. Louis, Mo.: St. Louis Air Force Station.

Diamond, Norma. 1988. The Maio and Poison: Interactions on China's Frontier. *Ethnology* 7:1–26.

Donnelly, Nancy D. 1986. Factors Contributing to a Split Within a Clientelistic Needlework Cooperative. In *The Hmong in Transition,* edited by Glen L. Hendricks, Bruce T. Downing, and Amos S. Deinard, 159–74. New York: Center for Migration Studies.

———. 1989a. Changing Lives of Refugee Hmong Women. Ph.D. dissertation, Department of Anthropology, University of Washington, Seattle. Ann Arbor: UMI Inc.

———. 1989b. *Seattle Schoolchildren Who Speak Asian Languages at Home: Residence by Census Tract, 1980, 1984, 1988.* Seattle: Information Services.

Dunnigan, Timothy, and Tou Fu Vang. 1980. Negotiating Marriage in Hmong Society, an Example of the Effect of Social Ritual on Language Maintenance. *Minnesota Papers in Linguistics and Philosophy of Language* 6, edited by Nancy Stenson, 28–47.

———. 1986. Antecedents of Hmong Resettlement in the United States. In *Hmong Art: Tradition and Change,* 5–9. Catalog of an exhibition held 24 February–5 May 1985. Sheboygan, Wis.: John Michael Kohler Arts Center.

Eisenstadt, S. M., and Louis Roniger. 1980. Patron-Client Relations as a Model of

Structuring Social Exchange. *Comparative Studies in Society and History* 22:42–77.

Ember, Lois. 1984. Yellow Rain: The Strange Case of the Hmong. *Chemical and Engineering News*, 9 January, 9–34.

Far Eastern Economic Review. 1960. 29(1):40.

——— . 1974. 81(27):39.

——— . 1975. 85(27):52.

Fass, Simon. 1985. Through a Glass Darkly: Cause and Effect in Refugee Resettlement Policies. *Journal of Policy Analysis and Management* 5(1):119–37.

——— . 1986. Innovations in the Struggle for Self-Reliance: The Hmong Experience in the United States. *International Migration Review* 20(2):351–82.

Finck, John, and Doua Yang. 1984. "Peace Has Not Been Made." Video, distributed by State of Rhode Island (Providence Plantations), Department of Social and Rehabilitation Services, Office of Refugee Resettlement, 600 New Lond Avenue, Cranston, R.I. 02920.

Geddes, William. 1971 [1967]. *Miao Year.* Film (16mm). Available for rental through Instructional Media Services, University of Washington, Seattle.

——— . 1976. *Migrants of the Mountains.* Oxford: Clarendon Press.

Goldstein, Beth L. 1986. Resolving Sexual Assault: Hmong and the American Legal System. In *The Hmong in Transition*, edited by Glen L. Hendricks, Bruce T. Downing, and Amos S. Deinard, 135–44. New York: Center for Migration Studies.

Graham, David Crockett. 1978. *The Tribal Songs and Tales of the Ch'uan Miao.* Taipei: Chinese Association for Folklore.

Hafey, Pamela. n.d.[1982]. *Southeast Asian Textiles.* Flier, collection of the author.

Hang, Doua. 1986. Tain Tuab Neeg: Connecting the Generations. In *The Hmong World I*, edited by Brenda Johns and David Strecker, 33–41. New Haven: Council on Southeast Asia Studies, Yale Center for International and Area Studies.

Hanks, Lucien M. 1977. The Corporation and the Entourage: A Comparison of Thai and American Social Organization. In *Friends, Followers, and Factions*, edited by Steffen W. Schmidt et al., 161–66. Berkeley: University of California Press.

Harris, Jane. 1982. Designs from Another World. *Journal-American* (Bellevue, Wash.), 28 June.

Heimbach, Ernest. 1979. *White Hmong-English Dictionary.* Ithaca, N.Y.: Southeast Asia Program, Cornell University.

Hendricksen, Georg. 1971. The Transactional Basis of Influence: White Men Among Naskapi Indians. In *Patrons and Brokers in the East Arctic*, edited by Robert Paine, 22–33. Toronto: University of Toronto Press.

Hirayama, Kasumi K., and Hisashi Hirayama. 1988. Stress, Social Supports, and Adaptational Patterns in Hmong Refugee Families. *Amerasia* 14(1):92–108.

Hurlich, Marshall, and Nancy D. Donnelly. 1984. Effects of Rapid Social Change on Ethnic Identity: The Hmong in the United States. Paper presented at the 83d Annual Meeting of the American Anthropological Association. Denver, Colo., 23 November.

Hurlich, Marshall, Neal R. Holtan, and Ronald G. Munger. 1986. Attitudes of Hmong Toward a Medical Research Project. In *The Hmong in Transition*, edited by Glen L. Hendricks, Bruce T. Downing, and Amos S. Deinard, 427–46. New York: Center for Migration Studies.

Johnson, Charles. 1981a. *Tus POJ NIAM thiab tus TSOV (The WOMAN and the TIGER): A Hmong Folk Tale in Hmong and Beginning ESL: Level 1*. Charles Johnson, series ed. St. Paul, Minn.: Linguistics Department, Macalester College.

———. 1981b. *Tus NEEG TXIAV TAWS, nws tus QAIB thiab nws POJ NIAM (The WOODCUTTER, his ROOSTER, and his WIFE): A Hmong Folk Tale in Hmong and Beginning ESL: Level 1*. Charles Johnson, series ed. St. Paul, Minn.: Linguistics Department, Macalester College.

Johnson, Charles, ed. 1985. *Dab Neeg Hmoob: Myths, Legends & Folk Tales from the Hmong of Laos*. St. Paul, Minn.: Linguistics Department, Macalester College.

Kohler Arts Center. 1986. *Hmong Art: Tradition and Change*. Sheboygan, Wis.: John Michael Kohler Arts Center.

Lande, Carl H. 1977. Introduction: The Dyadic Basis of Clientelism. In *Friends, Followers, and Factions*, edited by Steffen W. Schmidt, et al., xiii–xxxix. Berkeley: University of California Press.

Larteguy, Jean. 1979. *La fabuleuse aventure du people de l'opium*. Paris: Presses de la Cité.

Lee, Gary Yia. 1981. The Effects of Development Measures on the Socio-Economy of the White Hmong. Ph.D. dissertation, Department of Anthropology, University of Sydney, Australia.

Lemoine, Jacques. 1972. *Un Village Hmong Vert du Haut Laos*. Paris: Ecole Pratique des Hautes Etudes, Centre National de la Recherche Scientifique.

———. 1983. *L'initiation du mort chez les Hmong*. Bangkok: Pandora.

Levine, Kenneth, and Ivory Waterworth-Levine. 1982. *Becoming American*. Iris Films. 58-minute and 30-minute 16mm or video available through New Day Films, 121 West 27th St., Suite 902, New York, N.Y. 10001.

Lewis, Paul, and Elaine Lewis. 1984. *Peoples of the Golden Triangle: Six Tribes in Thailand*. London: Thames and Hudson Ltd.

Lin, Yueh-hwa. 1941. The Miao-Man Peoples of Kweichow. *Harvard Journal of Asiatic Studies* 5:261–345.

Long, Lynellen. 1988. The Floating World: Laotian Refugee Camp Life in Thailand. Ph.D. dissertation, Graduate School of Education, Stanford University. Ann Arbor: UMI Inc.

Lumet de Lajonquiere, E. 1904. *Ethnographie des territoires militaires, rédige sur l'ordre du general Coronnat, d'apres le travaux de MM. le lieutenant-colonel Diquet, le commandant Bonifacy, le commandant Réverony, le capitaine Fesch, etc.* Hanoi.

Mallinson, Jane. 1985. Blue Hmong Women's Skirts as Markers of Women's Roles. Master's thesis, Department of Anthropology, University of Washington, Seattle.

Mallinson, Jane, Nancy D. Donnelly, and Ly Hang. 1988. *Hmong Batik.* Seattle: Mallinson/Information Services.

Mason, Linda, and Roger Brown. 1983. *Rice, Rivalry, and Politics: Managing Cambodian Relief.* South Bend, Ind.: Notre Dame University Press.

McCoy, Alfred. 1970. French Colonialism in Laos, 1893–1945. In *Laos: War and Revolution,* edited by Nina Adams and Alfred McCoy, 67–99. New York: Harper Colophon Books.

Menschel, Neil. 1987. "Kialor prepares greens in bowl on kitchen floor as Tou and his father, Yong Koua, talk." Photograph. *Christian Science Monitor,* 12 August, p. 15.

Mickey, Margaret P. 1947. The Cowrie Shell Miao of Kweichow. *Papers of the Peabody Museum of American Archaeology and Ethnology,* Harvard University, 32(1). Cambridge, Mass.: Peabody Museum.

Mortland, Carol. 1988. Southeast Asians and the American Economy: Intervening Groups. Paper presented at the 87th Annual Meetings of the American Anthropological Association, Phoenix, Ariz., 18 November.

Mottin, Fr. Jean. 1980a. *55 Chants d'Amour Hmong Blanc (55 Zaj Kwvtxhiaj Hmoob Dawb).* Bangkok: The Siam Society.

————. 1980b. *History of the Hmong.* Bangkok: Odeon.

Office of Financial Management. n.d. [1982]. *Washington State Data Book 1981.* Olympia: State of Washington.

Office of Refugee Resettlement. 1981. *Report to the Congress: Refugee Resettlement Program for 1980.* Washington, D.C.: Department of Health and Human Services.

————. 1984–85. *The Hmong Resettlement Study.* Vol. 1: Final Report. Vol. 2: Economic Development and Employment Projects. Vol. 3: Exemplary Projects and Projects with Unique Features of Programmatic Interest. Site Reports: Providence; Portland; Orange County; Fresno; Minneapolis/St. Paul; Fort Smith; Dallas. Stephen Reder, Project Director. Washington, D.C.: U.S. Department of Health and Human Services.

Paine, Robert. 1971. Introduction. In *Patrons and Brokers in the East Arctic,* edited by Robert Paine, 3–21. Toronto: University of Toronto Press.

Peterson, Sally. 1988. Translating Experience and the Reading of a Story Cloth. *Journal of American Folklore* 101(399):6–22.

————. 1989. Seeking Spirits Among the Flowers: Signs and Non-signs in Hmong Design. Paper presented to the Annual Meetings of the Association of Asian Studies, Washington, D.C., 1 March.

Robinson, Court. In press. *Laotian Refugees in Thailand: The Thai and U.S. Response, 1975 to 1988.* Washington, D.C.: U.S. Committee for Refugees.

Ruey Yih-Fu. 1958. Terminological Structure of the Miao Kinship System. *Bulletin of the Institute of History and Philology,* Academia Sinica, Taipei (Taiwan), 29(2):613–39.

Rumbaut, Ruben G., and John R. Weeks. 1986. Fertility and Adaptation: Indochinese Refugees in the United States. *International Migration Review* 20(2):428–65.

Sanday, Peggy Reeves. 1981. *Female Power and Male Dominance: On the Origins of Sexual Inequality.* Cambridge and New York: Cambridge University Press.

Savina, F. M. 1930. *Histoire des Miao.* Hong Kong: Imprimerie de la Societé des Missions-Etrangères.

Schanche, Don. 1970. *Mister Pop.* New York: David McCay.

Scott, George, Jr. 1982. A New Year in a New Land: Religious Change Among the Lao Hmong Refugees in San Diego. In *The Hmong in the West,* edited by Bruce T. Downing and Douglas P. Olney, 63–85.

Seeley, Thomas D., Joan W. Nowicke, Matthew Meselson, Jeanne Guillemin, and Pongthep Akratanakul. 1985. Yellow Rain. *Scientific American* 253(3):128–37.

Smalley, William A. 1956. The Gospel and the Cultures of Laos. *Practical Anthropology* 3(3):46–57.

————. 1986. "Stages of Hmong Cultural Adaptation." In *The Hmong in Transition,* edited by Glen L. Hendricks, Bruce T. Downing, and Amos S. Deinard, 7–22. New York: Center for Migration Studies.

Swidler, Ann. 1986. Culture in Action: Symbols and Strategies. *American Sociological Review* 51:273–86.

Tapp, Nicholas. 1985. *Categories of Change and Continuity Among the White Hmong (Hmoob Dawb) of Northern Thailand.* Ph.D. thesis, Anthropology Department, School of Oriental and African Studies, University of London.

————. 1988. *Sovereignty and Rebellion: The White Hmong of Northern Thailand.* Singapore: Oxford University Press.

Thomas, Elaine. 1982. Hmong and Mien Textile Arts: Motif and Meaning. Unpublished manuscript (author's files).

United States Committee for Refugees. 1983. *Refugee Protection: An Analysis and Action Proposal.* Washington, D.C.: U.S. Committee for Refugees.

Vang, Lue, and Judy Lewis. 1984. *Grandmother's Path, Grandfather's Way.* Rancho Cordova, Cal.: Zellerbach Family Fund.

White, Kenneth, trans. 1983. *Kr'ua Ke (Showing the Way): A Hmong Initiation of the Dead, Recorded and Translated into French by Jacques Lemoine.* Bangkok: Pandora.

Wilson, Wendell L., and Michael A. Garrick. 1983. *Refugee Assistance Termination Study.* Olympia, Wash.: Office of Research and Data Analysis, Division of Administration and Personnel, Department of Social and Health Services.

Xiong, May, and Nancy D. Donnelly. 1986. My Life in Laos. In *The Hmong World 1,* edited by Brenda Johns and David Strecker, 201–43. New Haven: Yale Center for International and Area Studies, Council on Southeast Asia Studies.

Xiong, Xeev Nruag. n.d. [1985]. *Lub Neej Ib Vuag Dlua, 1975–1985* (A Family Temporarily Ripped Apart, 1975–1985). Winfield, Ill.: Hmong Literacy.

Yanagisako, Sylvia J., and Jane F. Collier. 1987. Toward a Unified Analysis of Kinship and Gender. In *Gender and Kinship: Essays Toward a Unified Analysis,* edited by Jane F. Collier and Sylvia J. Yanagisako, 14–50. Stanford: Stanford University Press.

Yang Dao. 1976 [1975]. *The Hmong of Laos in the Vanguard of Development* (Les Hmong du Laos Face au Developpement). Vientiane: U.S. Department of the Army. Reprint of Vientiane: Siaosavath Publishers.

Yang, Teng, et al. 1985. An *Evaluation of the Highland Lao Initiative: Final Report.* Washington, D.C.: Office of Refugee Resettlement, Department of Health and Human Services.

Yu, Elena S. H., and William T. Liu. 1986. Methodological Problems and Policy Implications in Vietnamese Refugee Research. *International Migration Review* 20(2):483–501.

INDEX

Adaptation: and individual identity, 4
Affairs, sexual, 119–22, 124
Age pyramid: Hmong in Laos, 19, 21; Hmong in U.S., 65, 67
Alienation: of girls from natal family, 120
American law: and catch-hand marriage, 143; and Hmong divorce, 180
American society: as perceived by Hmong, 15, 71–76; and Hmong definition of family, 189
American sponsors, 61, 201n.16; and domestic disputes, 171–72; and divorce, 181–82
AN. *See* Asian Needlecrafters
Arranged marriages, 132–33. *See also* Marriage
Asian Americans: Seattle demographics of, 62, 83–84, 202n.22
Asian Counselling and Referral Service, 108
Asian Needlecrafters, 89–95, 102, 108, 109; organizational structure of, 89–90; marketing practices of, 90; and deception, 93; and inventory problems, 97
Assistance to Families with Dependent Children, 79

Baby carriers, 44–45
Ball game, courtship, 65, 116, 178, 204n.1
Ban Vinai (refugee camp), 58
Batik, 88
Beacon Hill (Seattle), 61, 62, 83
Becoming American (film), 74
"Beginning of the World, The" (origin story), 36–37
Behavior: cultural patterning of, 8; and gender concepts, 12, 16; bidirectional, 205. *See also* Men's roles; Women's roles
Benefits: cut in federal, 60; for refugees, 75, 77. *See also* Welfare
Bilingual education, 83
Birth control, 85
Blue Hmong: dialect, *vii*; costume, 43–44
Boldness: women's, 16; in girls, 128; in boys, 142

BORA. *See* Washington State Bureau of Refugee Assistance
Boua Mu (mountain), 57
Boys' roles, 36, 142. *See also* Patrilineality; Training
Bride wealth, 132, 140–41, 154–60, 163; as protection for wives, 150, 152, 155, 158–59; in wedding negotiations, 151; unpaid, 156, 178; as price, 157–58; amounts, in U.S., 158; American attitudes inferred, 169; and divorce, 169
Business practices: and Hmong Artwork Association, 103

Cambodians: in Seattle, 83
Cash. *See* Money
Cash crop: in Laos, 21, 27
Catch-hand marriage, 141–43; and negotiations, 145. *See also* Elopement; Marriage
Census: in Laos, 19; in U.S., 62–63; of schoolchildren, 83–84, 202n.22
Central Intelligence Agency (C.I.A.), 50, 51, 55
Change. *See* Social change
Chao Fa (guerrilla force), 168
Chiang Kham (refugee camp), 58
Chiengmingmai (village), 160, 189
Childbirth: in Laos, 33–34
Childlessness: Hmong attitudes toward, 15, 71–72
Children: as reason for marriage, 33; survival of, in Laos, 34–35; behavior of, in U.S., 75–76; as population indicator, 83–84. *See also under* Training
Child support, 180
Chinese: in Seattle, 62, 83
Chinese traders: in Laos, 46
Choice. *See* Decision making
Christianity, Hmong, 49–50, 60, 80, 85–86; and textiles, 111; and sexuality, 121; and research needed, 192. *See also* Missionaries; Ritual; Secularism
Christian Missionary Alliance, 60, 197
C.I.A., 50, 51, 55

217